VOTING CHRISTIAN VALUES: 2012 ELECTION

TIMOTHY A. JACOBSON
B.S., M.A., J.D., LTC, U.S. ARMY (RET.)

VOTING CHRISTIAN VALUES: 2012 ELECTION

DEDICATION

This book is hereby dedicated to:

The God of Abraham, the God of our Founding Fathers.
"In Him we live, and move, and have our being"
(Acts 17:28, KJV).

My parents Rev. Gerald and Jean Jacobson,
and my brothers Thomas, Michael, and Daniel.

My wife Delores
and my daughters Rebecca, Kristin, and Kelsey.

SPECIAL HONOR

"Eye hath not seen, nor ear heard, neither have entered into the heart of man, the things which God hath prepared for them that love him" (1 Cor 2:8-10). On the day that she suffered the final stroke that silenced her forever, my mother was doing what she enjoyed most, quoting Scripture and singing hymns. The words "For to me, to live is Christ and to die is gain" (Phil 1:20-22) epitomized her life. She was consumed by love and passion for serving the Lord. She loved reading Scripture, "God's Word," and was able to quote countless passages. My father described her as "a walking concordance."

My father and mother were united in total commitment to loving and serving the LORD until the passing of my mother. Today, my father, a retired minister, missionary, and state prison chaplain with three master's degrees, works without pay as a volunteer chaplain at local hospitals. He is an absolutely wonderful, caring father and grandfather, completely devoted to the LORD and to his family.

AUTHOR

Timothy Jacobson is a Christian attorney and retired U.S. Army Lieutenant Colonel. His academic degrees include a Bachelor of Science, United Stated Military Academy, West Point, Master of Arts in Theology, Summa Cum Laude, Regent University, and Juris Doctor, Regent University. His 33 years of military service included 11 years active duty and 22 years National Guard and Reserves. He has lived throughout the United States, in Brazil as the son of a missionary, and in Germany as an Army Officer. He now lives with his wife Delores and youngest daughter in Ohio.

FAVORITE QUOTES

"For me to live is Christ, and to die is gain."
The Apostle Paul.

"God made me fast, and when I run, I feel His pleasure."
Eric Liddel, Chariots of Fire,
Olympic runner and missionary to China.

"Thanks be to God for the challenge and the victory."
West Point yearbook.

"Help me to never seek a crown, for
my reward is giving glory to you."
Keith Green, songwriter.

VOTING CHRISTIAN VALUES

Every vote is a vote for or against God and his laws. It is absolutely amazing how much Democrats are united in voting against Christian values. Democrats do not simply fail to do "the will of [the] Father" on moral issues they dismiss as "social issues" (same-sex marriage, abortion). They fail to do God's will in virtually all areas (healthcare, taxing the rich, national spending, national debt, etc.).

Rejection of God and His laws is rejection of Christ and proof that one is not a Christian. On Judgment Day Christ will reject many Americans who call themselves Christians because they failed to do "the will of [the] Father." Christ said,

> Not every one that saith unto me, "Lord, Lord,"
> shall enter into the kingdom of heaven; but he
> that doeth the will of my Father which is in
> heaven. Many will say to me in that day, "Lord,
> Lord, have we not prophesied in thy name? and
> in thy name have cast out devils? and in thy name
> done many wonderful works?" And then will I
> profess unto them, I never knew you: depart from
> me, ye that work iniquity (Matt. 7:21-23, KJV).

The best way to quickly see how Democrats are united in voting against Christian values is to go to www.FRCaction.org and view the scorecards developed by Family Research Council Action and Citizenlink, an affiliate of Focus on the Family, which show how members of Congress voted on Christian values.

During 2011, the average score for Republicans in the Senate was about 73%. The average score for Democrats was less than 2% (1.65%). No Democrat scored above 14%. 88% of Democrats scored an absolute 0%. In the House of Representatives, the average score for Republicans was about 89%. The average score for Democrats was about 9%. 91% of Democrats scored 10% or less.[1]

Scores for prior years show the same pattern i.e. very high for Republicans and extremely low for Democrats. Senator Obama and Senator Biden both scored 0% on the scorecard available during the 2008 election. They voted against Christian values every time they voted on the legislation evaluated by Family Research Council Action and Citizenlink.[2]

Democrats are riding the wrong horse at high speed in the wrong direction toward a cliff, completely unaware of the present and future consequences of their actions. Contrary to popular opinion, the most loving thing to do is not to remain silent, be tolerant, avoid divisive issues or avoid being critical or judgmental, but to forcefully and emphatically challenge Christians to love and serve God in greater obedience to the laws and principles that God has revealed through Scripture.

CHRISTIAN VOTER GUIDANCE

Christians who need voter guidance should go to www.FRCaction.org or google FRC Action (Family Research Council Action). Click on Voter Tools for the following:

1. Voter Registration: Tool for voter registration.

---

[1] "Vote Scorecard," Family Research Council Action, http://www.frcaction.org (accessed February 17, 2012).
[2] "Vote Scorecard," Family Research Council Action, http://www.frcaction.org (accessed July 9, 2008).

2. *__Presidential Voter Guide:__* Chart that compares presidential candidates.

3. *__Congressional Scorecard:__* Scorecards on how members of Congress voted.

4. State Groups: May provide state level voter guidance.

5. Legislation Tracker: Current legislation on listed topics.

6. Endorsements: FRC Action endorsements of candidates.

7. Contact Officials: Local and state elected officials.

Additional Christian voter guidance:

1. CitizenLink (www.Citizenlink.com). Affiliate of Focus on the Family. Developed congressional scorecards with FRC Action. Voter guidance on family issues.

2. National Right to Life (www.NRLC.org). Congressional scorecards and voter guidance related to abortion, healthcare, etc.

3. Heritage Foundation (www.Heritage.org). Click on ISSUES for detailed written briefs on economy, federal budget, national debt, deficit, taxes, entitlements, health care, Medicare, social security, welfare, family, marriage, education, energy, environment, immigration, terrorism, and many other topics.

Please support these ministries with part of your tithe.
Donate online.

Gifts to political action groups are not tax deductible.
Give anyway.

TABLE OF CONTENTS

CHAPTER 1.0

INTRODUCTION

ON GOD'S SIDE: During the American Civil War, a minister asked President Lincoln whether God was on their side. He answered by saying, "Sir, my concern is not whether God is on our side; my greatest concern is to be on God's side, for God is always right."[3] Every American needs to ask: "Am I on God's side?"

READERS: This book is only written for Christians (Protestants and Catholics) who believe that "all Scripture is inspired by God" and want to love and serve God through obedience to His laws and principles revealed through Scripture, through the words of Moses, King David, King Solomon, the prophets, Paul, and other authors of Scripture.

Many Americans believe that they have the right to do whatever is right in their own eyes and they treasure that freedom. This book is not written for them. This book is only written for Christians who want to take up their cross and follow Christ. Readers who need quick guidance may refer to the conclusion, which provides a detailed, comprehensive summary of the book.

PURPOSE: This book is written to challenge the apathy and ignorance of Americans regarding the heart and mind of God on politics and religion and the laws and principles He has revealed through Scripture. It is not written to make friends. It will inspire hatred and personal attacks. So be it. Life is not

---

[3] Carpenter, F.B. (1866), "Six Months at the White House," p. 282 (retrieved 2010-02-20). Quoted in "Abraham Lincoln and Religion," TheFreeDictionary, http://encyclopedia.thefreedictionary.com/ Abraham+Lincoln+ and+religion #endnote_rf-17.

about whatever best serves oneself. Life is about loving and serving God in obedience to the greatest commandment. The author has one challenge for those who disagree with the message of this book: prove it wrong with Scripture.

OBJECTIVES: As an Army officer, the author was trained to think first in terms of mission and objectives. Please join in affirming these objectives.

FIRST OBJECTIVE: The primary objective of this book is obedience to the greatest commandment, first stated by Moses: "Thou shalt love the Lord thy God with all thy heart, and with all thy soul, and with all thy might" (Deut. 6:5, KJV). The foundation of all other laws, it is the one law that should govern every thought and action.

SECOND OBJECTIVE: Christ restated the greatest commandment, and added the second greatest commandment:

> "Thou shalt love the Lord thy God with all thy heart, and with all thy soul, and with all thy mind." This is the first and great commandment. And the second is like unto it, "Thou shalt love thy neighbour as thyself." On these two commandments hang all the law and the prophets (Matt. 22:37-40, KJV).

This commandment is totally secondary to the greatest commandment. The foundation of all laws regarding men, it should govern all our thoughts and actions toward other men.

THIRD OBJECTIVE: The third objective of this book is to secure for our nation blessings that result from obedience to God's commandments. "Blessed is the nation whose God is the LORD...." (Psalm 33:11, KJV). "Righteousness exalt[s] a nation: but sin is a reproach to any people" (Prov. 14:34, KJV).

If my people, which are called by my name, shall
humble themselves, and pray, and seek my face,
and turn from their wicked ways; then will I hear
from heaven, and will forgive their sin, and will
heal their land (2 Chron. 7:14, KJV).

Americans need to "humble themselves, and pray,
and seek [God's] face, and turn from their wicked ways." True
repentance means turning from wrongdoing to obedience to
God's commandments. This brings God's forgiveness, healing,
and blessing to a nation. Americans cannot expect God to bless
America if they live and vote contrary to His laws. That makes
about as much sense as a man trying to violate the law of gravity
by jumping off a tall building without a parachute. He will not
violate the law; he will prove it by showing how it works on a
falling body.

FOURTH OBJECTIVE: The final but more
immediate objective of this book is to influence the 2012
election by challenging Christians to vote Christian values by
challenging the extreme ignorance of Americans regarding laws
that God created to govern men and governments, laws are
embodied in Scripture and the U.S. Constitution. Christian
values are Christ's values, which are the values of God, which
God has revealed through Scripture. Often what seems right to
even the most intelligent of men is totally contrary to God's
ways, because God's ways are higher than man's ways.
Scripture reveals the wisdom of God.

REASON FOR LIVING: Why are you living? What
makes life worth living? What gives life meaning? As a teenager
the author of this book dreamed about finding and sharing better
answers to these questions. This book is not that dream come
true; it is about voting Christian values. However, the reader will
learn what makes life worth living from this book because what
gives one reason for living gives one reason for voting Christian

values, and what informs one how to live a Christian life informs one how to vote Christian values.

Most Americans are taught that life centers around themselves, and that they have the right to do whatever best serves themselves. They determine facts and truth and decide right and wrong without reference to God or Scripture. They choose jobs or careers that best serve themselves, not God or others. They search for love, get married, and then divorce when their marriage partner no longer meets their needs. Scripture teaches that life centers around God, not man, and that men were not designed to live self-centered lives. Scripture commands men to love God with all their heart, mind, soul, and strength, and to love their fellow man with the same measure that they love themselves.

2008 ELECTION: During every national election, millions of Christians vote totally contrary to millions of other Christians. Pastors, priests, and other Christian leaders do likewise, countering each other's votes. During the 2008 presidential election, the presidential candidates and their vice-presidents all claimed to be Christians, but had totally contradictory voting records. Millions of African Americans (95%) voted for Senator Obama because he is African-American. Millions of women voted for Hillary Clinton because she is a woman. When Senator McCain chose Governor Palin as his Vice-President, many women switched their support from Senator Obama and Senator Biden to Senator McCain and Governor Palin. When the economic crisis suddenly got worse, millions of voters changed again, giving Senator Obama a lead that proved impossible to overcome. In other words, Americans voted for themselves based on race, gender, and the economy. They did not vote for whatever would best serve God, their fellow man, or their nation. They voted in violation of the two greatest commandments, by not loving God or their fellow man, and ignored the best interests of their nation.

13

QUESTIONS: The totally contrary voting of Christians raises many questions. This book will provide answers based upon simple, clear teachings of Scripture. Take time to briefly consider some of these questions.

POLITICS AND GOVERNMENT: What is the heart and mind of God on politics and government? Does God care about politics and government or, like many Christian leaders, does He only care about spiritual matters? Jesus said, "My kingdom is not of this world..." (John 18:36, KJV). He said, "Render to Caesar the things that are Caesar's, and to God the things that are God's" (Mark 12:16-18, KJV. See also Matt. 22:21; Luke 20:24-26). Does this mean that God is concerned about spiritual matters like salvation and sanctification, but not secular matters like politics and government?

CHURCH AND STATE: What is the heart and mind of God on separation of church and state? Would God agree with decisions of some American courts that exclude Him from schools, government, and the workplace? How is it possible that a nation founded as "One Nation Under God," founded on belief in God as the Creator of all things and all men, allows court decisions that exclude God and creation from schools, government, and the workplace to stand unchallenged and uncorrected by citizens or government?

POLITICAL PARTIES: What is the heart and mind of God on political parties? Does God take sides between Republicans or Democrats, or does he deliberately avoid taking sides? Who is on God's side more than the other, Republicans or Democrats? How and why?

ELECTIONS: What is the heart and mind of God on elections? Does God care how Christians vote, or does He only care about spiritual matters? Is every vote a vote for or against God, or does God simply not care how we vote? Do Christians have: (1) a right to vote however they want, (2) a right to do

14

whatever is right in their own eyes; (3) a duty to vote according to their conscience i.e. to do right as God gives them light to see right, or (4) a duty to vote in accordance with certain laws and principles?

If Christ was living in the United States today, how would He vote? Would he vote according to Biblical laws and principles? Does the totally contradictory voting of Christians prove ignorance of the laws and principles that God gave through Moses, King David, King Solomon, the prophets, Paul, and other authors of Scripture? Christ said, "Not every one that saith unto me, "Lord, Lord," shall enter into the kingdom of heaven; but he that doeth the will of my Father which is in heaven" (Matt. 7:21, KJV). Does "doing the will of the Father" require voting for Republicans in the 2012 election?

RESULT OF 2008 ELECTION: History will record the 2008 election as even more important than the 2012 election. However, most Americans probably cannot identify the most important result of the 2008 election. It is not that President Obama was the first African-American president; it has nothing to do with race. It is not "Obamacare, the totally unconstitutional national healthcare system which is already projected to cost double original estimates, costing more than the nation being at war for the remainder of its history. It is not because President Obama directed the Department of Justice to not enforce DOMA, the Defense of Marriage Act, which defines marriage as between one man and one woman. It is not because he is the most liberal, most socialist, most pro-abortion, pro-homosexual, pro-same-sex marriage president in the history of the United States, although it is directly related to all of that. It is because he replaced two U.S. Supreme Court justices with two very liberal female justices who will serve for life and legislate from the bench contrary to Scripture and contrary to the U.S. Constitution for countless years after he is no longer in office.

ORGANIZATION OF BOOK: This book is organized into sections. The first chapter is the introduction. Section 2 (Chapters 2.1 to 2.3) lays the foundation for voting Christian values. Section 3 (Chapters 3.1 to 3.4) addresses the jurisdiction of government and separation of church and state. Section 4 (Chapters 4.1 to 4.4) discusses biblical law (God's law) on moral issues. Section 5 (Chapters 5.1 to 5.3) addresses other hot political issues. Section 6 (Chapters 6.1 to 6.2) reviews Christian scorecards for members of Congress. Section 7 (Chapters 7.1 to 7.6) analyzes Christian voters guidance on presidential candidates. Section 8 (Chapters 8.1 to 8.2) discusses deception during the 2008 and 2012 presidential campaigns. Section 9 (Chapters 9.1 to 9.3) addresses the failure of Christian leaders, judgment on America, and what God desires for man. The tenth chapter, the conclusion, provides a detailed, comprehensive summary of the book.

FOUNDATION

SECTION REVIEW: This section lays the foundation for the book. The first chapter reviews the vital importance of Scripture as the foundation for this book and foundation for living the Christian life. The second chapter defines what it means to be a Christian. The third chapter discusses how biblical law provides guidance for living and voting Christian values.

CHAPTERS: Chapters in this section include the following:

2.1 One Foundation: Scripture
2.2 Defining "Christian"
2.3 Biblical Law

ONE FOUNDATION: SCRIPTURE

LEADING QUESTION: "What is the one thing that I want you to believe more than anything else?" I asked my three daughters. The answer, I explained, was not God or Christ, but Scripture. Why?

FIRST REASON: God reveals Himself to man through Scripture. Without Scripture every man must imagine God in his own mind, and everyone gets it wrong in so many ways. Why is knowledge of God so important? Understanding of God, the Creator of all things seen and unseen, is the foundation for understanding of the meaning and purpose of all things seen and unseen. Americans today, including Christians, are at an all time low for understanding of God and the meaning and purpose of their own lives. Also, on Judgment Day most Americans will face the wrath of a holy, righteous God, in part because they never understood God or what He requires of man.

SECOND REASON: Second, God uses Scripture to reveal Christ to man. It gives prophecy regarding Christ and tells the story of His birth, life, death, and resurrection. God uses Scripture not only to give facts about Christ, but also, by telling the story of the life of Christ, to give the perfect example of what it means to be a Christian, a follower of Christ. Christ also provides an example of someone who understood the importance of Old Testament Scripture and studied it so diligently that as a young boy He knew more than the priests in the temple. He quoted it throughout His ministry.

THIRD REASON: Third, Scripture reveals what is required to become a Christian, a follower of Christ, through the words of Christ, Matthew, Mark, Luke, John, Paul, Peter, and other authors of Scripture. The Apostle Paul refers to "the holy Scriptures, which are able to make thee wise unto salvation through faith which is in Christ Jesus" (2 Tim. 3:15, KJV). The chapter entitled "Defining Christian" discusses the elements of being a Christian.

FOURTH REASON: Fourth, God uses Scripture to give the facts regarding the history ("His story") of the world and of His workings with His people and others from creation to Christ's birth, life, death, and resurrection and to the time of Christ's return to earth in glory.

FIFTH REASON: Fifth, God gives Christians the guidance they need to live the Christian life through laws and principles revealed in Scripture, through the words of Moses, King David, King Solomon, the prophets, Christ, Paul, and other authors of Scripture. Paul said, "All Scripture is given by inspiration of God, and is profitable for doctrine, for reproof, for correction, for instruction in righteousness" (2 Tim. 3:16, KJV).

Without Scripture, every man does whatever is right in his own eyes, and even the most intelligent get it so very wrong. The words, "Every man did that which was right in his own eyes" (Judges 17:5-7; 21:24-25) describe a period of lawlessness in Israel (See Deut. 12:7-9; Prov. 12:15; 21:2). Proverbs states, "The way of a fool is right in his own eyes: but he that hearken[s] unto counsel is wise" (Prov.12:14-16) and "there is a way which seem[s] right unto a man, but the end thereof are the ways of death (Prov. 14:12; 16:25). God spoke through Isaiah saying, "For my thoughts are not your thoughts, neither are your ways my ways, saith the LORD. For as the heavens are higher than the earth, so are my ways higher than your ways, and my thoughts than your thoughts (Isa. 55:8-10). Jesus said, "Ye do err, not knowing the Scriptures, nor the power of God" (Matt. 22:29, KJV). Often what seems right to even the most intelligent of men is totally contrary to God's ways, because God's ways

19

are higher than man's ways. The perfect example is President Obama, as will be shown, a very intelligent man with the best of intentions who fights for policies totally contrary to God's laws.

CONCLUSION: Belief in Scripture is more important than belief in God or Christ because Scripture defines God, Christ, and what it means to be a Christian. Every law student, lawyer, and judge studies two aspects of every case: the facts and the law. God uses Scripture to give man the facts and the law needed for living the Christian life. Without Scripture even Christians have totally wrong and conflicting opinions of God, Christ, what it means to be a Christian, and what it means to live and vote Christian values. Scripture is a very special gift of God to man, given because God knew man desperately needed written guidance for godly living. Men seek freedom through rebellion against God's law, through doing whatever is right in their own eyes. But true freedom and blessings only come through obedience to God's laws. That is why King David said, "Thy word is a lamp unto my feet, and a light unto my path" (Psalms 119:105) and "I will walk at liberty: for I seek thy precepts" (Psalms 119:45, KJV).

DEFINING "CHRISTIAN"

REASON FOR CHAPTER: Most Americans cannot give an accurate definition of "Christian." Non-Christians have a totally flawed understanding what it means to be a Christian and what freedom of religion requires. Many Christians think that simply believing in Christ as Savior makes one a Christian. This is totally contrary to the teachings of Christ.

FIRST ELEMENT: There are several essential elements of being a Christian. First, a Christian is someone who, like all Jews and Muslims, believes in God. He understands that:

1. There is one true God, who always was, is, and ever shall be.
2. He never changes. He is the same yesterday, today, and tomorrow.
3. He created all things seen and unseen, and all laws that govern all things seen and unseen.
4. He creates each man in His own image, knitting him together in his mother's womb.

A Christian understands that God's moral laws are rooted in His unchanging character. They do not change or evolve. They are the same today as they were when our universe was created. These include laws that govern men and governments. The United States was founded upon these self-evident, common sense truths, revealed by God through creation and embodied in the Declaration of Independence and U.S. Constitution.

SECOND ELEMENT: Second, a Christian is someone who, unlike Jews or Muslims, believes in a triune God, one God in three persons: Father, Son, and Holy Spirit. This is not common sense. It is not revealed through creation. It is revealed through Scripture, and it takes a special gift of faith from God to believe.

Many Christians publicly profess their faith in the God the Father, Son, and Holy Spirit through the Apostles' Creed, which briefly summarizes key tenants of the Christian faith.

1. I believe in God, the Father almighty, creator of heaven and earth.
2. I believe in Jesus Christ, His only Son, our Lord.
3. He was conceived by the power of the Holy Spirit and born of the Virgin Mary.
4. He suffered under Pontius Pilate, was crucified, died, and was buried.
5. He descended to the dead. On the third day he rose again.
6. He ascended into heaven and is seated at the right hand of the Father.
7. He will come again to judge the living and the dead.
8. I believe in the Holy Spirit,
9. the holy Catholic Church, the communion of saints,
10. the forgiveness of sins,
11. the resurrection of the body,
12. and life everlasting. Amen.[4]

A Christian believes that Christ is the Son of God and the Messiah and Savior whose coming was prophesied to the people of Israel. He believes that Christ is fully God and fully man and that if He was not both He could not be the perfect, blameless "Lamb of God" who made payment in full for the sins of man through His death on the cross. However, belief in all the

---

[4] The *Catechism of the Catholic Church* gives this English translation of the Apostles' Creed. The Catechism maintains the traditional division into twelve articles. See http://en.wikipedia.org/wiki/Apostles%27_Creed.

foregoing does not make one a Christian. Satan and his demons believe in God; it does not make them Christians.

THIRD ELEMENT: Third, a Christian is a repentant sinner. "I love being Catholic, because I can do whatever I want and just go to confession," said a young lady. She is the perfect example of someone who is not a Christian because he or she is not repentant. No priest has the power to forgive the sins of anyone who is not repentant. Repentance means more than true regret for sin; it means turning from sin to obedience to God. King David provides the best example of true repentance:

> Have mercy upon me, O God, according to thy
>   lovingkindness: according unto the
>   multitude of thy tender mercies blot out
>   my transgressions.
> Wash me thoroughly from mine iniquity, and
>   cleanse me from my sin.
> For I acknowledge my transgressions: and my sin
>   is ever before me.
> Against thee, thee only, have I sinned, and done
>   this evil in thy sight: that thou mightest be
>   justified when thou speakest, and be clear
>   when thou judgest.
> Behold, I was shapen in iniquity; and in sin did
>   my mother conceive me.
> Behold, thou desirest truth in the inward parts:
>   and in the hidden part thou shalt make me
>   to know wisdom.
> Purge me with hyssop, and I shall be clean: wash
>   me, and I shall be whiter than snow.
> Make me to hear joy and gladness; that the bones
>   which thou hast broken may rejoice.
> Hide thy face from my sins, and blot out all mine
>   iniquities.
> Create in me a clean heart, O God; and renew a
>   right spirit within me.

Cast me not away from thy presence; and take
not thy Holy Spirit from me.
Restore unto me the joy of thy salvation; and
uphold me with thy free spirit.
Then will I teach transgressors thy ways; and
sinners shall be converted unto thee.
Deliver me from bloodguiltiness, O God, thou
God of my salvation: and my tongue shall
sing aloud of thy righteousness.
O Lord, open thou my lips; and my mouth shall
shew forth thy praise.
For thou desirest not sacrifice; else would I give
it: thou delightest not in burnt offering.
The sacrifices of God are a broken spirit: a
broken and a contrite heart, O God, thou
wilt not despise.
Do good in thy good pleasure unto Zion: build
thou the walls of Jerusalem.
Then shalt thou be pleased with the sacrifices of
righteousness, with burnt offering and
whole burnt offering: then shall they offer
bullocks upon thine altar. Psalm 51:1-19
(KJV).

Note that true repentance requires: (1) full acknowledgment of sin against God; (2) true regret for sin against God; (3) humble request for God's forgiveness; (4) cleansing and full restoration of relationship with God; (5) empowerment by God to do His will; (6) humble obedience to God's will.

FOURTH ELEMENT: Fourth, a Christian is someone who accepts Christ as Savior. He understands that God is holy, and that no man can meet God's standard of perfection. He understands that "all have sinned, and come short of the glory of God" (Rom 3:22-24). He understands that only Christ, the perfect Lamb of God, fully God and fully man, could make payment for man's sins. He understands that Christ died on the cross as payment in full for his sins, and that he can only be cleansed by faith in what Christ has done for him. "For God so loved the world, that he gave his only begotten Son, that whosoever believeth in him should not perish, but have everlasting life" (John 3:16, KJV). He knows that "a man is not justified by the works of the law, but by the faith of Jesus Christ" (Gal 2:16, KJV). Therefore he accepts Christ as his Savior, as the Lamb of God who made payment in full for his sins through death on the cross.

FIFTH ELEMENT: Fifth, a Christian is someone who accepts Christ as the Lord of his life. Christ said, "If any man will come after me, let him deny himself, and take up his cross, and follow me" (Mat. 16:23-25, KJV). He said, "And he that taketh not his cross, and followeth after me, is not worthy of me" (Matt. 10:38, KJV. See also Mark 8:34-35, Luke 9:22-24, KJV). Christ said, "My food is to do the will of Him who sent Me, and to finish His work" (John 4:34, NKJV). If a man believes in Christ and accepts Him as the Lord of his life, then he will take up his cross, dying to self, and follow Him.

Christ made it clear that one cannot be a Christian, a follower of Christ, and live contrary to God's commandments.

> Not every one that saith unto me, "Lord, Lord," shall enter into the kingdom of heaven; but he that doeth the will of my Father which is in heaven. Many will say to me in that day, "Lord, Lord, have we not prophesied in thy name? and in thy name have cast out devils? and in thy name done many wonderful works?" And then will I profess unto them, I never knew you: depart from me, ye that work iniquity (Matt. 7:21-23, KJV).

In other words, believing in Christ as Lord and Savior and doing great miracles in His name does not make one a Christian. A Christian is a follower of Christ who does "the will

25

of my Father." Doing God's will means living and in obedience to His commandments. This does not mean that anyone is saved by works. Man is saved by faith not works, but "faith without works is dead" (James 2:20, KJV; see also James 2:17, 25-26). A man who chooses to live contrary to God's commandments is not a Christian because he is not repentant and he has not accepted Christ as Lord and Savior.

SIXTH ELEMENT: Sixth, a Christian is empowered and guided by the Spirit of God (the Holy Spirit). Jesus made it clear that being saved required being "born again" and that this spiritual rebirth required not just baptism with water, but being "born of…the Spirit." He said, "Except a man be born of water and of the Spirit, he cannot enter into the kingdom of God. That which is born of the flesh is flesh; and that which is born of the Spirit is spirit. Marvel not that I said unto thee, Ye must be born again" (John 3:5-7, KJV).

When Christ gave the Great Commission to his disciples, he said, "All power is given unto me in heaven and in earth. Go ye therefore, and teach all nations, baptizing them in the name of the Father, and of the Son, and of the Holy Ghost: Teaching them to observe all things whatsoever I have commanded you…" (Matt. 28:18-20, KJV). Baptism in the name of the Spirit (Holy Ghost) had special meaning. Jesus said, "For John truly baptized with water; but ye shall be baptized with the Holy Ghost…. But ye shall receive power, after that the Holy Ghost is come upon you: and ye shall be witnesses unto me…unto the uttermost part of the earth" (Act 1:5-8, KJV). In other words, part of being saved involved being "baptized with the Holy Ghost", which resulted in being empowered by the Holy Spirit.

John states that believers in Christ would receive the "Spirit" ("Holy Ghost"). First he quotes Christ; then he explains the meaning of Christ's words (in parentheses): " 38 He that believeth on me, as the Scripture hath said, out of his belly shall flow rivers of living water. 39 (But this spake he of the Spirit, which they that believe on him should receive: for the Holy Ghost was not yet given; because that Jesus was not yet glorified)" (John 7:38-39, KJV). Acts 5:32 refers to the Holy Spirit as "the Holy Ghost, whom God hath given to them that obey him" [32] (Acts 5:32, KJV). In other words, being saved requires obedience to God's commandments, and God gives His Holy Spirit to those who are saved and therefore obedient to His will.

The Apostle Paul explains in great detail the role of the Spirit of God in empowering and guiding the believer to do the will of God.

> For they that are after the flesh do mind the things of the flesh; but they that are after the Spirit the things of the Spirit. For to be carnally minded is death; but to be spiritually minded is life and peace. Because the carnal mind is enmity against God: for it is not subject to the law of God, neither indeed can be. So then they that are in the flesh cannot please God. But ye are not in the flesh, but in the Spirit, if so be that the Spirit of God dwell in you. Now if any man have not the Spirit of Christ, he is none of his. And if Christ be in you, the body is dead because of sin; but the Spirit is life because of righteousness. But if the Spirit of him that raised up Jesus from the dead dwell in you, he that raised up Christ from the dead shall also quicken your mortal bodies by his Spirit that dwelleth in you. Therefore, brethren, we are debtors, not to the flesh, to live after the flesh. For if ye live after the flesh, ye shall die: but if ye through the Spirit do mortify the deeds of the body, ye shall live. For as many as are led by the Spirit of God, they are the sons of God (Rom 1:5-14, KJV).

SEVENTH ELEMENT: Seventh, a Christian is a person whose reason for living is Christ. Paul said, "For to me to live is Christ, and to die is gain"(Phil. 1:20-22). Christ said, "My

27

meat is to do the will of him that sent me, and to finish his work" (John 4:34, KJV). Christ and Paul provide perfect examples of the total devotion and commitment required by someone whose reason for living is loving and serving God.

Christ also said, "He that loveth father or mother more than me is not worthy of me: and he that loveth son or daughter more than me is not worthy of me"(Matt. 10:36-38, KJV). If loving and serving God is not a man's top priority and primary objective, his reason for living, then he is in violation of the greatest commandment: "Thou shalt love the Lord thy God with all thy heart, and with all thy soul, and with all thy might" (Deut. 6:5, KJV. See also Matt. 22:37-38; Luke 10:27). He is also in violation of the first of the ten commandments: "Thou shalt have none other gods before me" (Deut. 5:7, KJV).

The author defines a man's faith or religion as his reason for living. Everyone has a faith or religion, a reason for living. A man's true faith or religion is the true reason he lives and votes that way that he does. A man who claims to be a Christian and attends church weekly but lives and votes contrary to Christian values is not a Christian.

CONCLUSION: Contrary to popular opinion, a Christian is not simply someone who believes in God or someone who accepts Christ as Savior. A Christian is someone who: (1) believes one true God, the Creator of all things seen and unseen (2) believes in a triune God, one God in three persons: Father, Son, and Holy Spirit; (3) is a repentant sinner; (4) is saved by faith in Christ as his Savior; (5) accepts Christ as the Lord of his life; (6) is empowered and guided by the Holy Spirit; and (7) is a person whose reason for living is Christ.

BIBLICAL LAW: BASIC PRINCIPLES

REASON FOR CHAPTER: Why does a chapter entitled "Biblical Law" immediately follow a chapter entitled "Defining Christian?" A Christian is by definition a follower of Christ who wants to love and serve God by doing "the will of the Father" by being obedient to God's laws revealed through Scripture. In other words, Christians need Scripture to live the Christian life. That is why Christ said, "Ye do err, not knowing the Scriptures, nor the power of God"(Matt. 22:28-30, KJV).

Many Christians and Christian leaders are surprisingly ignorant regarding basic principles of biblical law. There is very little emphasis on biblical law in seminaries, and many men in the ministry have little interest in law, politics, business, jobs, the economy, etc. They live in a different world and fail to provide the guidance that God offers through Scripture regarding these areas. Many concentrate on the love of God and neglect His holiness and righteousness. They fail to properly challenge Americans who live in a fantasy world where a loving God would never punish "good" people. Christians and Christian leaders fail to realize that study of biblical law provides amazing, fascinating insight into the heart and mind of God in many areas of life where they desperately need His guidance.

OLD TESTAMENT LAW: Some Christians claim that Jesus showed that Old Testament law should no longer be applied when He forgave the woman caught in adultery. The Pharisees tried to trap Jesus, knowing that the law called for stoning. Jesus evaded their trap by writing in the sand until all of the woman's accusers left. Then He said "Neither do I condemn thee: go, and sin no more"(John 8:10-12, KJV). However, Jesus was not a government official with authority or responsibility to impose punishment. Even a judge would not have authority to render judgment and impose the death penalty without a trial. When Christ returns, he will judge everyone.

Many Christians believe that Old Testament law is part of the Old Covenant that God had with the nation of Israel, and that it was replaced by the New Testament or New Covenant, which does not require obedience to Old Testament law. Some clergy might point to verses that seem to imply that the law was just a tutor to point sinners to Christ. "So that the law is become our tutor to bring us unto Christ, that we might be justified by faith. But now faith that is come, we are no longer under a tutor" (Gal. 3:24-25, ASV). "No longer under a tutor" means no longer under the law. However, assuming that one can therefore ignore the law would be totally contrary to the teachings of Christ and Scripture. God cares just as much about obedience to His laws today as when he killed thousands of His own people for what many today would consider minor disobedience.

Many Christians and religious leaders do not understand how Old Testament law applies to modern times. Christ said, "Think not that I am come to destroy the law, or the prophets: I am not come to destroy, but to fulfill. For verily I say unto you, till heaven and earth pass, one jot or one tittle shall in no wise pass from the law, till all be fulfilled" (Matt. 5:17-18, KJV). The law and the prophets are the books of law and the prophets in the Old Testament. The "jot" and "tittle" are the smallest parts of the Hebrew alphabet, similar to the dot on an "i" and apostrophe in the English language. Christ made it clear that He did not come to destroy Old Testament law, but to fulfill it, and that not even the smallest part of the law would "pass" until it was "fulfilled." As one of my professors in graduate school said, God the Father was not converted by Christ the Son. Christ's coming did not do away with Old Testament law. It fulfilled Old Testament laws related to payment for sin, because

30

He was the Lamb of God who gave His life as payment for sin, but all other laws remained in full effect.

LOVING GOD: As noted in the Introduction, the most important biblical law is the Greatest Commandment, first stated by Moses: "Thou shalt love the Lord thy God with all thy heart, and with all thy soul, and with all thy might" (Deut. 6:5, KJV). Christ said: "Thou shalt love the Lord thy God with all thy heart, and with all thy soul, and with all thy mind. This is the first and great commandment" (Matt. 22:37-38, KJV; see Luke 10:27).

Many Old and New Testament passages state that loving God requires obedience to his commandments. "For this is the love of God, that we keep his commandments: and his commandments are not grievous" (1 John 5:3, KJV). "If ye love me, keep my commandments" (John 14:15, KJV). "He that hath my commandments, and keepeth them, he it is that loveth me: and he that loveth me shall be loved of my Father, and I will love him, and will manifest myself to him" John 14:21 (KJV). "Therefore thou shalt love the LORD thy God, and keep his charge, and his statutes, and his judgments, and his commandments, always" (Deut. 11:1, KJV). "In that I command thee this day to love the LORD thy God, to walk in his ways, and to keep his commandments and his statutes and his judgments, that thou mayest live and multiply: and the LORD thy God shall bless thee in the land whither thou goest to possess it" (Deut. 30:16, KJV). "But take diligent heed to do the commandment and the law, which Moses the servant of the LORD charged you, to love the LORD your God, and to walk in all his ways, and to keep his commandments, and to cleave unto him, and to serve him with all your heart and with all your soul" (Joshua 22:5, KJV).

Four of the most important commandments that deal with loving God are the first four of the Ten Commandments:

I am the LORD thy God, which brought thee out of the land of Egypt, from the house of bondage. [First Commandment] Thou shalt have none other gods before me. [Second Commandment] Thou shalt not make thee any graven …for I the LORD thy God am a jealous God, visiting the iniquity of the fathers upon the children unto the third and fourth generation of them that hate me, And shewing mercy unto thousands of them that love me and keep my commandments. [Third Commandment] Thou shalt not take the name of the LORD thy God in vain: for the LORD will not hold him guiltless that taketh his name in vain. [Fourth Commandment] Keep the sabbath day to sanctify it… (Deut. 5:6-15, KJV).

Note that God brings terrible judgment upon those who hate Him, "visiting the iniquity of the fathers upon the children unto the third and fourth generation of them that hate me," but shows great mercy toward those who love him, "shewing mercy unto thousands of them that love me and keep my commandments" (Deut. 5:9-10, KJV). Many passages state that God shows love and mercy to those who love Him and keep his commandments (Ex. 20:6; Deut. 5:10; 7:9; 11:1-2, 13-14, 22-23; 19:9; Josh. 22:5-6; Neh. 1:5; Dan. 9:4; John 14:21; 15:10). Deuteronomy 7:9 (KJV) states: "Know therefore that the LORD thy God, he is God, the faithful God, which keepeth covenant and mercy with them that love him and keep his commandments to a thousand generations."

LOVING MAN: After Christ quoted the greatest commandment, He added the second greatest commandment.

Jesus said unto him, Thou shalt love the Lord thy God with all thy heart, and with all thy soul, and with all thy mind. This is the first and great commandment. And the second is like unto it,

Thou shalt love thy neighbour as thyself. On
these two commandments hang all the law and
the prophets (Matthew 22:37-40, KJV).

Note Christ's final words: "On these two commandments
hang all the law and the prophets" (Matt. 22:40, KJV). The law
and the prophets are the books of law and books of the prophets
of the Old Testament, which contain Old Testament law. Thus
Christ affirmed that all Old Testament law, which remains in
effect, "hangs" on these two commandments.

The primary means of loving one's neighbor is
obedience to the many commandments given through Scripture
related to treatment of others. "And this is love, that we walk
after his commandments. This is the commandment, That, as ye
have heard from the beginning, ye should walk in it" (2 John
1:6, KJV). "By this we know that we love the children of God,
when we love God, and keep his commandments" (1 John 5:2,
KJV). Examples commandment related to loving one's
neighbor include the final six of the ten commandments.

[Fifth Commandment] Honour thy father and thy mother,
as the LORD thy God hath commanded thee; that thy
days may be prolonged, and that it may go well with
thee, in the land which the LORD thy God giveth thee.
[Sixth Commandment] Thou shalt not kill.
[Seventh Commandment] Neither shalt thou commit
adultery.
[Eighth Commandment] Neither shalt thou steal.
[Ninth Commandment] Neither shalt thou bear false
witness against thy neighbour.
[Tenth Commandment] Neither shalt thou desire thy
neigh[bor]s wife, neither shalt thou covet thy
neigh[bor]'s house, his field, or his manservant, or his
maidservant, his ox, or his ass, or any thing that is thy
neigh[bor]'s. (Deut. 5:16-21, KJV).

HIGHER STANDARD: After declaring that He came not to destroy Old Testament law, but to fulfill it, Christ introduced a higher standard. First He clarified the importance of obedience to even the "least commandments." Then he reviewed many points of Old Testament law, and showed that he required even higher standards.

> Whosoever...shall break one of these least commandments, and shall teach men so, he shall be called the least in the kingdom of heaven: but whosoever shall do and teach them, the same shall be called great in the kingdom of heaven.... Ye have heard that it was said...Thou shalt not kill; and whosoever shall kill shall be in danger of the judgment: "But I say unto you, That whosoever is angry with his brother without a cause shall be in danger of the judgment.... Ye have heard that it was said... Thou shalt not commit adultery: But I say unto you, That whosoever looketh on a woman to lust after her hath committed adultery with her already in his heart.... It hath been said, Whosoever shall put away his wife, let him give her a writing of divorcement: But I say unto you, That whosoever shall put away his wife, saving for the cause of fornication, causeth her to commit adultery: and whosoever shall marry her that is divorced commit[s] adultery. Again, ye have heard that it hath been said... Thou shalt not forswear thyself, but shalt perform unto the Lord thine oaths: But I say unto you, Swear not at all.... But let your communication be, Yea, yea; Nay, nay: for whatsoever is more than these cometh of evil. Ye have heard that it hath been said, An eye for an eye, and a tooth for a tooth: But I say unto you, That ye resist not evil: but whosoever shall smite thee on thy right cheek, turn to him the other also.... Ye have heard that it hath been said, Thou shalt love thy neighbour, and hate thine enemy. But I say unto you, Love your enemies, bless them that curse you, do good to them that hate you, and pray for them which

34

despitefully use you, and persecute you; That ye may be the children of your Father which is in heaven …. <u>Be ye therefore perfect, even as your Father which is in heaven is perfect</u> (Matt. 5:17-49, KJV).

Christ established higher standards for murder, adultery, divorce, justice and mercy, and loving one's enemies. Then He gave the clincher, the bottom line, the principle that should govern the life of every Christian: "Be ye therefore perfect, even as your Father which is in heaven is perfect" (Matthew 5:49, KJV). In other words, Christians are called to be perfect not only through complete obedience to the letter of Old Testament law (every jot and title), but also through complete obedience to the much higher standard of the true spirit and intent of the law, as taught and lived by Christ. No Christian can be perfect like God the Father, but every Christian is commanded by Christ to strive for perfection. This means getting up after falling, repenting of wrongdoing, and continuing to run the race which Christians are called to run, striving for perfection.

<u>CONCLUSION</u>: So what does all this have to do with politics and elections? God provides much needed guidance to man through biblical law revealed through Scripture. Without biblical law, man cannot properly discern right from wrong. Being a Christian means not just believing in Christ as Lord and Savior, but taking up one's cross and following Christ, dying to self and living for Christ, and being obedient to God's commandments. These include all Old Testament and New Testament laws not fulfilled by the coming of Christ. Christ only fulfilled laws regarding sacrifice, because He was the Lamb of God, the final, perfect sacrifice. Christ made it perfectly clear that He did not come to abolish the law, but to fulfill it, and gave an even higher standard for obedience to biblical law revealed through the Old Testament, the only Scripture that existed at the time of Christ. Being a Christian requires voting for candidates that support God's laws revealed through Scripture.

35

JURISDICTION

SECTION REVIEW: This section reviews the importance of jurisdiction, one of the most important principles of law, to all Americans. The first chapter addresses the jurisdiction of the federal government of the United States. The second chapter discusses jurisdiction of church and state and the requirement that all Americans, Christian and non-Christian, properly acknowledge God.

CHAPTERS: Chapters in this section include the following:
3.1 Jurisdiction of U.S. Government: Foundation
3.2 Jurisdiction of U.S. Government: Constitution
3.3 Jurisdiction: Church and State
3.4 Jurisdiction: Rights and Freedoms

JURISDICTION FEDERAL GOVERNMENT: FOUNDATION

REASON FOR CHAPTER: Why does a chapter entitled Jurisdiction immediately follow a chapter on Biblical Law? Answer: Because government does not have authority to enforce all biblical law. The U.S. Constitution, the highest law of the land, defines the jurisdiction of the U.S. government.

LAW AND GOVERNMENT: Consider the importance of law to government. The legislative branch makes laws. The executive branch enforces the laws. The judicial branch decides cases and controversies with respect to application of the laws. In other words, the federal government makes, enforces, and decides cases or controversies regarding federal laws.

DEFINITION OF JURISDICTION: Jurisdiction is one of the most important legal principles taught in law school. Black's Law Dictionary gives an insightful definition of jurisdiction for the judicial branch of government. "A term of large and comprehensive import, and embraces every kind of judicial action...." It is the "power and authority of a court to hear and determine a judicial proceeding."[5] Black's Law Dictionary actually takes a couple pages to fully define the broad subject of jurisdiction. Readers of this book only need to know that the jurisdiction of the federal government is the "power and authority" that it has under the Constitution to make, enforce, and make judgments regarding application of federal law. In other words, the United States Constitution defines the responsibility and limits of power of the United States government.

---

[5] Henry Campbell Black, Black's Law Dictionary, 5th Ed., 1979, p 766.

BASIC DUTY OF GOVERNMENT: Understanding of the most basic, fundamental duty of government is essential to understanding of the jurisdiction of government. "YOU CANNOT DICTATE MORALITY" read the full-page newspaper advertisement in large, bold letters. It was many years ago, but I could never forget it. Many Americans, like Senator Biden, believe that abortion should be legal because no one has the right to "legislate morality" or to impose their morality on someone else. When asked when life began, Senator Obama said the answer to that question was "above his pay grade." But it was not above his pay grade to decide that the unborn child must die if not wanted by the mother. He actually said that he would not want one of his daughters to be punished by being forced to give birth to an unwanted child. Were Senators Obama and Biden right or wrong? Does government have the jurisdiction (power and authority) to dictate morality?" Anyone who cannot properly answer these simple questions cannot begin to understand the role, jurisdiction, or limits of authority of government.

In his letter to the Romans, the Apostle Paul helps one more clearly understand the jurisdiction of government. Romans 13:1-7 states:

> Let every soul be in subjection to the higher powers: for there is no power but of God; and the powers that be are ordained of God. Therefore he that resist[s] the power, withstand[s] the ordinance of God: and they that withstand shall receive to themselves judgment. For rulers are not a terror to the good work, but to the evil. And would thou have no fear of the power? do that which is good, and thou shalt have praise from the same: for he is a minister of God to thee for good. But if thou do that which is evil, be afraid; for he bear[s] not the sword in vain: for he is a

38

minister of God, an avenger for wrath to him that doeth evil. Wherefore ye must needs be in subjection, not only because of the wrath, but also for conscience' sake. For this cause ye pay tribute also; for they are ministers of God's service, attending continually upon this very thing. Render to all their dues: tribute to whom tribute is due; custom to whom custom; fear to whom fear; honor to whom honor (Rom 13:1-7, ASV).

In other words, government officials are "ministers of God" with jurisdiction (power, authority, and responsibility) to impose morality and punish evildoers. The primary reason they have a duty to punish criminal acts is not because they harm other citizens or because punishment best serves the accused, the victim, others, or the government, but because the criminal acts are morally wrong, they demand justice, and it is their God-given duty to ensure justice in accordance with God's laws as they are revealed through Scripture.

CAPITAL PUNISHMENT: An excellent example of the foregoing is God's commandment, given through Moses, regarding capital punishment for murder. Some Christians oppose capital punishment because they consider it murder or "cruel and unusual punishment." This passage proves how wrong they are in the eyes of God.

Whoso kill[s] any person, the murderer shall be put to death by the mouth of witnesses: but one witness shall not testify against any person to cause him to die. Moreover ye shall take no satisfaction for the life of a murderer, which is guilty of death: but he shall be surely put to death. And ye shall take no satisfaction for him that is fled to the city of his refuge, that he should come again to dwell in the land, until the death of the priest. So ye shall not pollute the land wherein ye are: for blood it

39

defile[s] the land: and the land cannot be cleansed of the blood that is shed therein, but by the blood of him that shed it. Defile not therefore the land which ye shall inhabit, wherein I dwell: for I the LORD dwell among the children of Israel (Num. 35:30-34, KJV).

God demands that a murderer be put to death to cleanse the defilement of the land by the murder. If the murderer is not put to death, the nation remains defiled in the eyes of God by the murder and lack of justice. Government officials are ministers of God with a duty to ensure justice in the eyes of God through application of nothing less than the death penalty to citizens convicted of murder. Other verses show that accidental killing does not merit the death penalty.

DECLARATION OF INDEPENDENCE: To have the best possible understanding of the jurisdiction of the federal government of the United States, it best to start not with the United States Constitution, but with the Declaration of Independence. This may sound strange, but the reasons will become clear after reading both documents. See Appendix for full text of the Declaration of Independence.

The first sentence of the Declaration of Independence announces its purpose: to "declare the causes which impel them to the separation" from Great Britain. The first sentence cites, as justification, the "Laws of nature and Nature's God."[6] The founding fathers understood that: (1) God created all things seen and unseen and all laws that govern all things seen and unseen; (2) these laws justified the Declaration of Independence from Great Britain; and (3) these laws were the legal foundation for the establishment of a new, independent nation.

---

[6] "Declaration of Independence," U.S. National Archives & Records Administration, http://www.archives.gov/exhibits/charters/declaration.html.

The first cause for separation cited refers to God as the Creator who continues to create all men equal. This belief is based upon Scripture. God told the prophet Jeremiah:"Before I formed thee in the belly I knew thee; and before thou [came] forth out of the womb I sanctified thee, and I ordained thee a prophet unto the nations" (Jer. 1:5, KJV). Job said, "Did not he that made me in the womb make him? and did not one fashion us in the womb?" (Job 31:15, KJV). King David said, "I will praise thee; for I am fearfully and wonderfully made: marvelous are thy works; and that my soul know[s] right well. My substance was not hid from thee, when I was made in secret, and curiously wrought in the lowest parts of the earth. Thine eyes did see my substance, yet being unperfected; and in thy book all my members were written, which in continuance were fashioned, when as yet there was none of them" (Ps. 139: 14-16, KJV). See also Beck. 11:5; Isa. 44:2, 24; 49:1-5; Jer. 1:5; Luke 1:15,41-44.

The first cause for separation then states that God gives every man "certain unalienable Rights, that among these are Life, Liberty and the pursuit of Happiness."[7] It states "that to secure these rights, Governments are instituted among Men, deriving their just powers from the consent of the governed" and "that whenever any Form of Government becomes destructive of these ends, it is the Right of the People to alter or to abolish it, and to institute new Government, laying its foundation on such principles and organizing its powers in such form, as to them shall seem most likely to effect their Safety and Happiness."[8] "Unalienable Rights" are God-given rights which no man or government has the right to take away from any man. It is the violation of these rights, which God gives to every man, that justify the Declaration of Independence from Great Britain and the formation of a new government.

---

[7] Ibid.
[8] Ibid.

The Declaration states that "Governments long established should not be changed for light and transient causes" but when there is a "long train of abuses and usurpations...it is their right, it is their duty, to throw off such Government, and to provide new Guards for their future security."[9] These "new Guards" are the protections embodied in the U.S. Constitution.

The next section of the Declaration of Independence gives an incredibly long list of the "repeated injuries and usurpations" of the "King of Great Britain...all having in direct object the establishment of an absolute Tyranny over these States."[10] These abuses justified the Declaration of Independence from Great Britain.

> He has refused his Assent to Laws, the most wholesome and necessary for the public good.
> He has forbidden his Governors to pass Laws of immediate and pressing importance, unless suspended in their operation till his Assent should be obtained; and when so suspended, he has utterly neglected to attend to them.
> He has refused to pass other Laws for the accommodation of large districts of people, unless those people would relinquish the right of Representation in the Legislature, a right inestimable to them and formidable to tyrants only.
> He has called together legislative bodies at places unusual, uncomfortable, and distant from the depository of their public Records, for the sole purpose of fatiguing them into compliance with his measures.
> He has dissolved Representative Houses repeatedly, for opposing with manly firmness his invasions on the rights of the people.
> He has refused for a long time, after such dissolutions, to

[9] Ibid.
[10] Ibid.

cause others to be elected; whereby the Legislative powers, incapable of Annihilation, have returned to the People at large for their exercise; the State remaining in the mean time exposed to all the dangers of invasion from without, and convulsions within.

He has [endeavored] to prevent the population of these States; for that purpose obstructing the Laws for Naturalization of Foreigners; refusing to pass others to encourage their migrations hither, and raising the conditions of new Appropriations of Lands.

He has obstructed the Administration of Justice, by refusing his Assent to Laws for establishing Judiciary powers.

He has made Judges dependent on his Will alone, for the tenure of their offices, and the amount and payment of their salaries.

He has erected a multitude of New Offices, and sent hither swarms of Officers to harass our people, and eat out their substance.

He has kept among us, in times of peace, Standing Armies without the Consent of our legislatures.

He has affected to render the Military independent of and superior to the Civil power.

He has combined with others to subject us to a jurisdiction foreign to our constitution, and unacknowledged by our laws; giving his Assent to their Acts of pretended Legislation:

For Quartering large bodies of armed troops among us:

For protecting them, by a mock Trial, from punishment for any Murders which they should commit on the Inhabitants of these States:

For cutting off our Trade with all parts of the world:

For imposing Taxes on us without our Consent:

For depriving us in many cases, of the benefits of Trial by Jury:

For transporting us beyond Seas to be tried for pretended offences

For abolishing the free System of English Laws in a [neighboring] Province, establishing therein an Arbitrary government, and enlarging its Boundaries so as to render it at once an example and fit instrument for introducing the same absolute rule into these Colonies:

For taking away our Charters, abolishing our most valuable Laws, and altering fundamentally the Forms of our Governments:

For suspending our own Legislatures, and declaring themselves invested with power to legislate for us in all cases whatsoever.

He has abdicated Government here, by declaring us out of his Protection and waging War against us.

He has plundered our seas, ravaged our Coasts, burnt our towns, and destroyed the lives of our people. He is at this time transporting large Armies of foreign Mercenaries to [complete] the works of death, desolation and tyranny, already begun with circumstances of Cruelty & perfidy scarcely paralleled in the most barbarous ages, and totally unworthy the Head of a civilized nation.

He has constrained our fellow Citizens taken Captive on the high Seas to bear Arms against their Country, to become the executioners of their friends and Brethren, or to fall themselves by their Hands. He has excited domestic insurrections amongst us, and has [endeavored] to bring on the inhabitants of our frontiers, the merciless Indian Savages, whose known rule of warfare, is an undistinguished destruction of all ages, sexes and conditions.

In every stage of these Oppressions We have Petitioned for Redress in the most humble terms: Our repeated Petitions have been answered only by repeated injury. A Prince whose character is thus marked by every act which may define a Tyrant, is unfit to be the ruler of a free people.[11]

---

[11] Ibid.

After listing the many abuses of the King of Great Britain, the Declaration of Independence briefly states the efforts the Colonies made to resolve their problems with Great Britain, and the total lack of positive response to their efforts.

The final section of the Declaration of Independence states,

> We, therefore, the Representatives of the united States of America, in General Congress, Assembled, <u>appealing to the Supreme Judge of the world</u>...solemnly publish and declare, That these United Colonies are, and of Right ought to be <u>Free and Independent States</u>; that they are <u>Absolved from all Allegiance to the British Crown</u>, and that <u>all political connection</u> between them and the State of Great Britain, is and ought to be <u>totally dissolved</u>; and that as Free and Independent States, they have full Power to levy War, conclude Peace, contract Alliances, establish Commerce, and to do all other Acts and Things which Independent States may of right do. [12]

The appeal to the "Supreme Judge of the world" is an appeal to God. The last sentence of the Declaration of Independence states, "And for the support of this Declaration, with a firm reliance on the protection of divine Providence, we mutually pledge to each other our Lives, our Fortunes and our sacred Honor."[13] "Firm reliance on the protection of divine Providence" means firm reliance on God.

CONCLUSION: So what does the Declaration of Independence tell us about the Founding Fathers? They had a biblical worldview. They understood that: (1) God created all things seen and unseen and all laws that govern all things seen

---

[12] <u>Ibid.</u>
[13] <u>Ibid.</u>

45

and unseen; (2) God creates all men equal with "certain unalienable Rights that [...include] Life, Liberty and the pursuit of Happiness;" (3) "to secure these rights, Governments are instituted among Men, deriving their just powers from the consent of the governed;" (4) "whenever any...Government becomes destructive of these ends, it is the Right of the People to alter or to abolish it, and to institute new Government;" (5) this new government must be established in accordance with God's laws to protect the God-given unalienable rights of all men.[14]

---

[14] Ibid.

JURISDICTION FEDERAL GOVERNMENT: CONSTITUTION

REASON FOR CHAPTER: To protect the God-given unalienable rights of life, liberty, and the pursuit of happiness, and to protect citizens from the abuses of power of the King of Great Britain, the Founding Fathers drafted a Constitution which made the federal government of the United States a government of enumerated powers. Each branch of government only had the powers granted to it by the Constitution. All other powers were reserved to the states. This book will concentrate on the parts of the Constitution that state what powers are granted to the federal government, not on administrative sections.

The Constitution is divided into a preamble and seven articles. The short preamble states:

> We the People of the United States, in Order to form a more perfect Union, establish Justice, insure domestic Tranquility, provide for the common [defense], promote the general Welfare, and secure the Blessings of Liberty to ourselves and our Posterity, do ordain and establish this Constitution for the United States of America.[15]

The preamble states the general purpose of the Constitution. It does not grant any powers to any branch of the federal government. If, for example, "promote the general Welfare" granted any authority, it would grant almost unlimited authority to all branches of the federal government, which would destroy the intent of the signers to create a government of

---

[15] "Constitution of the United States," U.S. National Archives & Records Administration, http://www.archives.gov/exhibits/charters/constitution.html.

enumerated powers where each branch only had those powers granted to it by the Constitution.

The first three articles of the Constitution grant powers to the three branches of the federal government. The first, longest, most important article grants powers to a Congress. Article I is divided into ten sections. Section 1 states, "All legislative Powers herein granted shall be vested in a Congress of the United States, which shall consist of a Senate and House of Representatives." Sections 2-7 state how members of Congress are elected, serve, are paid, etc. See Appendix B for text.

Section 7 addresses raising taxes, "All Bills for raising Revenue shall originate in the House of Representatives; but the Senate may propose or concur with Amendments as on other Bills." The remainder of Section 7 reviews how bills are voted upon, passed, and become law. See Appendix B for text.

Section 8 states powers granted to Congress. Note that there is no mention of education, healthcare, or any other social programs.

> *The Congress shall have Power To lay and collect Taxes, Duties, Imposts and Excises, to pay the Debts and provide for the common Defence and general Welfare of the United States; but all Duties, Imposts and Excises shall be uniform throughout the United States;*
> *To borrow Money on the credit of the United States;*
> *To regulate Commerce with foreign Nations, and among the several States, and with the Indian Tribes;*
> To establish an uniform Rule of Naturalization, and uniform Laws on the subject of Bankruptcies throughout the United States;
> To coin Money, regulate the Value thereof, and of foreign Coin, and fix the Standard of Weights and Measures;

To provide for the Punishment of counterfeiting the Securities and current Coin of the United States;
To establish Post Offices and post Roads;
To promote the Progress of Science and useful Arts, by securing for limited Times to Authors and Inventors the exclusive Right to their respective Writings and Discoveries;
To constitute Tribunals inferior to the supreme Court;
To define and punish Piracies and Felonies committed on the high Seas, and Offences against the Law of Nations;
To declare War, grant Letters of Marque and Reprisal, and make Rules concerning Captures on Land and Water;
To raise and support Armies, but no Appropriation of Money to that Use shall be for a longer Term than two Years;
To provide and maintain a Navy;
To make Rules for the Government and Regulation of the land and naval Forces;
To provide for calling forth the Militia to execute the Laws of the Union, suppress Insurrections and repel Invasions;
To provide for organizing, arming, and disciplining, the Militia, and for governing such Part of them as may be employed in the Service of the United States, reserving to the States respectively, the Appointment of the Officers, and the Authority of training the Militia according to the discipline prescribed by Congress;
To exercise exclusive Legislation in all Cases whatsoever, over such District (not exceeding ten Miles square) as may, by Cession of particular States, and the Acceptance of Congress, become the Seat of the Government of the United States, and to exercise like Authority over all Places purchased by the Consent of the Legislature of the State in which the Same shall be, for the Erection of Forts, Magazines, Arsenals, dock-Yards, and other needful Buildings;--And

To make all Laws which shall be necessary and proper for carrying into Execution the foregoing Powers, and all other Powers vested by this Constitution in the Government of the United States, or in any Department or Officer thereof.

Section 9 states limitations on the powers of Congress. Section 10 states rules regarding states (treaties, duties on imports or exports, etc.). See Appendix B for text of these sections.

The second article of the Constitution grants powers to the President, the executive branch of the government. It is divided into four sections. Section 1 states how the President is elected, serves, is paid, etc. See Appendix B for text. Section 2 states powers granted to the President. Note that there is no mention of education, healthcare, or any other social programs.

The President shall be Commander in Chief of the Army and Navy of the United States, and of the Militia of the several States, when called into the actual Service of the United States; he may require the Opinion, in writing, of the principal Officer in each of the executive Departments, upon any Subject relating to the Duties of their respective Offices, and he shall have Power to grant Reprieves and Pardons for Offences against the United States, except in Cases of Impeachment.
He shall have Power, by and with the Advice and Consent of the Senate, to make Treaties, provided two thirds of the Senators present concur; and he shall nominate, and by and with the Advice and Consent of the Senate, shall appoint Ambassadors, other public Ministers and Consuls, Judges of the supreme Court, and all other Officers of the United States, whose Appointments are not herein otherwise provided for, and which shall be established by Law: but the Congress may by Law vest the Appointment of such inferior Officers,

as they think proper, in the President alone, in the Courts of Law, or in the Heads of Departments.

The President shall have Power to fill up all Vacancies that may happen during the Recess of the Senate, by granting Commissions which shall expire at the End of their next Session.

Section 3 states how President will work with Congress (State of Union, etc.). Section 4 states grounds for impeachment of the President, Vice President, and all "civil Officers of the United States." See Appendix B for text.

The third article of the Constitution grants powers to the Supreme Court and federal courts, the judicial branch of the federal government. It is divided into three sections. Section 1 states how the judges will serve, be paid, etc. Section 3 addresses treason against the United States. Only Section 2 states powers of the courts: Note that there is no mention of education, healthcare, or any other social programs.

The judicial Power shall extend to all Cases, in Law and Equity, arising under this Constitution, the Laws of the United States, and Treaties made, or which shall be made, under their Authority;--to all Cases affecting Ambassadors, other public Ministers and Consuls;--to all Cases of admiralty and maritime Jurisdiction;--to Controversies to which the United States shall be a Party;--to Controversies between two or more States;-- between a State and Citizens of another State;--between Citizens of different States;--between Citizens of the same State claiming Lands under Grants of different States, and between a State, or the Citizens thereof, and foreign States, Citizens or Subjects.

In all Cases affecting Ambassadors, other public Ministers and Consuls, and those in which a State shall be Party, the supreme Court shall have original Jurisdiction. In all the other Cases before mentioned, the

51

supreme Court shall have appellate Jurisdiction, both as to Law and Fact, with such Exceptions, and under such Regulations as the Congress shall make.
The Trial of all Crimes, except in Cases of Impeachment, shall be by Jury; and such Trial shall be held in the State where the said Crimes shall have been committed; but when not committed within any State, the Trial shall be at such Place or Places as the Congress may by Law have directed.

The fourth article of the Constitution addresses issues related to the states. It is divided into four sections. The fifth article of the Constitution states the rules regarding proposal and ratification of amendments to the Constitution. The sixth article declares "this Constitution, and the Laws of the United States which shall be made in Pursuance thereof…the supreme Law of the Land; and the Judges in every State shall be bound thereby…." It also states that "Senators and Representatives…and the Members of…State Legislatures, and all executive and judicial Officers…of the United States and of the…States, shall be bound by Oath or Affirmation, to support this Constitution; but no religious Test shall ever be required as a Qualification to any Office…"[16] The seventh and final article of the Constitution only deals with details of ratification of the Constitution by the states in 1787.

BILL OF RIGHTS: In 1789 Congress ratified the first ten amendments to the Constitution, known as the "Bill of Rights."[17] Although all of the amendments are important for protection of freedoms enjoyed by Americans, this book will only concentrate on the few cited herein.

---

[16] Ibid.
[17] "Bill of Rights," U.S. National Archives & Records Administration, http://www.archives.gov/exhibits/charters/constitution.html.

The vitally important First Amendment protects the freedoms of religion, speech, and assembly.

Congress shall make no law respecting an establishment of religion, or prohibiting the free exercise thereof; or abridging the freedom of speech, or of the press; or the right of the people peaceably to assemble, and to petition the Government for a redress of grievances.

The Second Amendment protects the right to bear arms. "A well regulated Militia, being necessary to the security of a free State, the right of the people to keep and bear Arms, shall not be infringed." Note that the absolute "right of the people to keep and bear Arms" which "shall not be infringed" is linked to defense of the state.

The Sixth Amendment states, "In all criminal prosecutions, the accused shall enjoy the right to a speedy and public trial, by an impartial jury…and to have the Assistance of Counsel for his [defense]." Note that these rights apply to criminal cases, not civil cases.

The Ninth Amendment states, "The enumeration in the Constitution, of certain rights, shall not be construed to deny or disparage others retained by the people." In other words, the fact that the Constitution and Bill of Rights list and describe certain rights does not mean these are their only rights.

The tenth amendment simply states the vitally important principle that "powers not delegated to the United States by the Constitution, nor prohibited by it to the States, are reserved to the States respectively, or to the people."[18] All rights not given by the Constitution to the federal government are "reserved to the states." This vitally important amendment is additional

---

[18] Ibid.

confirmation that the federal government only has those powers that are specifically granted to it by the Constitution.

CONCLUSION: So what the Constitution say about the jurisdiction of the federal government? First, it is a government of enumerated powers; each branch only has those powers granted by the Constitution. Article I grants powers to Congress (Senate and House of Representatives). Article II grants powers to the executive branch (President). Article III grants powers to the judicial branch (Supreme Court and federal courts). No part of the Constitution grants any authority regarding education, healthcare, or any other social programs. Detailed discussion of all powers granted to the federal government is beyond the scope of this book. It concentrates on the primary problem, the exercise of powers never granted by the Constitution.

The first ten amendments to the Constitution are known as the Bill of Rights. The first protects the freedoms of religion, speech, and assembly. The second grants the right to bear arms. The sixth grants the right to a criminal defense attorney, etc. The ninth protects other rights of the people. The tenth makes it clear that the federal government only has those powers granted to it by the Constitution, and that all other powers are reserved to the states.

JURISDICTION: CHURCH AND STATE

REASON FOR CHAPTER: Why does a chapter entitled "Jurisdiction: Church and State" follow a chapter entitled "Jurisdiction: Federal Government"? Answer: Jurisdiction of church and state is a major issue deserving separate treatment from basic principles of jurisdiction. Most Americans do not understand the limits of power and authority of church and government.

SEPARATION OF CHURCH AND STATE: Most Americans believe in separation of church and state, but differ sharply in what they believe it means. Many believe that the words "separation of church and state" are in the U.S. Constitution. They are not. They were first used by Thomas Jefferson to refer to the need to keep the church free from interference by government and to not have a state church improperly ruled by the government as in England. Over one hundred years later, they were used by the Supreme Court to define the limits of authority of church and state. Today many Americans believe in separation of church and state in a way that would be anathema to the Founding Fathers. Democrats have reversed the meaning of Jefferson's words, using them to justify action against the church and to silence Christian leaders, a violation of their rights to freedom of religion and freedom of speech. See Bill of Rights, Appendix C.

BELIEF IN GOD: Today many Americans believe that separation of church means that teachers and elected officials cannot rightfully be expected to believe in God or creation because these are matters of personal faith that do not belong in public schools, government, or the workplace. This is totally contrary to Scripture, common sense, and the beliefs of the

Founding Fathers.

Belief in God and creation does not require faith. It only requires a modicum of common sense. "We hold these truths to be self-evident, that all men are created equal, that they are endowed by their Creator with certain unalienable Rights...." (Declaration of Independence, Appendix A.) The United States was founded upon belief in God and creation. The Founding Fathers understood that belief in God, creation, and God's laws were common sense, self-evident truths. The most amazing common sense, self-evident truth embraced by the founding fathers was that God continues to create all men within their mothers, and to endow them with certain God-given unalienable rights which no man or government can rightfully take from another man. The Founding Fathers believed that it was the violation of these rights that justified the Declaration of Independence, Revolutionary War, and establishment of the United States of America.

Anyone who does not believe in God and creation is a fool. No fool should be trusted with any teaching or leadership position. King David said, "The fool has said in his heart, 'There is no God.'" (Psalm 14:1-3; 53:1-3). In other words, only an absolute fool refuses to acknowledge the existence of God. Scripture teaches through King Solomon and other authors of Proverbs, that the fear of God is the beginning of wisdom.

Belief in God does not constitute endorsement of any religion. Many religions believe in God, and many individuals who are not part of any known religion believe in God. Belief in Christ is totally different. Neither Scripture nor the Founding Fathers stated that knowledge of Christ is a common sense, self-evident truth. God has not revealed Christ through creation. It takes acceptance of a gift of faith from God to believe in Christ because the cross is foolishness to man but the wisdom and power of God (1 Cor. 1:18-25). Belief in Christ as the Son of God is a tenant of one religion—Christianity.

56

ACKNOWLEDGMENT OF GOD: Do Christian and non-Christian teachers, professors, employers, judges, and government leaders have a right to impose their personal belief in God and creation upon their students, employees, courts, and citizens? Yes! Absolutely! All Americans have a duty to acknowledge God as the Creator of all things seen and unseen and of the laws that govern all things seen and unseen.

Why do all Americans, especially those in teaching or leadership positions, have a duty to acknowledge God? First, it is not because the Founding Fathers or Declaration of Independence acknowledged God. No one has any obligation to acknowledge anything just because the Founding Fathers acknowledged it. Second, it is not because Scripture acknowledges God. Scripture acknowledges Christ as Lord and Savior, but non-Christians cannot be required to acknowledge Christ as Savior. However, Scripture does explain why the Founding Fathers and the Declaration of Independence properly acknowledged God.

In his letter to the Romans, the Apostle Paul wrote,

For the wrath of God is revealed from heaven against all ungodliness and unrighteousness of men, who hold the truth in unrighteousness; Because that which may be known of God is manifest in them; for God hath shewed it unto them. For the invisible things of him from the creation of the world are clearly seen, being understood by the things that are made, even his eternal power and Godhead; so that they are without excuse: Because that, when they knew God, they glorified him not as God, neither were thankful; but became vain in their imaginations, and their foolish heart was darkened. Professing themselves to be wise, they became fools…"

(Romans 1:18-22, KJV).

First, many Americans believe that they have complete freedom to choose whether or not to believe in God. They do not. No man has any excuse for failure to believe in God because God has revealed the "invisible things" about Himself, including His "eternal power and Godhead," to all men so "they are without excuse." These "invisible things" about God are "clearly seen, being understood by the things that are made." In other words, God reveals Himself to man through creation. Also, "that which may be known of God is manifest in them" (in all men). God personally reveals Himself to all men.

Second, many Americans live as though they do not presently answer to God for their actions. They are wrong. The "wrath of God **is** revealed" (present tense) against "all ungodliness and unrighteousness of men." In other words, Americans are suffering the wrath of God today.

Third, Americans fail to understand why they suffer God's wrath. They suffer because they "glorified him not as God, neither were thankful." In other words, they suffer because they failed to properly acknowledge God and be thankful for His many blessings.

Fourth, Americans fail to understand how they suffer the wrath of God. "Because… they glorified him not as God, neither were thankful" they "became vain in their imaginations, and their foolish heart was darkened. Professing themselves to be wise, they became fools…" Those words describe many Americans today. They think they are wise, but they are absolute fools. They cannot see the light of the truth because their hearts are darkened. They have become vain and foolish in their thinking.

Vain and foolish thinking are not the only ways Americans suffer God's judgment. The "wrath of God is revealed from heaven against all ungodliness and unrighteousness of men." In other words, Americans suffer the wrath of God for "all ungodliness and unrighteousness."

Consider the extreme ignorance and absolute foolishness of teachers and professors who believe that they can properly teach their students without teaching the self-evident, common sense truths embodied in the Declaration of Independence i.e. that God is the Creator of all things seen and unseen, to include all students, and the Creator of all laws that govern all things seen and unseen, to include all laws of mathematics and science, and laws that govern men and governments.

God has ordained that man must live by faith. Every man has a faith or religion that is his reason for living. The most important thing taught in schools is not reading, writing, arithmetic, or other academic subjects. It is faith. Today students are taught to not acknowledge or have faith in God and not to respect, fear, love or serve God or lead God-centered lives. They are taught that life is a meaningless product of evolutionary chance and that they should have faith in themselves, lead self-centered lives, and do whatever is right in their own eyes, without reference to God or His unchanging moral laws, laws rooted in His unchanging character.

Consider the extreme ignorance of judges who have studied law for years, but refuse to acknowledge the Supreme Lawgiver, the God who created the laws that govern all things seen and unseen. They are fools who cannot be trusted to render wise judgments. Examples are liberal justices on the Supreme Court who rule totally contrary to God's laws.

Consider extreme foolishness of government leaders who fail to properly acknowledge God. They cannot be trusted to enact, enforce, or properly adjudicate laws in accordance with God's laws. Examples include members of Congress who vote totally contrary to God's laws.

<u>FREEDOM OF SPEECH, FREEDOM OF RELIGION</u>: Democrats have repeatedly tried to enact laws to silence Christians, to eliminate their competition during national elections. No group of Americans has more restrictions on its freedom of speech and freedom of religion than Christians. The U.S. Supreme Court actually approved laws designed for organized crime for use against anti-abortion protestors. During 2008, Democrats tried to enact legislation to silence Christian and conservative talk shows. A law nicknamed the LBJ law because President Lyndon Baines Johnson signed it to silence his critics, threatens the tax-exempt status of any church or religious organization that endorses any candidate. Every religious leader has a duty to provide moral guidance to his congregation regarding all areas of life, to include politics. The Founding Fathers would be absolutely shocked to learn that pastors have been silenced in the name of "separation of church and state." Today most judges fail to realize that these laws are clear violations of freedom of speech and freedom of religion.

The author of this book had the honor of asking U.S. Supreme Court Justice Anthony Scalia one question during his visit to Regent University. He asked why the Supreme Court permitted the voice of moral leaders to be silenced. Justice Scalia asked if he would give the same rights to an ACLU attorney. When he said that he would be inclined to do so, Scalia said that he did not have a logical problem, but that the hands of the Supreme Court were tied by Congress, meaning by the LBJ law. Justice Scalia should be respected for his response. Many liberal judges show little respect for laws enacted by Congress or state legislatures. However, the author respectfully disagrees. The Supreme Court is one of the three branches of the federal government with responsibility to serve as part of the checks and balances established by the Founding Fathers. It has a duty to correct Congress when they enact a law that is so clearly a violation of the U.S. Constitution's protections of freedom of religion and freedom of speech. See Bill of Rights, Appendix C.

CONCLUSION: The Founding Fathers of the United States had a godly, biblical understanding of the jurisdiction of church and state clearly reflected in the Declaration of Independence, which began with what they clearly understood to be the only proper justification for declaration of independence from Great Britain. That justification was based upon understanding that: (1) God created all things seen and unseen and all the laws that govern all things seen and unseen; (2) God continues to create all men equal, with certain God-given unalienable rights; and (3) only repeated extreme violation of these rights justified declaration of independence and the establishment of a new government.

Today most Americans, to include most lawyers and judges, have a totally wrong understanding of the jurisdiction of church and state and the simple self-evident common sense truths that this nation was founded upon. They exclude God, creation, and God's laws from politics, government, schools, and the workplace. They completely fail to recognize that all Americans have an absolute duty to properly acknowledge God in politics, government, schools, and the workplace in the same way that our nation's Founding Fathers acknowledged Him. They also completely fail to understand that failure to properly acknowledge, respect and fear God reduces one to vain thinking and absolute foolishness because darkened hearts cannot see the light of truth. They fail to recognize this because they have already suffered the judgment of God due to their failure to properly acknowledge Him in all areas.

The greatest fools are those who have studied science or law but cannot see the Creator or Supreme Lawgiver; they cannot see the forest because there are so many trees. Many government leaders do great harm to our beloved nation by failing to acknowledge God, ask for His much needed guidance and blessings, and making, enforcing, and judging laws in accordance with God's laws. Many teachers and professors do

61

great injury to and handicap their students by teaching them that they can determine truth and right and wrong without God or His laws. All Americans, especially teachers and government leaders, have a duty to properly acknowledge God, pray for His guidance and blessings, and live and vote in accordance with His laws.[19]

If President Obama is reelected and Democrats have a majority in the House and Senate, Congress will enact laws to further restrict the freedom of speech and freedom of religion of Christians. If President Obama is reelected, he will appoint liberal federal judges and/or Supreme Court Justices who do not understand or respect the limits of authority imposed on government by the Constitution and legislate from the bench to further restrict the freedom of speech and freedom of religion of Christians and other Americans.

---

[19] George Washington would not allow his troops to curse, for fear of losing God's blessings. All Americans should be familiar with the beautiful painting of General Washington during the Revolutionary War, kneeling in the snow, praying for God's guidance and blessing. Americans need godly Christian leaders like George Washington in government.

JURISDICTION: RIGHTS AND FREEDOMS

REASON FOR CHAPTER: Why is chapter on Jurisdiction: Rights and Freedoms included in the section on Jurisdiction? First, parts of the U.S. Constitution grant specific rights to all Americans. Many of these rights are embodied in the first ten amendments to the U.S. Constitution, known as the Bill of Rights. Second, many Americans mistakenly believe that they have many rights under the Constitution which they do not have. This greatly impacts politics, government, and the federal laws that Americans live under.

RIGHTS TO LIFE, LIBERTY, AND THE PURSUIT OF HAPPINESS: The U.S. Constitution does not grant any American the rights to life, liberty, or the pursuit of happiness. The Declaration of Independence properly acknowledges that these are God-given inalienable rights which no man or government can rightfully take from any man.[20]

RIGHTS TO FREEDOM OF SPEECH AND FREEDOM OF RELIGION: The First Amendment to the Constitution grants every American the rights to freedom of speech and freedom of religion. It states:

> Congress shall make no law respecting an establishment of religion, or prohibiting the free exercise thereof; or abridging the freedom of speech, or of the press; or the right of the people peaceably to assemble, and to petition the Government for a redress of grievances.[21]

---

[20] "Declaration of Independence," U.S. National Archives & Records Administration, http://www.archives.gov/exhibits/charters/declaration.html
[21] "Bill of Rights," U.S. National Archives & Records Administration, http://www.archives.gov/exhibits/charters/constitution.html.

The "LBJ law," which threatens the tax-exempt status of any church or religious organization that endorses any candidate, is totally unconstitutional. The Obama Administration's mandate that forces Catholic and other religious institutions to provide contraceptives, abortions, abortive drugs, and other medical products or procedures that violate their deeply held religious or moral convictions is the most egregious violation of the First Amendment to the U.S. Constitution by a President in the history of the United States.[22]

RIGHT TO AN ATTORNEY: The Sixth Amendment to the Constitution grants every American accused of a crime the right to a criminal defense attorney. There is no right to an attorney for civil cases. The Sixth Amendment states:

> In all criminal prosecutions, the accused shall enjoy the right to a speedy and public trial, by an impartial jury of the State and district wherein the crime shall have been committed, which district shall have been previously ascertained by law, and to be informed of the nature and cause of the accusation; to be confronted with the witnesses against him; to have compulsory process for obtaining witnesses in his favor, and to have the Assistance of Counsel for his defence.[23]

RIGHT TO BEAR ARMS: The Second Amendment to the Constitution grants every American the rights to bear arms. The Second Amendment states: "A well regulated Militia, being necessary to the security of a free State, the right of the people to keep and bear Arms, shall not be infringed."[24]

---

[22] "Where Do the Candidates Stand on Life: Mitt Romney, Barack Obama," National Right to Life Committee, http://www.nrlc.org.
[23] "Bill of Rights."
[23] "Where Do the Candidates Stand on Life: Mitt Romney, Barack Obama."
[24] Ibid.

RIGHT TO EDUCATION: The U.S. Constitution does not grant any American the right to an education. The United States government has no constitutional authority to make any laws regarding what person or organization provides or pays for education. The federal government has no authority to grant college student loans. Many state constitutions may grant citizens the right to a public education paid for by other citizens, but there is no right to any education under the Constitution of the United States.

RIGHT TO HEALTHCARE: The U.S. Constitution does not grant any American the right to any healthcare paid for by other Americans. The United States government has no constitutional authority to make any laws regarding what persons or organizations provide or pay for healthcare. See chapters on Obamacare and Supreme Court.

RIGHT TO WOMEN'S HEALTHCARE: The U.S. Constitution does not grant any American woman the right to any healthcare paid for by other Americans. The United States government has no constitutional authority to make any laws regarding what persons or organizations provide or pays for a women's healthcare. See chapters on War on Women, Obamacare, and Supreme Court.

CONCLUSION: The Bill of Rights, the first ten amendments to the Constitution, grants all Americans the rights of freedom of religion, freedom of speech, right to bear arms, right to a criminal defense attorney, and many other rights enumerated therein. However, no part of the U.S. Constitution grants any American any right to education or healthcare paid for by other Americans.

The federal government of the United States is a government of enumerated powers. Each branch of the government only has those powers granted to it by the U.S. Constitution. No part of the Constitution grants any branch of the federal government any authority to make any laws regarding what persons or organizations provide or pay for education or healthcare. The basic principles in this chapter apply to many other areas.

BIBLICAL LAW ON HOT POLITICAL TOPICS

SECTION REVIEW: This section reviews biblical law on hot political topics. Biblical law is God's law revealed through Scripture. Biblical law reveals the heart and mind of God on difficult subjects that sharply divide Americans. The first chapter reviews biblical law on homosexuality and gay marriage. The second chapter addresses biblical law on abortion. The third chapter discusses biblical law on government and the economy. The fourth chapter reviews biblical law on taxing the rich.

CHAPTERS: Chapters in this section include the following:
4.1 Homosexuality and Same-Sex Marriage
4.2 Abortion
4.3 Government and the Economy
4.4 Fairness: Taxing the Rich

BIBLICAL LAW:
HOMOSEXUALITY AND SAME-SEX MARRIAGE

INTRODUCTION: This chapter tackles homosexuality and same-sex marriage because a candidate's position on these issues should be a deciding factor for Christians. Homosexuals include Lesbians, Gays, Bisexuals, and Transvestites (LGBT). Scripture very clearly reveals the heart and mind of God and His laws on homosexuality, laws rooted in His unchanging character. A candidate's position on these topics clearly reveals the heart and mind of the candidate in relation to the heart and mind of God and His laws.

No President in the history of the United States has been a stronger supporter of homosexuality and same-sex marriage than President Obama. Democrats are far more supportive of homosexuality and same-sex marriage than Republicans. This can be quickly proven by reference to the voting records of members of Congress.[25] For the first time in history, Democrats will make same-sex marriage a part of their party platform. A Pew Research Center poll found that 65% of Democrats now support same-sex marriage (40% in 2004); only 29% of Democrats oppose it.[26]

"The American people in general, especially younger voters, seem to be moving in that direction, and Democrats probably see this as a way to get ahead of that parade," said Michael Franc, Vice President of Government Studies as The

---

[25] "Vote Scorecard," Family Research Council Action, http://www.frcaction.org (accessed July 9, 2008).
[26] Bethany Monk, "Same-Sex Marriage to Become Plank in DNC Platform," Citizenlink, July 31, 2012, http://www.citizenlink.com.

Heritage Foundation.[27] One exception is African-Americans. The Coalition of African-American Pastors announced a national campaign against same-sex marriage.[28] Most other Christian leaders remain silent, detached from reality, irrelevant, complete failures not only at providing moral leadership, but also at making it clear what it means to be a Christian.

Scripture reveals the heart and mind of God on homosexuality and same-sex marriage through the story of creation in Genesis, laws of God given through Moses in Leviticus, and letters from the Apostle Paul to Timothy and to the Romans and Corinthians.

SCRIPTURE: Genesis 2:18-24 (KJV):

And the LORD God said, It is not good that the man should be alone; I will make him an help meet for him. And out of the ground the LORD God formed every beast of the field, and every fowl of the air; and brought them unto Adam to see what he would call them: and whatsoever Adam called every living creature, that was the name thereof. And Adam gave names to all cattle, and to the fowl of the air, and to every beast of the field; but for Adam there was not found an help meet for him. And the LORD God caused a deep sleep to fall upon Adam, and he slept: and he took one of his ribs, and closed up the flesh instead thereof; And the rib, which the LORD God had taken from man, made he a woman, and brought her unto the man. And Adam said, This is now bone of my bones, and flesh of my flesh: she shall be called Woman, because she was taken out of Man. Therefore

---

[27] Ibid.
[28] Ibid.

shall a man leave his father and his mother, and shall cleave unto his wife: and they shall be one flesh."

COMMENTARY: Genesis 2:18-24 is the story of God's creation of man, then woman from man to be a suitable companion for man, and finally marriage as a special union between one man and one woman wherein "they shall be one flesh." Note that God created woman very different from man, to make her a suitable companion for man. Another man would not be a suitable companion. Note that in God's design for marriage, the man leaves his father and mother (his family), to form a special "one flesh" union with his wife, which we call marriage, and to start a new family. The new marriage couple is then responsible to be obedient to the dominion mandate to "be fruitful and multiply," which is impossible in a same-sex marriage.

SCRIPTURE: Leviticus 18:22-26 (KJV):

"Thou shalt not lie with mankind, as with womankind: it is abomination. Neither shalt thou lie with any beast to defile thyself therewith: neither shall any woman stand before a beast to lie down thereto: it is confusion. Defile not ye yourselves in any of these things: for in all these the nations are defiled which I cast out before you: And the land is defiled: therefore I do visit the iniquity thereof upon it, and the land itself vomiteth out her inhabitants. Ye shall therefore keep my statutes and my judgments, and shall not commit any of these abominations; neither any of your own nation, nor any stranger that sojourneth among you."

COMMENTARY: In Leviticus 18:22-26 Moses recites commandments directly from God to the Israelites. God

70

commands that men not have sexual relations with other men or beasts because is an "abomination." He states that it defiles the men who do it and their nations. God punishes a nation defiled by these sins. God warns the Israelites to keep His statutes and judgments, to not commit these abominations, and to not even allow a stranger who lives among them to "commit any of these abominations." The word "abomination" is used to describe something that is extremely offensive to God, an extreme perversion of His design and law.

SCRIPTURE: Leviticus 20:13-16 (KJV):

"If a man also lie with mankind, as he lieth with a woman, both of them have committed an abomination: they shall surely be put to death; their blood shall be upon them. And if a man take a wife and her mother, it is wickedness: they shall be burnt with fire, both he and they; that there be no wickedness among you. And if a man lie with a beast, he shall surely be put to death: and ye shall slay the beast. And if a woman approach unto any beast, and lie down thereto, thou shalt kill the woman, and the beast: they shall surely be put to death; their blood shall be upon them."

COMMENTARY: In Leviticus 20:13-16 God states His law regarding two men having sex. God declares it is an "abomination" (extreme perversion) which must be punished by death. The same penalty applies to a man who has sex with his wife and her mother and to a man or woman who has sex with an animal. This does not mean that we should impose the death penalty for sodomy. It does mean we should not support candidates who are so strongly opposed to God and His laws.

SCRIPTURE: Romans 1:16-32 (KJV):

71

"For I am not ashamed of the gospel of Christ: for it is the power of God unto salvation to every one that believeth; to the Jew first, and also to the Greek. For therein is the righteousness of God revealed from faith to faith: as it is written, The just shall live by faith. For the <u>wrath of God is revealed from heaven against all ungodliness and unrighteousness of men, who hold the truth in unrighteousness</u>; <u>Because that which may be known of God</u> is manifest in them<u>; for God hath shewed it unto them</u>. <u>For the invisible things of him from the creation of the world are clearly seen</u>, being understood by the things that are made, even his eternal power and Godhead; <u>so that they are without excuse</u>: Because that, <u>when they knew God, they glorified him not as God, neither were thankful; but became vain in their imaginations, and their foolish heart was darkened</u>. <u>Professing themselves to be wise, they became fools</u>, And changed the glory of the uncorruptible God into an image made like to corruptible man, and to birds, and fourfooted beasts, and creeping things. <u>Wherefore God also gave them up to uncleanness through the lusts of their own hearts, to dishonour their own bodies between themselves</u>: <u>Who changed the truth of God into a lie, and worshipped and served the creature more than the Creator, who is blessed for ever. Amen. For this cause God gave them up unto vile affections: for even their women did change the natural use into that which is against nature</u>: And <u>likewise also the men, leaving the natural use of the woman, burned in their lust one toward another; men with men working that which is unseemly, and receiving in themselves that recompence of their error which was meet. And even as they did not like to retain God in</u>

72

their knowledge, God gave them over to a
reprobate mind, to do those things which are not
convenient; Being filled with all unrighteousness,
fornication, wickedness, covetousness,
maliciousness; full of envy, murder, debate,
deceit, malignity; whisperers, Backbiters, haters
of God, despiteful, proud, boasters, inventors of
evil things, disobedient to parents, Without
understanding, covenantbreakers, without natural
affection, implacable, unmerciful: Who knowing
the judgment of God, that they which commit
such things are worthy of death, not only do the
same, but have pleasure in them that do them."

COMMENTARY: In Romans 1:16-32 Paul reveals the
heart and mind of God on homosexuality and other ungodliness
and unrighteousness. First, he states that God reveals His wrath
against "all ungodliness and unrighteousness of men, who hold
the truth in unrighteousness." Then he explains why men choose
ungodliness and unrighteousness and suffer the wrath of God:
(1) First, because they know what can be known about God
because God has shown it to them. (2) Second, because the
"invisible things" of God are "clearly seen" because they are
understood from observing the things that God created. These
"invisible things" of God that are "clearly seen" include His
"eternal power and Godhead" so they are "without excuse." (3)
Third, because although they knew God, they did not glorify
Him as God and were not thankful, but became "vain in their
imaginations" and their "foolish heart was darkened." Claiming
to be wise, they became fools, and exchanged the glory of
"uncorruptible God" for an image of "corruptible man," etc.
Then Paul explains what God did to these ungodly, unrighteous
fools: (1) First, He gave them up to their own lusts, to dishonor
their bodies "between themselves" because they rejected the
truth of God for a lie, and "worshiped and served" God's
creation more than the Creator. (2) Second, he gave them up to
"vile affections." Women changed the "natural use" of their

73

bodies for that "against nature." Men likewise rejected "natural use of the woman," "burned in their lust" for other men, and did "unseemly" things with other men. As a result they received due punishment for their wrongdoing. (3) Third, because they rejected God, He gave them up to a "reprobate mind," to do thing which are "not convenient." Then Paul lists the wrongdoing of these reprobate men and women: "all unrighteousness, fornication, wickedness, covetousness, maliciousness; full of envy, murder, debate, deceit, malignity; whisperers, backbiters, haters of God, despiteful, proud, boasters, inventors of evil things, disobedient to parents, without understanding, covenantbreakers, without natural affection, implacable, unmerciful." Finally, Paul ends by saying that they not only did all these evil things, but actually took pleasure in doing them, although they knew the "judgment of God" meant they were deserving of death for their wrongdoing."

SCRIPTURE: 1 Corinthians 6:9-10 (New KJV):

"Do you not know that the unrighteous will not inherit the kingdom of God? Do not be deceived. Neither fornicators, nor idolaters, nor adulterers, nor homosexuals, nor sodomites, nor thieves, nor covetous, nor drunkards, nor revilers, nor extortioners will inherit the kingdom of God" (1 Cor. 6:9-10, NKJV). [29]

COMMENTARY: 1 Corinthians 6:9-10 states that the "unrighteous will not inherit the kingdom of God" and that this includes "homosexuals" and "sodomites."

SCRIPTURE: 1 Timothy 1:9-10 (NKJV):

"knowing this: that the law is not made for a righteous person, but for *the* lawless and

---

[29] Holy Bible, New King James Version, 1982, Thomas Nelson, Inc..

74

insubordinate, for *the* ungodly and for sinners, for *the* unholy and profane, for murderers of fathers and murderers of mothers, for manslayers, for fornicators, for <u>sodomites</u>, for kidnappers, for liars, for perjurers, and if there is any other thing that is contrary to sound doctrine,"

<u>COMMENTARY</u>: 1 Timothy 1:9-10 shows that God considers homosexuals who commit sodomy to be "lawless...insubordinate...ungodly...sinners...unholy and profane."

<u>CONCLUSION</u>: Scripture is very clear about marriage and homosexuality. God created man male and female, and marriage to be a special union between one man and one woman (Genesis 2:18-24). He designed the family as the most fundamental unit in society, critical to its stability and proper function. Homosexuality and same-sex marriage are extreme perversions of God's design for man, woman, sex, marriage, and family. Homosexual acts are abominations to God deserving of the death penalty. There is absolutely no way that any individual or nation can ignore God's design for sex, marriage, and family without severe consequences.

Homosexuals call those who oppose them "homophobic," berating them with totally false accusations of fear of homosexuals. The opposite may be true. They may rightfully have greater fear and respect for God than man, and rightfully feel some of the same disgust for the extreme sexual perversion of homosexuality that God feels toward those who have so greatly perverted his design for man, woman, marriage, and family. Friends of the homosexual movement demonstrate greater fear of man than God, extreme ignorance, and extreme foolishness.

A candidate's positions on same-sex marriage and homosexuality should be deciding factors in voting because these sins are extremely offensive to God and because this subject area is so critically important to the future of our nation. President Obama and Democrats are far more supportive of the homosexual lifestyle and same-sex marriage than Republicans. See Vote Scorecards of Focus on the Family Action and Family Research Council Action and campaign website of President Obama.[30] Any American who votes for any Democrat or in any way helps Democrats gain control of the Presidency, Congress or any other political office will answer to God for supporting a lifestyle so offensive to Him that He deems it worthy of the death penalty. Any American who does not believe that he deserves to face the wrath of God for this is an absolute fool living in a fantasy world. Holy, holy, holy is the Lord God Almighty. Blessed be the name of the Lord.

---

[30] "Vote Scorecard," Family Reseach Council Action, http://www.frcaction.org (accessed July 9, 2008).

BIBLICAL LAW: ABORTION

INTRODUCTION: The second chapter in this section addresses abortion because a candidate's position on abortion should be a deciding factor for Christians. Scripture reveals the heart and mind of God and His laws, which are rooted in His unchanging character. A candidate's position on abortion reveals the heart and mind of the candidate in relation to the heart and mind of God and His laws.

In the history of the United States, no President has been a stronger supporter of abortion than President Obama. He has a 0% rating with National Right to Life and a 100% rating with "pro-choice" organizations. In the face of a government shutdown due to budget problems, he absolutely refused to cut federal funds to Planned Parenthood, the nation's number one abortion provider. When states have defunded Planned Parenthood, he has repeatedly stepped in to fund them will millions of dollars from millions of U.S. taxpayers who consider abortion to be murder. He has appointed federal judges and Supreme Court Justices and others who strongly support abortion. He has signed legislation forcing other nations to support abortion in order to be eligible for U.S. foreign aid. He has voted not only to support abortion, but also partial birth abortion—the killing of a partially born child. Even more amazing, he has supported the after-birth killing of a child who survives abortion. As an Illinois State Senator, Obama voted three times and spoke twice on the Senate floor against the Illinois "Born-Alive Infants Protection Act" (BAIPA).[31]

---

[31] "Where Do the Candidates Stand on Life: John McCain, Barack Obama," "Senator John McCain Record on Abortion in the United States Senate," and "Senator Barack Obama Record on Abortion, United States Senate, Illinois

Most Democrats are pro-abortion, whereas most Republicans are anti-abortion. See voting scorecards of Focus on the Family Acton and Family Research Council. Most Democrats in Congress voted to support all pro-abortion policies supported by President Obama, except the after-birth killing of a child that survives abortion. When Democrats have a majority in Congress, they chair the Senate Judiciary Committee and block the nomination of pro-life Christian judges to the Supreme Court and Federal Courts.

Question: Is abortion a woman's right to choose to control her own body, or is it murder of an innocent, completely helpless child? What does Scripture say about the heart and mind of God on this subject? Scripture provides answers through the words of Abraham, Moses, King David, Job, Isaiah, Jeremiah, Luke, the Apostle Paul, and other authors of Scripture.

SCRIPTURE: Exodus 21:22-23 (KJV):

"If men strive, and hurt a woman with child, so that her fruit depart from her, and yet no mischief follow: he shall surely be punished, according as the woman's husband will lay upon him; and he shall pay as the judges determine. And if any mischief follow, then thou shall give him life for life."

COMMENTARY: In Exodus 21:22-23 God speaks to Moses, giving His law regarding death of an unborn child, revealing His heart and mind on abortion. If there is no "mischief" and the death of the unborn child is purely an accident, then the man who caused the unborn child's death is fined as determined by the husband and judge. However, if

State Senate," National Right to Life, Committee, http://www.nrlc.org (accessed August 28, 2008).

"mischief" is involved, then the penalty for killing the unborn child is the death penalty. The value of the life of the unborn child is the same as the value of the man guilty of the "mischief," hence the penalty of "life for life." In this passage God makes it perfectly clear that the penalty for deliberate killing an unborn child should be the death penalty. This does not mean that God would want us to impose the death penalty on anyone guilty of abortion. It does mean that we should change our laws to outlaw abortion. Cases involving the life of the mother pose a separate moral issue.

The Hebrew word for the unborn child in Ex. 21:22 is used throughout the Old Testament to refer to children before and after birth ("hareh," word 2030, Strong's Exhaustive Concordance of the Bible, James Strong, Ed.). See Gen. 16:11; 17:10,12,14; 19:36; 38:24,25; Ex. 21:22; 22:22; Lev. 12:2,5; 1 Sam. 4:19; 2 Sam. 11:5; 2Kin. 8:12; 15:16; Isa. 26:17,18; 49:15; 54:1; Jer. 31:8; Hos. 13:16; Am. 1:13. In other words, a child is a child, a human life, before and after birth.

SCRIPTURE: Psalm 127:3 (KJV): "Lo, children are an heritage of the LORD: and the fruit of the womb is his reward."

Deuteronomy 7:12-13 (KJV):

"Wherefore it shall come to pass, if ye hearken to these judgments, and keep, and do them, that the LORD thy God shall keep unto thee the covenant and the mercy which he sware unto thy fathers: And he will love thee, and bless thee, and multiply thee: he will also bless the fruit of thy womb, and the fruit of thy land, thy corn, and thy wine, and thine oil, the increase of thy kine, and the flocks of thy sheep, in the land which he sware unto thy fathers to give thee."

79

COMMENTARY: Psalm 127:3 states that children, the "fruit of the womb," are a "reward" and "heritage of the LORD." Deuteronomy 7:12-13 shows that one of God's blessings upon His people if they are obedient to his commandments is the "fruit of thy womb," the gift of having children. All children are a blessing from God, and with the blessing comes responsibility for proper care of the child, before and after birth.

SCRIPTURE: Psalm 139:13-16 (NKJV): [32]

"For You formed my inward parts; You covered me in my mother's womb. I will praise You, for I am fearfully *and* wonderfully made; marvelous are Your works, and *that* my soul knows very well. My frame was not hidden from You, when I was made in secret, *and* skillfully wrought in the lowest parts of the earth. Your eyes saw my substance, being yet unformed, and in Your book they all were written, the days fashioned for me, when *as yet there were* none of them."

Job 31:15 (KJV): "Did not he that made me in the womb make him? And did not one fashion us in the womb?"
Isaiah 44:2 (KJV): "The LORD that made thee, and formed thee from the womb, which will help thee...."
Isaiah 44:24 (KJV): "The LORD...that formed thee from the womb, I am the LORD that maketh all things; that stretcheth forth the heavens alone; that spreadeth abroad the earth by myself...."
Isaiah 49:1,5 (KJV): "The LORD hath called me from the womb.... And now, saith the LORD that formed me from the womb to be his servant, to bring Jacob again to him ...."

---

[32] Holy Bible, New King James Version, 1982, Thomas Nelson, Inc.

Jeremiah 1:5 (KJV): "Before I formed thee in the belly I knew thee; and before thou camest forth out of the womb I sanctified thee, and I ordained thee a prophet unto the nations."

COMMENTARY: These verses affirm that God forms each person within the womb. Psalm 139:13-16, written by King David, is one of the most beautiful passages in the Bible. It states, "You formed my inward parts...I am fearfully *and* wonderfully made.... I was made in secret, *and* skillfully wrought." These words imply that every person is formed by God within the womb, "fearfully and wonderfully made...skillfully wrought." Then David states that God "saw my substance, being yet unformed, and in Your book they all were written, the days fashioned for me, when *as yet there were* none of them." These words tell us that God sees every day of everyone's life before He forms them in the womb.

Job 31:15 uses the words "fashion us in the womb." Isaiah 49:5 states that God "formed" Isaiah "to be his servant, to bring Jacob" (Israel) back to him. Jeremiah 1:5 states that God "knew" Jeremiah before He formed him in the womb, and "sanctified" and "ordained" him to be "a prophet unto the nations." These passages inform us that God forms each person in the womb and that he creates people with a purpose, to serve Him.

The Declaration of Independence affirms that God creates "all men" and endows them with the right to life, describing these as "self-evident" truths. "We hold these truths to be self-evident, that all men are created equal, that they are endowed by their Creator with certain unalienable Rights, that among these are Life, Liberty and the pursuit of Happiness."

SCRIPTURE: Luke 1:13-15 (KJV):

"But the angel said unto him, Fear not, Zacharias: for thy prayer is heard; and thy wife Elisabeth shall bear thee a son, and thou shalt call his name

John. And thou shalt have joy and gladness; and many shall rejoice at his birth. For he shall be great in the sight of the Lord, and shall drink neither wine nor strong drink; and he shall be filled with the Holy Ghost, even from his mother's womb."

Luke 1:30-31 (KJV): "And the angel said unto her, Fear not, Mary: for thou hast found favour with God. And, behold, thou shalt conceive in thy womb, and bring forth a son, and shalt call his name JESUS."

COMMENTARY: These passages contain prophecy of angels about the conception and birth of Jesus and John the Baptist. In Luke 1:13-15 the angel states that John will be filled with the Spirit of God before birth, within his mother's womb. In Luke 1:30-31 the angel tells Mary that she will conceive and give birth to Jesus. These passages show that God controls conception and birth, and that he forms a person within the womb for a purpose. Luke 1:13-15 also raises the question: How could anyone kill a child who could be filled the Spirit of God in the womb?

SCRIPTURE: Luke 1:41-44 (KJV):

"And it came to pass, that, when Elisabeth heard the salutation of Mary, the babe leaped in her womb; and Elisabeth was filled with the Holy Ghost: And she spake out with a loud voice, and said, Blessed art thou among women, and blessed is the fruit of thy womb. And whence is this to me, that the mother of my Lord should come to me? For, lo, as soon as the voice of thy salutation sounded in mine ears, the babe leaped in my womb for joy."

Luke 18:15-16 (KJV): "And they brought unto him also infants, that he would touch them: but when his disciples saw it, they rebuked them. But Jesus called them unto him, and said, 'Suffer little children to come unto me, and forbid them not: for of such is the kingdom of God.'"

COMMENTARY: Luke 1:41-44 is the story of the meeting of Mary, when she was pregnant with Jesus, with Elisabeth, when she was pregnant with John the Baptist. John the Baptist "leaped...for joy" within his mother's womb when he heard the voice of the mother of Jesus. How can anyone abort a child that is able to recognize the voice of the mother of Jesus and jump for joy within his mother's womb?

The Greek word for the unborn child in Luke 1:41-44 is used in the New Testament to refer to children before and after birth ("brephos" word 1025, The Word Study Concordance, George Wigram and Ralph Winter, Ed. 1972 & 1978. It is used to refer to baby Jesus wrapped in swaddling clothes (Luke 2:12) and lying in a manger (Luke 2:16), the little children (infants) brought to Jesus (Luke 18:15), young children (Acts 7:19), a young child (2 Tim 3:15), and newborn babies (1 Pet. 2:2). In other words, a child is a child before and after birth.

SCRIPTURE: Genesis 18:10-15 (KJV):

And he said, I will certainly return unto thee according to the time of life; and, lo, Sarah thy wife shall have a son. And Sarah heard it in the tent door, which was behind him. Now Abraham and Sarah were old and well stricken in age; and it ceased to be with Sarah after the manner of women. Therefore Sarah laughed within herself, saying, "After I am waxed old shall I have pleasure, my lord being old also?" And the LORD said unto Abraham, Wherefore did Sarah laugh, saying, Shall I of a surety bear a child,

83

which am old? Is any thing too hard for the LORD? At the time appointed I will return unto thee, according to the time of life, and Sarah shall have a son. Then Sarah denied, saying, I laughed not; for she was afraid. And he said, "Nay; but thou didst laugh."

Romans 4:19 (KJV): "And being not weak in faith, he considered not his own body now dead, when he was about an hundred years old, neither yet the deadness of Sarah's womb."

COMMENTARY: Genesis 18:10-15 and Romans 4:19 are about Abraham and Sarah. The key words in Genesis 18:10-15 are: "Is any thing too hard for the LORD?" God made Sarah, who was very old and no longer able to have children, conceive and bear a child, to fulfill His promise to give Abraham many descendents. Note that Sarah "laughed within herself", but the LORD who sees the heart and mind knew that she had laughed. Romans 4:19 is about Abraham faith that he would have a child with Sarah as promised by God, even though he was about a hundred years old and his wife was barren. This passage shows that God is able to miraculously cause conception and birth regardless of the age or physical condition of the father or mother.

CONCLUSION: Scripture is clear on abortion. In Exodus 21:22-23 God tells Moses that the penalty for the deliberate killing of an unborn child is the death penalty. This does not mean that God would want us to assume jurisdiction to impose the death penalty on everyone one guilty of abortion. However, it does mean that they are nevertheless deserving of death under God's laws and that we should therefore change our laws to outlaw abortion. Cases involving the life of the mother pose a separate moral issue, but that does not justify using "life of the mother" as an excuse for the murder of unborn children.

The Declaration of Independence affirms that God creates "all men" and endows them with certain God-given inalienable rights, which include the right to life. The founding fathers of the United States understood these "self-evident" truths as common-sense teachings of Scripture. Job 31:15; Isaiah 44:2; 44:24; 49:5 and Jeremiah 1:5 affirm that God forms each person within the womb. In Psalm 139:13-16 King David teaches that everyone is "formed" and "fearfully and wonderfully made" and "skillfully wrought" by God within the womb, and that God sees every day of a person's life before He forms him or her in the womb. Genesis 18:10-15 and Romans 4:19 show that God is able to cause conception and birth regardless of the age of the father and mother. Psalm 127:3 and Deuteronomy 7:12-13 teach that children are a blessing from the Lord. That blessing brings responsibility for proper care of the child, before and after birth.

Luke 1:13-15; 30-31 prophesizes the conception and birth of Jesus and John the Baptist, showing that God controls conception and birth and forms a person within the womb for a purpose. Luke 1:13-15 and 1:41-44 raise the question: How could anyone kill an unborn child who is filled the Spirit of God and be able to recognize the voice of the mother of Jesus and jump for joy within the womb?

The Hebrew word used in the Old Testament and the Greek word used in the New Testament to refer to unborn children are the same words used to refer to children after birth. In other words, a child is a child before and after birth, as precious as baby Jesus lying in a manger (Luke 2:12,16) and the little children brought to Jesus (Luke 18:15-16).

Many ancient cultures practiced child sacrifice. Most Americans cannot begin to understand how any people could be so cruel and evil to sacrifice children on stone alters to secure the blessings of their false gods. If any group of Americans sacrificed a child on an altar today, most Americans would be horrified and demand the death penalty. Abortion is child sacrifice. In the world today, unwanted children are sacrificed on the alter of convenience by an ungodly, godless people who do whatever is right in their own eyes and seek first not to love and serve God but to serve themselves.

A candidate's stand on abortion reveals his ability to acknowledge simple but inconvenient truths regarding the beginning of human life. When Senator McCain was asked when life begins, he said, "At conception," acknowledging a simple scientific fact. When Senator Obama was asked the same question, he avoided giving a direct answer by saying, "The answer to that question is above my pay grade." However, it was never above his pay grade to decide on the murder of unborn or partially born children.

Scripture reveals the heart and mind of God and His laws, which are rooted in His unchanging character. A candidate's stand on abortion speaks volumes about them; it reveals their heart and mind and the condition of their moral compass. Comparing a candidate's position on abortion with Scripture reveals whether or not the candidate's heart and mind are in sync with God and His laws, or whether the candidate simply does whatever is right in his own eyes.

Every American who voted for President Obama and other Democrats has the blood of thousands of American children on his hands. He answers to God for every murder, and there is absolutely no mercy from God where there is no true repentance from man. True repentance more than regret; it requires turning from sin to obedience to God.

BIBLICAL LAW:
GOVERNMENT AND ECONOMY

INTRODUCTION: The next president and Congress may greatly expand the role of the federal government, greatly increase individual and/or corporate taxes required to support the government, and greatly decrease the freedom that Americans enjoy. Most Republicans advocate a smaller federal government, lower taxes, and greater freedom. Most Democrats want a government that does more to help the people, which means more socialism, more redistribution of wealth, higher taxes and less freedom for citizens of the larger, more powerful government, all in violation of the powers granted to the federal government by the U.S. Constitution.

Most readers probably need clarification by what is meant by "less freedom." Greater taxes to pay for more government benefits means most Americans must work longer each year just to pay their taxes. More government benefits means the government is taking more by force from most taxpayers to very ineffectively process and redistribute the funds to other taxpayers in the form of government benefits. In other words, taxpayers are forced to pay the school tuition, doctor bills and other bills of other taxpayers and much of the money they are forced to pay is spent paying for the larger government needed to ineffectively manage the government programs. So having a government that does more to take care of its people means Americans work longer each year just to pay their taxes and have less "liberty" and less of their own money to spend however they wish in their personal "pursuit of happiness." In other words, they have less of two of three God-given inalienable rights the United States government was established to protect. Also, more money flowing through government to schools and businesses means more improper government control of and less freedom for schools and businesses. It also means more fraud, more government waste, and more improper influence of government officials.

All this raises the question: Does Scripture give any hint about God's ideal for government? First, consider 1 Samuel 8:4-22.

SCRIPTURE: 1 Samuel 8:4-22 (KJV):

Then all the elders of Israel gathered themselves together, and came to Samuel unto Ramah, and said unto him, "Behold, thou art old, and thy sons walk not in thy ways: now make us a king to judge us like all the nations." But the thing displeased Samuel, when they said, "Give us a king to judge us." And Samuel prayed unto the LORD. And the LORD said unto Samuel, "Hearken unto the voice of the people in all that they say unto thee: for they have not rejected thee, but they have rejected me, that I should not reign over them. According to all the works which they have done since the day that I brought them up out of Egypt even unto this day, wherewith they have forsaken me, and served other gods, so do they also unto thee. Now therefore hearken unto their voice: howbeit yet protest solemnly unto them, and shew them the manner of the king that shall reign over them." And Samuel told all the words of the LORD unto the people that asked of him a king. And he said, "This will be the manner of the king that shall reign over you: He will take your sons, and appoint them for himself, for his chariots, and to be his horsemen; and some shall run before his

88

chariots. And he will appoint him captains over thousands, and captains over fifties; and will set them to ear his ground, and to reap his harvest, and to make his instruments of war, and instruments of his chariots. And he will take your daughters to be confectionaries, and to be cooks, and to be bakers. And he will take your fields, and your vineyards, and your oliveyards, even the best of them, and give them to his servants. And he will take the tenth of your seed, and of your vineyards, and give to his officers, and to his servants. And he will take your menservants, and your maidservants, and your goodliest young men, and your asses, and put them to his work. He will take the tenth of your sheep: and ye shall be his servants. And ye shall cry out in that day because of your king which ye shall have chosen you; and the LORD will not hear you in that day." Nevertheless the people refused to obey the voice of Samuel; and they said, "Nay; but we will have a king over us; that we also may be like all the nations; and that our king may judge us, and go out before us, and fight our battles." And Samuel heard all the words of the people, and he rehearsed them in the ears of the LORD. And the LORD said to Samuel, "Hearken unto their voice, and make them a king."

COMMENTARY: 1 Samuel 8:4-22 tells the story about when the elders of Israel told Samuel that the people wanted a king "like all other nations." God told Samuel to warn them how much a king would take i.e. their sons, daughters, fields, vineyards, menservants, maidservants, best young men, and taxes. In other words, God was not just warning them about the king. He was warning them about having a government that would demand so much from them. The Israelites would also have less freedom to spend their own money as they chose, because a greater portion of their income would be taken from them to pay taxes to support the government. Taxes would be 10%, the exact same amount due in tithes to God.

SCRIPTURE: Genesis 4:9 (KJV): "And the LORD said unto Cain, Where is Abel thy brother? And he said, I know not: Am I my brother's keeper?"

COMMENTARY: These are not words used by Christ, but words used by Cain immediately after he killed his brother Abel. They have absolutely nothing to do with the role of government.

SCRIPTURE: Matthew 22:37-40 (KJV):

Jesus said unto him, "Thou shalt love the Lord thy God with all thy heart, and with all thy soul, and with all thy mind. This is the first and great commandment. And the second is like unto it, Thou shalt love thy neighbour as thyself. On these two commandments hang all the law and the prophets."

COMMENTARY: Christ declared the second greatest commandment to be, "Thou shalt love thy neighbour as thyself." During the 2008 election, Senator Obama probably intended to refer to this concept, the duty to love one's fellow man as oneself, when he used the words, "I am my brother's keeper." However, he completely failed to understand that this is a command given by God to individuals and does not describe the purpose of government or grant any authority to government. More specifically, it does not give government authority to take money by force from those who have lawfully earned that money and give it to the poor in the form of benefits. That is not love. Love is by definition an act of the will. Christ's command gives individuals a duty to love one's fellow man as oneself, and this is an act of the will of the individual who chooses to be obedient to the command and to love his fellow man as he loves himself.

SCRIPTURE: Exodus 23:1-3 (TNIV): "Do not show favoritism to the poor in a lawsuit."[33]

COMMENTARY: Exodus 23:3 states that the government must ensure equal justice for the rich and the poor, and this also means it should not make judgments in favor of the poor just because they are poor. The government should show impartiality not partiality toward the poor, because the government does not have authority, responsibility, or jurisdiction to favor or care for the poor.

SCRIPTURE: Leviticus 19:15 (KJV): "Ye shall do no unrighteousness in judgment: thou shalt not respect the person of the poor, nor honor the person of the mighty: but in righteousness shalt thou judge thy neighbour."

COMMENTARY: Leviticus 19 contains laws, which God directed Moses to give to the Israelites. Leviticus 19:15 states that one should not "respect" (favor) the poor in judgments. In other words, this verse also states that the government must ensure equal justice for the poor, and not make judgments in favor of the poor. Government should show impartiality not partiality toward the poor, because the government does not have authority, responsibility, or jurisdiction to favor or care for the poor.

SCRIPTURE: Romans 13:1-7 (New KJV):

Let every soul be subject to the governing authorities. For there is no authority except from God, and the authorities that exist are appointed

---

[33] Holy Bible, Today's New International Version, 2001, 2005, International Bible Society.

91

by God. Therefore whoever resists the authority resists the ordinance of God, and those who resist will bring judgment on themselves. For rulers are not a terror to good works, but to evil. Do you want to be unafraid of the authority? Do what is good, and you will have praise from the same. For he is God's minister to you for good. But if you do evil, be afraid; for he does not bear the sword in vain; for he is God's minister, an avenger to execute wrath on him who practices evil. Therefore you must be subject, not only because of wrath but also for conscience' sake. For because of this you also pay taxes, for they are God's ministers attending continually to this very thing. Render therefore to all their due: taxes to whom taxes are due, customs to whom customs, fear to whom fear, honor to whom honor.

COMMENTARY: Romans 13:1-7 is one of the most important passages in Scripture about government. First, Paul states the command that everyone must "be subject to the governing authorities." Second, he states the reasons for this command, that "there is no authority except from God" and that all "authorities that exist are appointed by God." Third, he draws a conclusion based upon this rule, that anyone who resists authority resists God's law and "bring[s] judgment on themselves." This general rule and conclusion apply to "all authorities that exist" (parents, employers, etc.), but Paul's concentration in this passage is on government authorities. Fourth, Paul states that Rulers are "God's ministers" for good, but they do "not bear the sword in vain" because they are God's "avenger to execute wrath" on those who do evil. Fifth, Paul concludes that one must be subject to government authorities, not just for fear of their "wrath," but for "conscience' sake" (because it is the right thing to do). Sixth, Paul makes one final conclusion, that one should therefore give taxes, customs, fear, and honor to the authorities as is due to them.

All authorities are "appointed by God" and are "God's ministers." If God wants everyone to fear and honor government authorities, then what does God think about how some Americans treat elected officials? Governor Clinton won a presidential election with the phrase, "It's the economy, stupid." The word stupid was used to belittle the first President Bush, a man of great honor and dignity. Many Democrats, talk show hosts, and others mocked the second President Bush, in complete disobedience to this Scriptural directive.

CONCLUSION: Scripture discusses the role of government. Romans 13:1-7 states that all "authorities that exist are appointed by God," and that anyone who resists the authorities resists God's law and brings "judgment on themselves." Rulers are "God's ministers" for good. They do "not bear the sword in vain" because they are God's "avenger to execute wrath" on evildoers. One must be subject to government authorities not just for fear of their "wrath," but because it is the right thing to do. All citizens must pay taxes and give proper respect to government officials.

Exactly what part of Scripture gives government any responsibility or authority to care for the poor or the middle class or anyone else? Answer: No part. In "Matthew 22:37-40 Christ gives the command to "love thy neighbor as thyself." This commandment is given to individuals; it does not grant any authority to government. Obedience requires a very personal act of the will of the individual who chooses to love his neighbor. The purpose of government is not to provide or care for citizens, but to protect life and liberty and thereby enable the pursuit of happiness.

Exodus 23:3 and Leviticus 19:15 both direct government to ensure equal justice for the poor, and not make judgments in favor of the poor. Government should show impartiality not partiality toward the poor, because the government does not have authority, responsibility, or jurisdiction to favor the poor.

In 1 Samuel 8:8-20 God told Samuel to warn the people that a king would take their sons, daughters, fields, vineyards, menservants, maidservants, best young men, and 10% in taxes, the same amount due in tithes to God. God clearly recommends the smallest possible government, which gives the people greater freedom to keep and spend their own earnings. The founding fathers of the United States understood God's ideal, which is embodied in the U.S. Constitution, of smaller government, lower taxes, and greater personal freedom and responsibility for all citizens. They were fiercely independent men who greatly treasured their freedom and would not trade it for government benefits.

During the 2008 election, Senator Obama often quoted the words "I am my brother's keeper" to explain what motivates him to government service. However, these are not words used by Christ, but words used by Cain after killing his brother Abel (Gen. 4:9). They have nothing to do with government. During the 2008 election, Senator McCain warned that Senator Obama would greatly increase government spending and debt. He did. Senator's Obama stated that the cost of health care alone would be $150 billion dollars per year. That was much greater than the annual cost of the war in Iraq, and the cost would go on forever, and continue to rise sharply (5% annual increase in health care costs per year per Nightly Business Report, September 24, 2008), and that is just one of the many costly programs that Obama wanted to initiate.

The objective of President Obama and Democrats to increase the size and cost of government to provide more benefits to citizens violates the limited powers granted to the federal government by the U.S. Constitution. During the Republican Primary election, Senator Rick Santorum repeatedly stated that when he was born 60% of government spending was

94

on defense, but that today over 60% of government spending is on social programs. The spending on social programs is unconstitutional. The federal government is a government of enumerated powers; each branch only has those powers granted to it by the Constitution. No part of the Constitution grants any power to establish social programs. This is discussed in greater detail in the chapter on Obamacare (national healthcare).

If reelected, President Obama and Democrats will continue to increase the size and cost of government, a cost which must be passed on to the taxpayers one way or another, through individual or corporate taxes. Taxpayers are the source of income for government and corporations. Taxes on corporations will be passed on to taxpayers in the form of higher costs for sales and services.

BIBLICAL LAW: TAXING THE RICH

INTRODUCTION. "Fairness" is one of the primary themes of President Obama and Democrats during the 2012 election. It sounds so American, so right for a nation "with liberty and justice for all." All they ask in the name of fairness is that rich Americans pay their "fair" share of taxes. So why in the world would Republicans object? Who is right and why?

Current official U.S. federal income tax rates range from 10% for the lowest income group to 35% for the highest income group (see "2011 Tax Rate Schedules" on page 98 of 2011 Form 1040 Instructions booklet). However, actual tax rates are very different for all groups, due to countless tax deductions and credits that, contrary to the totally false impression given by President Obama and many Democrats, benefit the poor and middle classes even more than the wealthy. The end result is that about 49% of Americans, mostly lower and middle income, pay no federal income tax.

Most very wealthy Americans also pay less than the official rate, which for them is a much higher rate of 35%. President Obama and Governor Romney (both highest income tax group) paid about 21% and 14% respectively. Governor Romney pays a lower rate in part because investments are taxed at a much lower rate than income for higher income taxpayers. Investments may be taxed at a lower rate because money is first taxed as income and then taxed again if any profit is made from investment of the same money.

How much federal taxes are actually paid by the rich, the middle class, and the poor? The lowest 20% (average income $15,900) earn 4% of the national income but pay only 1% of the taxes. The second 20% (average income $37,400) earn 8% of the income but pay only 4% of the taxes. The third 20% (average income $58,500) earn 13% of the income but pay only 9% of the taxes. The fourth 20% (average income $85,200) earn 20% of the income and pay 17% of the taxes. The next 10% (average income $120,700) earn 14% of the income and pay 14% of the taxes. The next 5% (average income $161,100) earn 10% of the income and pay 11% of the taxes. The next 4% (average income $277,200) earn 13% of the income but pay 17% of the taxes. The top 1% (average income 1,558,500) earn 18% of the income but pay 27% of the taxes. In other words, the bottom 60% of Americans pay much less than their share of federal taxes (14%), and the greatly and vilified top 1% pay far more than their share (27%).[34]

The foregoing only considers federal income tax. When you consider all taxes paid by Americans i.e. state and local income taxes, real estate taxes, sales taxes, fuel taxes, and all other taxes, then the poor and middle class Americans pay more than above, and wealthy Americans pay far more.

What is the heart and mind of God on taxes? Does Scripture give any hint about where God stands on this hot political issue? First, consider God's commands through Moses in Leviticus:

> And all the tithe of the land, whether of the seed
> of the land, or of the fruit of the tree, is the
> Lord's: it is holy unto the Lord. And if a man will
> at all redeem ought of his tithes, he shall add
> thereto the fifth part thereof. And concerning the
> tithe of the herd, or of the flock, even of

---

[34] Catherine Mulbrandon, "How Much Taxes Are Paid by the Poor, Middle Class and Rich," VisualizingEconomics, February 2, 2012, http://visualizingeconomics.com/2010/02/12/. Source of figures is Congressional Budget Office most recent figures (2005), http://www.cbo.gov/ftpdocs/88xx/doc8885/EffectiveTaxRates.shtml.

whatsoever passeth under the rod, the tenth shall
be holy unto the Lord (Leviticus 27:30-32).

Note that the God's tithe or "tax rate" was a tenth (10%)
for everyone, both the rich and the poor. See also Deut. 12:5-11;
14:22-28; Num. 18:24-28; Mal. 3:8-10; Heb. 7:1-4.

Second, consider 1 Samuel 8:8-20. See prior chapter for
more complete quote (1 Samuel 8:4-22).

SCRIPTURE: 1 Samuel 8:8-20 (KJV):

And Samuel told all the words of the LORD unto
the people that asked of him a king. And he said,
"This will be the manner of the king that shall
reign over you: He will take your sons, and
appoint them for himself, for his chariots, and to
be his horsemen; and some shall run before his
chariots. And he will appoint him captains over
thousands, and captains over fifties; and will set
them to ear his ground, and to reap his harvest,
and to make his instruments of war, and
instruments of his chariots. And he will take your
daughters to be confectionaries, and to be cooks,
and to be bakers. And he will take your fields,
and your vineyards, and your oliveyards, even the
best of them, and give them to his servants. And
he will take the tenth of your seed, and of your
vineyards, and give to his officers, and to his
servants. And he will take your menservants, and
your maidservants, and your goodliest young
men, and your asses, and put them to his work.
He will take the tenth of your sheep: and ye shall
be his servants. And ye shall cry out in that day
because of your king which ye shall have chosen
you; and the LORD will not hear you in that
day."

COMMENTARY: In 1 Samuel 8:8-20 God tells Samuel to warn the people that a king would take their sons, daughters, fields, vineyards, menservants, maidservants, best young men, and taxes. Taxes would be 10%, the same amount due in tithes to God.

CONCLUSION: Countless times during the 2012 election President Obama and other Democrats have made it clear that they want to raise taxes on the "rich" to force them to pay their fair share to relieve the unfair tax burden on the "middle class." Why is this wrong?

First, about 49% of Americans, mostly middle and lower class, do not pay any federal taxes. In other words, they are not paying their fair share of taxes. Second, God's "tax rate" for tithes is exactly the same rate for the rich and the poor: 10%. Second, God warned that a king would charge exactly the same rate for the rich and the poor: 10%. Thus it would seem that in the eyes of God a flat tax rate that is exactly the same for both the rich and the poor would be the "fairest" rate. This presumes that there would be little or no tax deductions or tax credits. Third, God warned the Israelites about the heavy burden that a king would impose, when the tax rate would be only 10%, which is far less than most Americans pay today. Furthermore, God warned about all the other burdens that having a king and government like other nations would impose upon the Israelites. It seems quite clear from a careful reading of 1 Samuel 8:8-20 that God would strongly recommend the smallest possible federal government as envisioned by the founding fathers of our nation and as required by the highest law of the land: the Constitution.

Exodus 23:3 and Leviticus 19:15, quoted in the prior chapter, direct government to ensure equal justice for the poor, and not make judgments in favor of the poor. Government should show impartiality not partiality toward the poor, because the government does not have authority, responsibility, or jurisdiction to favor the poor. Also, the U.S. Constitution makes the federal government a government of enumerated powers, where each branch only has those powers which are granted to it by the Constitution. There is absolutely no part of the Constitution that authorizes the social programs which now comprise most of the federal budget. Reduction or elimination of these programs would permit much lower tax rates and make it possible to eliminate the federal deficit and federal debt.

So how could federal tax laws be improved to ensure more "fairness" in taxation of all Americans? One option would be a flat tax where all Americans pay the exact same rate. Most tax deductions and tax credits would be eliminated for all income levels. This would ensure that everyone paid their fair share and would greatly reduce tax fraud, tax preparation time, and the size, cost and workload of the Internal Revenue Service. A second but much more likely option would be to maintain current tax rates but eliminate most tax deductions and tax credits for all tax brackets. This would reduce tax fraud, tax preparation time, and the job of the Internal Revenue Service. A third but much less likely option would be to totally eliminate the federal income tax and totally fund the federal government with sales taxes. This would eliminate the need to complete a federal tax return and greatly reduce tax fraud and the size, cost and function of the Internal Revenue Service.

HOT POLITICAL TOPICS

SECTION REVIEW: This section reviews other hot political topics. The first chapter tackles Obamacare, the national healthcare law enacted by President Obama. The second chapter discusses the totally fabricated war on women started by President Obama to win votes during the 2012 presidential campaign. The third chapter discusses hate crimes and freedom of religion.

CHAPTERS: Chapters in this section include the following:
5.1 Obamacare (National Healthcare)
5.2 War on Women
5.3 Hate Crimes and Freedom of Religion

OBAMACARE (NATIONAL HEALTHCARE)

INTRODUCTION: On March 23, 2010, President Obama "signed the Patient Protection and Affordable Care Act (Obamacare) into law, which will provide federal funding for health plans that pay for abortion on demand and lead to large-scale rationing of lifesaving medical treatments."[35]

Governor Romney said, "Obamacare will violate that crucial first principle of medicine" 'Do no harm.'"[36] He believes the Obama health care law, which would open the door to federal subsidies for abortion coverage and rationing of lifesaving medical care, should be repealed.[37]

RESULTS OR CONSEQUENCES OF OBAMACARE: Exactly what are the results or consequences of Obamacare for Christians?

1. ABORTION: "Obamacare is a massive expansion of taxpayer-subsidized abortion.[38] In other words, American taxpayers who believe that abortion is murder are forced to pay higher taxes to fund millions of abortions. After describing in great detail President Obama's very lengthy and "abysmal

---

[35] "National Right to Life Endorses Governor Mitt Romney," "Where Do the Candidates Stand on Life: Mitt Romney, Barack Obama," Carol Tobias, "Statement by Carol Tobias, National Right to Life President," April 12, 2012, State Senate," National Right to Life, Committee, http://www.nrlc.org.
[36] "Where Do the Candidates Stand on Life: Mitt Romney, Barack Obama."
[37] "National Right to Life Endorses Governor Mitt Romney" and Carol Tobias, "Statement by Carol Tobias, National Right to Life President."
[38] Bruce Hausknecht, "Obamacare Decision Next Week: What's at Stake?", June 22, 2012, http://www.citizenlink.com. See Citizenlink website at http://www.citizenlink.com/2012/10/29/pro-life-group-proves-that-obamacare-subsidizes-abortion/.

record on life,"[39] Carol Tobias, President of National Right to Life, said,

> But even more far-reaching than all of this, is how the president is impacting our health care system. In 2012, Congress passed and President Obama signed into law, the Patient Protection and Affordable Care Act, also known as ObamaCare. Today, every fifth child dies from abortion; that number will go even higher because of ObamaCare. This program will enshrine abortion and rationing of health care in our society for generations to come if it isn't stopped.[40]

2. <u>RELIGIOUS FREEDOM</u>: The mandate from the Health and Human Services (different from individual mandate to buy insurance), a byproduct of Obamacare, "requires most religious organizations and their private employers to provide employee healthcare coverage for drugs, medical procedures and other services against their deeply held religious beliefs."[41] These drugs and medical procedures may include abortion, abortion inducing drugs, contraceptives, sterilization, reproductive counseling, etc.[42] Andy Newland, Vice President of Hercules Industries, said the mandate requires business owners to compromise their beliefs.

> We never imagined the federal government would order our family business to provide

[39] Carol Tobias, "Statement by Carol Tobias, National Right to Life President."

[40] Ibid.

[41] Bruce Hausknecht, "Obamacare Decision Next Week: What's at Stake?"

[42] Bethany Monk, "HHS Contraception Mandate Deadline Falls Wednesday," July 31, 2012, http://www.citizenlink.com; "President Obama to Freedom of Religion: Nertz to You!", Family Reseach Council Action, August 6, 2012, http://www.frcaction.org.

insurance for drugs we object to covering. If you put yourself back to when the Founders founded America, it seems so contradictory to their intention that Americans be free to live out their beliefs in a country that was created for freedom from religious persecution.[43]

Newland said the mandate prevents families from bringing their moral and principles into their business. "What ethical and moral principles do you use to run your business? We'll end up with no ethical or moral principals at all."[44]

Emily Hardman, Communications Director for Becket Fund for Religious Liberty, said that the mandate is "a violation of those individuals with religious beliefs... People don't have to give up their faith when they enter their business."[45]

The only organizations exempted from the mandate are seminaries and churches that only employ and serve members of their own faith (and plans "grandfathered" under the rule). Catholic universities and hospitals are not exempt.[46] They are forced to violate their deeply held religious beliefs.

Fines for non-compliance can be as much as $100 per day per employee, an amount that can bankrupt a business.[47] In other words, to survive in the United States, Christian businesses or organizations will be forced by the government to violate their deeply held moral and religious beliefs.

3. LIMITS ON GOVERNMENT: The "individual mandate" of Obamacare (different from mandate of Health and Human Services) requires all Americans to buy health insurance

---

[43] Ibid.
[44] Ibid.
[45] Ibid.
[46] Ibid.
[47] "President Obama to Freedom of Religion: Nertz to You!"

or pay a penalty.[48] This mandate is totally contrary to the U.S. Constitution, the highest law of our nation, as explained below.

4. COST TO TAXPAYERS: The incredibly high cost of Obamacare to U.S. taxpayers will continue to rise dramatically. In 2010 the Congressional Budget Office estimated the ten-year cost of Obamacare to be $944 billion. In 2011 it estimated $1,442 billion. In 2012 it estimated $1,856 billion. See Forbes Magazine article at footnote.[49]

5. COST TO STATES: Obamacare requires states to demand "massive dollars" from state taxpayers to fund Obamacare. States must raise $33.5 billion from 2014 to 2020.[50]

6. REDISTRIBUTION OF WEALTH: Obamacare is a massive, monumental federal redistribution of wealth program that any good socialist or communist would take great pride in having created. Totally contrary to the U.S. Constitution, it forces American taxpayers to pay the healthcare bills of other Americans. How massive is the redistribution? The Los Angeles Times reports that California will receive about $15 billion from American taxpayers.[51] How would you feel if the government forced you to pay for all the healthcare bills of your neighbors? How can any elected or appointed government official be so incredibly stupid to think that healthcare is a right, and that the government has the right to force any American to pay the healthcare bills of other Americans? What about the food bills, the rent or mortgage bills, the home heating bills, the college education bills, the legal bills, etc. Exactly where do you draw the line and why?

---

[48] Bruce Hausknecht, "Obamacare Decision Next Week: What's at Stake?"
[49] Avik Roy, "CBO: Obamacare Will Spend More, Tax More, and Reduce the Deficit Less Than We Previously Thought," August 27, 2012, http://www.forbes.com.
[50] Bruce Hausknecht, "Obamacare Decision Next Week: What's at Stake?"
[51] Ibid.

U.S. CONSTITUTION: Question: Exactly what part of the U.S. Constitution mentions healthcare and gives the federal government authority to legislate national healthcare? Answer: Absolutely no part. The federal government of the United States is a government of enumerated powers. Each branch of government only has the powers granted to it by the Constitution. All other powers are reserved to the states. Healthcare is not even mentioned in the Constitution. The federal government has absolutely no authority to enact national healthcare.

Exactly what part of the Constitution is wrongfully used to justify legislation regarding many subject areas not even mentioned in the Constitution? Answer: The Interstate Commerce Clause. Article 1, Section 8, states: "The Congress shall have Power...To regulate Commerce with foreign Nations, and among the several States, and with the Indian Tribes."[52] The author of this book used the nation's most popular bar-preparation materials to prepare for the bar examination that enabled him to practice law. The law professor advising law school graduates throughout the United States said, "If you have any question about whether or not the Interstate Commerce Clause authorizes the federal government to do something, the answer is: 'Yes!'" In other words, the federal government wrongfully uses the Interstate Commerce Clause to justify legislation in many areas not authorized by the Constitution.

SUPREME COURT RULING: On June 28, 2012 the United States Supreme Court ruled Obamacare to be constitutional. Justice Kennedy was expected to be the deciding vote between liberals and conservatives. However, in a shocking turn of events that surprised even the experts, Chief Justice

---

[52] Constitution of the United States, U.S. National Archives & Records Administration, 8601 Adelphi Road, College Park, MD, 20740-6001, • 1-86-NARA-NARA • 1-866-272-6272; http://www.archives.gov/exhibits/charters/constitution.html.

Roberts, a conservative appointed by President George W. Bush, joined four liberal justices in ruling Obamacare constitutional. Neither Justice Kennedy nor the conservative justices were able to convince Chief Justice Roberts to rejoin conservatives in ruling Obamacare unconstitutional. To see entire text of 193-page majority opinion, go to reference in footnote.[53]

SCOTUS stands for Supreme Court of the United States. SCOTUSblog is sponsored by Bloomberg Law. SCOTUSblog summarized the majority opinion of the Affordable Care Act in one paragraph.

> In Plain English: The Affordable Care Act, including its individual mandate that virtually all Americans buy health insurance, is constitutional. There were not five votes to uphold it on the ground that Congress could use its power to regulate commerce between the states to require everyone to buy health insurance. However, five Justices agreed that the penalty that someone must pay if he refuses to buy insurance is a kind of tax that Congress can impose using its taxing power. That is all that matters. Because the mandate survives, the Court did not need to decide what other parts of the statute were constitutional, except for a provision that required states to comply with new eligibility requirements for Medicaid or risk losing their funding. On that question, the Court held that the provision is constitutional as long as states would only lose new funds if they didn't comply with the new requirements, rather than all of their funding.[54]

---

[53] "The Supreme Court's Obamacare Decision: Full Text," The Atlantic, June 28, 2012, http://www.theatlantic.com/politics/archive/2012/06/the-supreme-courts-obamacare-decision-full-text/259102/.

In an article entitled "Roberts: Our Decision Isn't About Whether Obamacare Is Sound Policy," Chief Justice Roberts explained the ruling upholding the Affordable Care Act:

> We do not consider whether the Act embodies sound policies. That judgment is entrusted to the Nation's elected leaders. We ask only whether Congress has the power under the Constitution to enact the challenged provisions. In this case we must again determine whether the Constitution grants Congress powers it now asserts, but which many States and individuals believe it does not possess. Resolving this controversy requires us to examine both the limits of the Government's power, and our own limited role in policing those boundaries. [55]

In other words, Chief Justice Roberts first and foremost made it abundantly clear that his decision did not mean that he approved of the legislation by Congress as good policy for the nation. That was the responsibility of elected members of Congress. The question remains: Why did Chief Justice John Roberts decide to join liberal justices in ruling Obamacare constitutional? The Catholic World News explained his decision as follows:

> The US Supreme Court has upheld the constitutionality of President Obama's sweeping

[54] Derek Thompson, "The Health Care Decision Explained in 1 Paragraph on SCOTUSblog," The Atlantic, June 28, 2012, http://www.theatlantic.com/business/archive/2012/06/the-health-care-decision-explained-in-1-paragraph-on-scotusblog/259097/.

[55] Chief Justice Roberts, "Roberts: Our Decision Isn't About Whether Obamacare Is Sound Policy," Talking Points Memo Livewire, June 28, 2012, http://livewire.talkingpointsmemo.com/entries/roberts-our-decision-isnt-about-whether-obamacare-is.

health-care reform legislation. Writing for the majority in a hotly contested 5-4 decision, Chief Justice John Roberts said that the individual mandate—the requirement that every citizen must purchase health insurance—was in effect a tax. "Because the Constitution permits such a tax, it is not our role to forbid it, or to pass upon its wisdom or fairness," he wrote.

The June 28 ruling does not affect the lawsuits brought by Catholic institutions to challenge the law's requirement that all health-care insurance programs must include coverage for contraception. Those suits will continue to move forward. The US bishops' conference responded to the Supreme Court decision by urging Congress to change the law, saying that it should be amended to eliminate funding for abortion, ensure conscience rights, and provide protection for immigrants. The statement noted that the US bishops have not sought to overturn the legislation entirely.[56]

Chief Justice Roberts ruled that Obamacare (The Affordable Care Act) was constitutional because "the requirement that every citizen must purchase health insurance—was in effect a tax" and "the Constitution permits such a tax." In other words, he ruled Obamacare constitutional because the Constitution grants Congress the power to levy taxes.

As noted in the same quote from the Catholic World News, the dissenting justices, in a joint opinion, said: "In our view, the act before us is invalid in its entirety."[57] To view the

[56] "Supreme Court Upholds Obama Health-care Reform," Catholic World News, June 28, 2012, http://www.catholicculture.org/news/headlines/index.cfm?storyid=14767.
[57] Ibid.

minority opinion in its entirety, see reference at footnote.[58] For more information on the ruling, see "ObamaCare and the Power to Tax" from the Wall Street Journal,[59] "Obamacare: Dissenting Justices Opinion" from the Lorinov's Blog,[60] "Obamacare Dissenting Opinion the Original Majority Opinion?" from the Kansas Citian.[61]

CONCLUSION: Was Chief Justice Roberts correct in ruling that Obamacare (The Affordable Care Act) was constitutional because the Constitution grants Congress the power to levy taxes? Absolutely not! He was wrong because the Constitution does not grant Congress the power to force Americans to pay taxes for any purpose not authorized by the Constitution. The Constitution does not even mention healthcare. It does not grant any branch of the federal government authority to levy taxes for healthcare. Congress cannot forcefully take money from one American to pay the healthcare bills of another American.

The minority opinion held that Obamacare (The Affordable Care Act) was "invalid in its entirety." Was the minority opinion correct? Absolutely, because the federal government of the United States is a government of enumerated powers. Each branch of government only has the powers

---

[58] "SCOTUS Obamacare Ruling: The Dissenting Opinion in it's entirety," Patriots for America, June 28, 2012, http://patriotsforamerica.ning.com/forum/topics/scotus-obamacare-ruling-the-dissenting-opinion-in-it-s-entirety.

[59] ."ObamaCare and the Power to Tax," Wall Street Journal, June 28, 2012, http://online.wsj.com/article/SB100014240527023035615045774952424733 19890.html.

[60] Lorinov, "Obamacare: Dissenting Justices Opinion," Lorinov's Blog, June 28, 2012, http://roblorinov.wordpress.com/2012/06/28/obamacare-dissenting-justices-opinion/.

[61] Ed Whelan, "Obamacare Dissenting Opinion the Original Majority Opinion?," Kansas Citian, June 28, 2012, http://thekansascitian.blogspot.com/2012/06/obamacare-dissenting-opinion-original.html.

granted to it by the Constitution. Healthcare is not even mentioned in the Constitution. The federal government has absolutely no authority to enact national healthcare. Trying to use the Interstate Commerce Clause or the taxing clauses of the Constitution to justify legislation of national healthcare totally violates the intent of the Founding Fathers to establish a government of limited, enumerated powers and renders the reservation of all other powers to the states quite meaningless.

So what are the consequences of Obamacare for Christians? First, Christians are forced to pay higher federal and state taxes to pay the healthcare bills of other Americans and to fund the killing of millions of unborn or partially born American children. Second, Christians are forced to buy heath insurance or be fined. Third, Christian organizations are forced, against their deeply held moral and religious beliefs, to perform or support abortions, abortive drugs, sterilization, contraceptives, etc. Organizations that fail to comply may be fined and forced into bankruptcy.

WAR ON WOMEN

INTRODUCTION: During the 2012 election, Democrats accused Republicans of waging war on women. They accused Republicans of trying to deny women much needed healthcare i.e. contraceptives, abortions, abortive drugs, etc. They also accused Republicans of trying to wrongfully deny federal funds to Planned Parenthood, a provider of women's services to thousands of Americans.

WHO STARTED THE WAR AND WHY: Question: Exactly who took the first actions that led to the accusation of Republicans waging a war on women and why? Answer: President Obama, to win votes. In 2012, an election year, President Obama ordered Catholic health organizations (and others), contrary to their religious beliefs, to provide free contraceptives to women. Why would President Obama order Catholic leaders to act contrary to their firmly held religious beliefs during an election year? Answer: He wanted to mobilize women against Republicans and motivate them to get out the vote for Him. Did it work? Yes, very well.

WOMEN'S HEALTHCARE FUNDING: Exactly why were Democrats wrong to accuse Republicans of discriminating against women by not providing health care that they are entitled to under the Constitution? First, no Republican was trying to deny any woman the right to buy contraceptives. Second, it is a violation of the freedom of religion clause to compel Catholic organizations to provide contraceptives, abortions, and abortive drugs contrary to their religious beliefs. Third, no part of the U.S. Constitution gives the federal government authority to compel taxpayers to pay for any healthcare. The federal government only has those powers granted to it within the

Constitution. Healthcare is not mentioned. The Interstate Commerce Clause is wrongfully used to justify government action in this and many other areas not even mentioned in the Constitution. Fourth, it is morally wrong. It is theft to forcefully take lawfully earned money from one taxpayer to pay the medical bills of another taxpayer. No citizen has a right to the services of a doctor paid for by other taxpayers. No exception. No excuse. It is a matter of principle, something many Americans have a hard time grasping. The end does not justify the means.

PLANNED PARENTHOOD FUNDING: Some Republicans have, as accused, tried to block federal funding of Planned Parenthood, a major provider of women's healthcare. So why are Democrats so very wrong to accuse Republicans of wrongdoing. First, Planned Parenthood is the nation's greatest provider of abortions. Millions of Americans rightfully regard abortion as murder of unborn or partially born children. Forcing these taxpayers to pay for the murder of children is morally wrong. Second, for reasons stated above, no part of the U.S. Constitution gives the federal government authority to compel taxpayers to pay for any healthcare for any other Americans.

CONCLUSION: During 2012, Democrats accused Republicans of waging war on women. How is it possible that they can profit so greatly from such a blatant lie? Why do so many women reward the lies with their support? Why can't anyone discern the real issue, which is money. Why do Americans want to force taxpayers who believe that abortion is murder to pay for abortions? Why do they want to force Catholic organizations to provide contraceptives and abortions contrary to their deeply held moral and religious beliefs? How is it possible that President Obama and Democrats care so little about the U.S. Constitution, the highest law of the land, which they swore to uphold. Why do they completely ignore the limits of power imposed upon the federal government. Why do they care so little about the God given inalienable rights of so many

Americans, the rights to life, liberty, and freedom of religion?

HATE CRIMES AND FREEDOM OF RELIGION

INTRODUCTION: What is the position of God on hate crimes laws? Why did Congress not enact hate crimes laws during the first two hundred years of our nation's history? Scripture contains countless laws. Why are there no hate crimes laws? Were God and our nation's Founding Fathers simply unaware of the need for laws to protect men from discrimination based upon sexual orientation?

Government has jurisdiction to enforce criminal laws against murder, theft, and slander, three of the ten commandments. However, government does not have jurisdiction to force anyone to love God, love their fellow man, honor their father and mother, or to not covet their neighbor's wife or property. In other words, government has jurisdiction over criminal actions, but not over hearts and minds.

2004 PRESIDENTIAL ELECTION: During the 2004 presidential election, the NAACP ran a strong political advertisement against President George W. Bush by attacking him for his opposition to a hate crimes law. The voice of the little black girl, whose father had been dragged to death behind a truck in a southern state by two racist white men, said that when she heard about President Bush's opposition to the hate crimes law, it was as though her father had been dragged to his death again. The political advertisement completely failed to mention or acknowledge that as Governor of Texas, George W. Bush would have supported the death penalty for these men, just as he did with others less deserving of the death penalty. There was absolutely no need for a hate crimes law to ensure justice for these men. They were guilty of premeditated, aggravated, first degree murder, and according to biblical law and the laws of every state with the death penalty, they should have been put to death, not given life in prison.

2008 PRESIDENTIAL CAMPAIGN: During the 2008 presidential election, President Obama's campaign website posted this quote by Senator Obama:

> While we have come a long way since the Stonewall riots in 1969, we still have a lot of work to do. Too often, the issue of LGBT rights is exploited by those seeking to divide us. But at its core, this issue is about who we are as Americans.[62]

See the LGBT (Lesbian Gay Bisexual Transvestite) link under "People" on the campaign website of President Obama.[63] Senator Obama promised to sign a bill "to overturn the statutory ban on homosexuals serving in the military."[64] He said that as President he would sign a "federal hate crimes law that included protections based upon sexual orientation and 'gender identity'."[65] He said, "I will place the weight of my administration behind enactment of the Matthew Sheppard Act to outlaw hate crimes and a fully inclusive Employment Nondiscrimination Act.[66]

RELIGIOUS PERSECUTION: So why should anyone be concerned about Hate Crimes laws? What bad consequences could possibly result from having laws which punish

---

[62] LGBT (Lesbian Gay Bisexual Transvestite) link under "People" on 2008 campaign website of President Obama at http://pride.barackobama.com.
[63] Ibid.
[64] "Values Voter Guide for 2008 Presidential Candidates," Family Research Council Action, http://www.frcaction.org (July 9, 2008).
[65] Ibid.
[66] Michael Foust, "Obama: If Elected I Will Use the Bully Pulpit for Gay Causes," Baptist Press, Feb 28, 2008, http://www.bpnews.netbpnews.asp?id=27510 as quoted in October 2008 letter from James Dobson, Ph.D., Founder and Chairman of Focus on the Family. Full letter at Citizenlink, http://www.citizenlink.com.

discrimination based upon sexual orientation? A quick look at Europe gives a picture of where the United States is headed.

1. A British pastor said that homosexuality was a sin. He was arrested.[67]

2. A bishop in the Church of England refused to hire a gay man as a youth official. He was convicted of unlawful discrimination.[68]

3. A Christian couple told a Muslim that Jesus was the Son of God. They were convicted of a hate crime. Later the case was dismissed.[69]

4. A Christian grandmother wrote a letter to the Norwich city council expressing her disapproval of a gay-pride event. She was investigated.[70]

5. An elderly Christian couple in Cornwall, England refused to rent a room with one double bed to two gay men. They were fined about $2,850 each and have been continually harassed by phone calls and homosexual couples wanting to rent from them.[71] The 71 year old husband had a heart attack. Even a gay British politician defended them:

Mr. and Mrs. Bull have been tagged as homophones, taken to court, forced to justify

---

[67] Jeff Johnston, "The Penalty for Diversity," January 28, 2011, Citizenlink, http://www.citizenlink.com. See also "UK Pastor Arrested Over Comments on Homosexuality," Citizenlink, http://www.citizenlink.com/2010/05/citizenlink-uk-pastor-arrested-over-comments-on-homosexuality/.

[68] Ibid. See also British Broadcasting Company, http://news.bbc.co.uk/2/hi/uk_news/wales/6904057/stm.

[69] Ibid. See also Paul Bracchi, "It May Have Been a Victory for Free Speech, But Why Did Breakfast Insult of Muslim's Faith Case Ever Come to Court?", DailyMail, http://www.dailymail.co.uk/news/article-1234680/ It-victory-free-speech-did-breakfast-insult=Muslims-faith-case-come-court.html.

[70] Ibid. See also "So-Called Hate Speech," Citizenlink, http://www.citizenlink.com/2010/03/citizenlink-so-called-hate-speech/.

[71] Ibid.

their literal interpretation of the Bible, told by the Judge involved that their views are out of date and, finally, given a punishment which will place a significant strain upon their business finances. In the end, the penalty for holding a diverse viewpoint has been extreme.[72]

One of the gay men said,

We're really pleased that the judge has confirmed what we already know—that…our civil partnership has the same status in law as marriage between a man and a woman, and that regardless of each person's religious beliefs, no one is above the law.[73]

The United States is headed in the same direction. Consider this quote:

Cities and states all over the U.S. have passed laws giving special protections based on sexual orientation and gender identity. More and more schools teach children about homosexuality— even against parents' wishes. A judge declares belief in one-man-one-woman marriage "irrational." And groups like the Alliance Defense Fund constantly have to battle for the rights of freedom of speech, freedom of religion and freedom of association.[74]

Consider the extreme consequences of federal hate crimes laws for all Americans. They punish hateful thoughts as

---

[72] Ibid. See also "Widdecombe and Gay Tory Defend Cornish BB Owners, The Christian Institute, http://www.christian.org.uk/news/widdecombe-and-gay-tory-defend-cornish-bb-owners/.
[73] Ibid.
[74] Ibid.

crimes, totally contrary to biblical principles and the U.S. Constitution. Americans could go to jail just for repeating words which God the Father spoke to Moses in Leviticus, or words that the Apostle Paul used in his letter to the Romans. In Sweden a minister was placed in prison for giving a sermon that discussed Scripture regarding homosexuality.

There would also be severe consequences for all American schools, churches, and places of employment. Schools and employers would be required to conduct diversity training that would teach students and employees that the homosexual lifestyle, which God told Moses was an abomination, is an acceptable lifestyle. They would also be warned about the possible consequences of any criticism of this lifestyle i.e. counseling, disciplinary action, legal action, or job termination. Employers and possibly churches would be required to not discriminate on the basis of sexual orientation in hiring or treatment of workers. In other words, churches may be required to hire homosexuals and be careful not say anything critical about a lifestyle that is an abomination to God and, worst of all, not repeat any of the words which God spoke to Moses or Paul wrote to the Romans. Doing so might land them in jail, just like the Swedish pastor.

CONCLUSION: Hate crimes laws are wrong because they criminalize thoughts, not just actions. Governments have authority to punish wrongful actions, not thoughts that they deem wrong. The punishment should not be greater or lesser based upon the race or sexual orientation of the victim. Being a racist or hating homosexuals are not crimes punishable by government. A holy God will ensure full justice for every evil thought and word, but government has no jurisdiction over the hearts and minds of men.

A government that tries to exercise jurisdiction over the hearts and minds of men becomes an oppressor and wrongfully deprives men of their God given inalienable rights to freedom of speech and freedom of religion. Government officials are "minister of God" with a duty to punish evildoers. Hate crimes laws written to protect men from discrimination based upon sexual orientation empower government officials to protect evildoers and punish Christians with fines and prison time for simply trying to live according to Christian values. American Christians will face greatly increased persecution for living Christian values.

CHRISTIAN VOTER GUIDANCE

SECTION REVIEW: This section reviews Christian Voter Guidance available during 2012 for members of Congress. The first chapter reviews congressional vote scorecards developed by Family Research Council and Citizenlink, an affiliate of Focus on the Family (formerly known as Focus Action). The second chapter reviews congressional vote scorecards developed by National Right to Life.

CHAPTERS: Chapters in this section include the following:
6.1 Congressional Scorecards: FRC Action and Citizenlink
6.2 Congressional Scorecards: National Right to Life

CONGRESSIONAL SCORECARDS: FRC ACTION AND CITIZENLINK

INTRODUCTION: The best way to evaluate a candidate is not to look at what he said or promised when trying to get elected, but how he actually voted. Voting records reveal extreme differences between Republicans and Democrats. Most Republicans vote Christian values most of the time. Most Democrats vote against Christian values most of the time. The extreme degree to which this is true is almost beyond belief, but clearly proven by scorecards that show exactly how elected officials voted on issues that required the application of Christian values.

Each year Family Research Council Action (FRC Action) and Citizenlink, an affiliate of Focus on the Family (formerly called Focus Action) produce a "Vote Scorecard" that shows how members of Congress voted on "the most clear-cut, pro-family votes." This chapter will review the scorecards published during two election years: 2008 and 2012. During 2008, FRC Action and Focus Action published a scorecard for 100th Congress, First Session that covered votes cast during 2007.[75] During 2012, FRC Action and Citizenlink published a scorecard for 112th Congress, First Session that covered votes cast during 2011.[76] Go to http://www.frcaction.org to view scorecards and see exactly how every member of Congress voted.

---

[75] FRC Action and Focus on the Family Action, "Vote Scorecard, 110th Congress, 1st Session," http://www.frcaction.org (accessed July 9, 2008).
[76] FRC Action and Citizenlink, "Vote Scorecard, 112th Congress, 1st Session," http://www.frcaction.org (accessed February 17, 2012).

2008 SENATE SCORECARD: The 2008 scorecard reveals extreme disparity between the voting records of Republicans and Democrats in the U.S. Senate. Senator Obama and Senator Biden scored 0%. Republicans scored an amazingly high average of 86%. Most Republicans scored 100% (58%; 29 of 50). They voted on all 7 pro-family issues, and always voted with the recommendation of Focus Action and FRC Action. Ten Republicans (20%) scored 85-99%. Seven Republicans (14%) scored 57-71%. One Republican (2%) scored 42% (Senator McCain). Three Republicans (6%) scored 28% (Senators Collins and Snowe of Connecticut and Spector of Pennsylvania). No Republican scored lower than 28%. Democrats scored an average of only 8.02%, less than one-tenth the average score of Republicans.[77]

Most Democrats scored 0% (67%; 33 of 49). They voted against the position of Focus Action and FRC Action, against Christian values, on all 7 issues. Eleven Democrats (22%) scored 14%. One Democrat (2%) scored 28%. Three Democrats (6%) scored 42%. One Democrat (2%) scored 85% (Senator Nelson of Nebraska). No Democrat scored 100%.[78]

Senators were evaluated on 7 critical "pro-family" issues. The legislation included:
Issue 1: An amendment to the Lobby Reform Act to protect grassroots organizations from unfair regulation of lobbying activities;[79]
Issue 2: The Embryonic Stem Cell Research Act, a bill funding embryonic stem cell research that required destruction of human embryos;[80]

---

[77] FRC Action and Focus on the Family Action, "Vote Scorecard, 110th Congress, 1st Session," http://www.frcaction.org (accessed July 9, 2008).
[78] Ibid.
[79] Ibid.
[80] Ibid.

Issue 3: An amendment to the State Children's Health Insurance Program to allow states to provide health insurance for unborn children;[81]

Issue 4: An amendment to the State, Foreign Operations and Related Programs Appropriations Act to prevent funding of international groups "that support or participate in coercive abortion or involuntary sterilization programs;"[82]

Issue 5: An amendment to the same Act that would have funded international organizations "that perform and promote abortions as a method of family planning;[83]

Issue 6: A "thought crimes amendment" to the Department of Defense Authorization that "would establish federal 'hate crimes' for certain violent acts based on the actual or perceived race, religion, disability, gender identity or sexual orientation of any person;"[84] and

Issue 7: Confirmation of Judge Southwick, nominated by President Bush, to the U.S. Court of Appeals.[85]

Senate Republicans sponsored all 4 bills, amendments or motions supporting Christian values. No Democrat sponsored any pro-Christian, pro-family values legislation, but they did sponsor 3 bills or amendments contrary to Christian values. Most Senate Democrats supported all anti-Christian legislation opposed by Republicans (Issues 1,2,4,5,6). They opposed all pro-Christian values legislation supported by Republicans (Issue 3) and opposed confirmation of conservative federal judge who supports Christian values (Issue 7).

Most Senate Republicans opposed: (1) laws regulating lobbying that inhibit Christian organizations from providing information to the public on matters before Congress (Issue 1); (2) federal funds for embryonic stem cell research that require

---

[81] Ibid.
[82] Ibid.
[83] Ibid.
[84] Ibid.
[85] Ibid.

destruction of human embryos (Issue 2); (3) federal funds for international groups that support abortion or involuntary sterilization (Issues 4,5); (4) hate crimes laws that wrongfully criminalize thoughts not just actions regarding "race, religion, disability, gender identity or sexual orientation" (Issue 6). Most Republicans supported: (1) confirmation of a federal judge who supports Christian values (Issue 7) and (2) laws that permit states to have health insurance for unborn children (Issue 3).

2008 HOUSE OF REPRESENTATIVES SCORECARD: The 2008 scorecard also reveals extreme disparity between the voting records of Republicans and Democrats in the U.S. House of Representatives. Republicans scored an average of 87%. Most Republicans scored 100% (53%; 108 of 203). They voted on all 11 pro-family issues, and they always voted with the recommendation of Focus Action and FRC Action. 54 Republicans (27%) scored 76-99%. 26 Republicans (13%) scored 51-75%. Nine Republicans (4.4%) scored 26-50%. Five Republicans (2%) scored 1-25% (Congressman Shays of Connecticut, Castle of Delaware, Kirk of Illinois, Gilchrest of Maryland, and Frelinghuysen of New Jersey). Only one Republican (0.5 %) scored 0% (Congressman Norwood of Georgia).[86]

Democrats scored an average of only 10%, about one-eighth the average score of Republicans. Almost half of the Democrats scored 0% (46%; 109 of 235). They always voted against the position of Focus Action and FRC Action, against Christian values, on all issues. 72 Democrats (another 31%) scored only 6%, barely above 0. 29 Democrats (12%) scored 12-25%. 9 Democrats (4%) scored 26-50%. 9 Democrats (4%) scored 51-75%. Only 5 of 235 Democrats (2%) scored 76-99% (Congressman Marshall of Georgia, Ellsworth of Indiana, Peterson of Minnesota, and Taylor of Mississippi Lincoln Davis of Tennessee. Only 2 of 235 Democrats (1%) scored 100%

---

[86] Ibid.

(Congressmen McIntyre and Shuler of North Carolina).[87]

Representatives were evaluated on 16 "pro-family" issues. The legislation included:

Issue 1: A motion to recommit the Embryonic Stem Cell Research Act that would ensure that taxpayer funds were not used for human cloning."[88]

Issue 2: The Embryonic Stem Cell Research Act, which would fund stem cell research that required destruction of human embryos.[89]

Issue 3: A motion to recommit the Head Start Reauthorization bill that would remove a provision that "prevents faith-based organizations from hiring according to their faith.[90]

Issue 4: Federal Hate Crimes Act, a "thought crimes bill" that "would establish federal 'hate crimes' for certain violent acts based on the actual or perceived race, religion, disability, gender identity or sexual orientation of any person."[91]

Issue 5: Human Cloning Protection Act, a bill that would allow "the creation of cloned human embryos for destructive research."[92]

Issue 6: Embryonic Stem Cell Research Act, a bill funding embryonic stem cell research that required destruction of human embryos.[93]

Issue 7: An amendment to the State, Foreign Operations and Related Programs Appropriations Act that would require "a third of HIV/AIDs prevention funding to be spent for 'abstinence-until-marriage' and 'be-faithful' programs.[94]

---

[87] Ibid.
[88] Ibid.
[89] Ibid.
[90] Ibid.
[91] Ibid.
[92] Ibid.
[93] Ibid.
[94] Ibid.

Issue 8: A amendment to the State, Foreign Operations and Related Programs Appropriations Act that would allow "taxpayer funded contraceptives to be given to international organizations that perform and promote abortions as a method of family planning."[95]

Issue 9: An amendment to same Act that would have "upheld the prohibition against federal funding of international organizations that perform and promote abortions as a method of family planning."[96]

Issue 10: State, Foreign Operations and Related Programs Appropriations Act, a bill that undermines the funding of "abstinence-until-marriage" and "be-faithful" programs and the prohibition of federal funding of "international organizations that perform or promote abortions as a method of family planning."[97]

Issue 11: An amendment to the Financial Services and General Government Appropriations Act that restricts funding of needle exchange programs in the District of Columbia.[98]

Issue 12: An amendment to the same Act that "strips the Federal Communications Commission of the authority to reinstitute" the…"Fairness Doctrine"…that would "order broadcasters to give equal air time to both sides of controversial issues."[99]

Issue 13: Another amendment to the same Act that would prevent federal funds from being used by the District of Columbia for domestic partner benefits.[100]

Issue 14: An amendment to the Labor, Health and Human Services and Education Appropriations Act that would restrict use of federal funds for abortions by withholding $331 million appropriated to Planned Parenthood, the nation's leading abortion provider, for "family planning services."[101]

---

[95] Ibid.
[96] Ibid.
[97] Ibid.
[98] Ibid.
[99] Ibid.
[100] Ibid.

Issue 15: The Children's Health and Medicine Protection Act, a bill that reauthorizes and expands the State Children's Health Insurance Program. It undermines health coverage for unborn children, allows states to provide family planning services for individuals not eligible for Medicaid, and undermine abstinence education.[102]

Issue 16: The Employment Non-Discrimination Act, it provides special protection for homosexuals not given to other employees and radically transforms workplace discrimination law.[103]

In the House of Representatives, Republicans sponsored 7 pro-family, pro-Christian bills, amendments, or motions, and Democrats sponsored 8 contrary to Christian values. A Republican and a Democrat jointly sponsored only 1 of the 16 issues. Most Democrats in the House supported all anti-Christian values legislation supported by Republicans and opposed all pro-Christian values legislation supported by Republicans.

Most Republicans in the House, like Republicans in the Senate, opposed: (1) federal funds for embryonic stem cell research that requires the destruction of human embryos (Issues 2,6); (2) federal funds for groups that support abortion (Issues 8,9,10); (3) hate crimes laws which wrongfully criminalize thoughts not just actions regarding "race, religion, disability, gender identity or sexual orientation" (Issue 4). House Republicans also opposed: (1) use of taxpayer funds for cloning human embryos for destructive research (Issues 1,5); (2) legislation that prevents faith-based organizations from hiring according to their faith for the Head Start Program (Issue 3); (3) a law which would require part of HIV/AIDs prevention funding to be spent for "abstinence-until-marriage" and "be-faithful"

---

[101] Ibid.
[102] Ibid.
[103] Ibid.

programs (Issues 7,10); (4) restrictions on funds for needle exchange programs in the District of Columbia (Issue 11); (5) the 'Fairness Doctrine,' which would inhibit Christian broadcasters by forcing them to give equal time to both sides of issues (Issue 12); (6) use of federal funds by the District of Columbia for domestic partner benefits (Issue 13); (7) use of federal funds for abortions by Planned Parenthood (Issue 14); (8) allowing states to fund family planning for those not eligible for Medicaid and requiring states to fund family planning as part of Medicaid (Issue 15); (9) granting special consideration on the basis of "sexual orientation" not extended to other employees in the workplace (Issue 16). House Republicans supported state health coverage for unborn children and state abstinence education programs (Issue 15).

2012 SENATE SCORECARD: The 2012 scorecard reveals extreme disparity between the voting records of Republicans and Democrats in the U.S. Senate. The average score for Republicans was 73%. The average score for Democrats was less than 2% (1.65%). No Democrat scored above 14%. 88% of Democrats scored an absolute 0%.[104]

Senators were evaluated on 7 "pro-family" issues. The legislation included:

Issue 1: An amendment to the FAA Authorization Bill that would repeal Obamacare, the national health care law called the Patient Protection and Affordable Care Act, a law that funded abortion, denied conscience protections, and instituted health care rationing.[105]

Issue 2: A Continuing Resolution to fund abortion in the District of Columbia that did not exclude funding for Planned Parenthood.[106]

---

[104] FRC Action and Citizenlink, "Vote Scorecard, 112th Congress, 1st Session," http://www.frcaction.org (accessed February 17, 2012).
[105] Ibid.
[106] Ibid.

Issue 3: An amendment to the Department of Defense and Full Year Continuing Appropriations Act of 2011 that would prevent funding of the health care act (Patient Protection and Affordable Care Act), a law that funded abortion, denied conscience protections, and instituted health care rationing.[107]

Issue 4: An amendment to the Department of Defense and Full Year Continuing Appropriations Act of 2011 that would prevent funding of Planned Parenthood, the nation's largest abortion provider.[108]

Issue 5: A vote on John McConnell for U.S. District Judge. Nominated by President Obama, there was evidence that he would not be an impartial judge and that he would legislate from the bench. [109]

Issue 6: A vote on Goodwin Liu for U.S. Court of Appeals Circuit Judge. Nominated by President Obama, there was evidence that he would be an activist judge and replace the Constitution with personal views.[110]

Issue 7: A bill that would authorize the President to make appointments to thousands of government positions without Senate confirmation.[111]

2012 HOUSE OF REPRESENTATIVES SCORECARD: The 2012 scorecard also reveals extreme disparity between the voting records of Republicans and Democrats in the U.S. House of Representatives. The average score for Republicans was about 89%. The average score for Democrats was about 9%. 91% of Democrats scored 10% or less.[112]

Representatives were evaluated on 10 "pro-family" issues. The legislation included:

---

[107] Ibid.
[108] Ibid.
[109] Ibid.
[110] Ibid.
[111] Ibid.
[112] Ibid.

Issue 1: The Repealing the Job-Killing Health Care Law would repeal Obamacare, the national health care law called the Patient Protection and Affordable Care Act, a law that funded abortion, denied conscience protections, and instituted health care rationing.[113]

Issue 2: An amendment to the Full-Year Continuing Appropriations Act that would prevent funding of Planned Parenthood, the nation's largest abortion provider.[114]

Issue 3: A Continuing Resolution with funding for abortion in the District of Columbia and funding for Planned Parenthood.[115]

Issue 4: The Scholarships for Opportunity and Results Act would reauthorize the D.C. Opportunity Scholarship Program to allow students in the District of Columbia to attend the school of their choice.[116]

Issue 5: An amendment to the Department of Defense and Full Year Continuing Appropriations Act of 2011 that would prevent funding of Obamacare, the national health care law called the Patient Protection and Affordable Care Act, a law that funded abortion, denied conscience protections, and instituted health care rationing.[117]

Issue 6: An amendment to the Department of Defense and Full Year Continuing Appropriations Act of 2011 that would prevent funding of Planned Parenthood, the nation's largest abortion provider.[118]

Issue 7: The No Taxpayer Funding of Abortion Act was an amendment that would permanently prevent federal funds from paying for abortions and health care plans that covered abortions and protect conscience rights of health care providers who objected to doing abortions.[119]

---

[113] Ibid.
[114] Ibid.
[115] Ibid.
[116] Ibid.
[117] Ibid.
[118] Ibid.
[119] Ibid.

Issue 8: The Foxx amendment to change Obamacare, the national health care law called the Patient Protection and Affordable Care Act, to bar federal funding of abortions and use for educating medical students on how to perform abortions.[120]

Issue 9: An amendment to the Department of Defense Appropriations Act of 2012 that would prevent Pentagon funds from being used contrary to Defense of Marriage Act.[121]

Issue 10: Another amendment to the same Act that would prohibit funding of Navy a directive allowing chaplains to perform same-sex marriages in violation of the Defense of Marriage Act.[122]

CONCLUSION: The scorecards jointly produced by Family Research Council Action (FRC Action) and Citizenlink, an affiliate of Focus on the Family (formerly Focus on the Family Action) show how members of Congress voted on "the most clear-cut, pro-family votes." The 2008 Senate scorecard showed that Senator Obama and Senator Biden scored 0%. Senate Republicans scored an average of 86%. Most Republicans scored 100% (58%; 29 of 50). Senate Democrats scored an average of only 8.02%, less than one-tenth the average score of Republicans. Most Democrats scored 0% (67%; 33 of 49).

In the House of Representatives, Republicans scored an average of 87%. Most Republicans scored 100% (53%; 108 of 203). Democrats scored an average of only 10%, about one-eighth the average score of Republicans. Almost half of the Democrats scored 0% (46%; 109 of 235). 72 Democrats (another 31%) scored only 6%, barely above 0. In other words, 77% of Democrats (181 if 235) scored either 0% or 6%.

---

[120] Ibid.
[121] Ibid.
[122] Ibid.

On the 2012 Senate scorecard, the average score for Republicans was 73%. The average score for Democrats was less than 2% (1.65%). No Democrat scored above 14%. 88% of Democrats scored an absolute 0%. In the House of Representatives, the average score for Republicans was about 89%. The average score for Democrats was about 9%. 91% of Democrats scored 10% or less.

Knowing these facts raises a couple questions. How can anyone who calls himself a Christian vote for any Democrat knowing that Democrats are so united in voting against Christian values? How can any Christian do anything that would help put Democrats in power, knowing that they would govern totally contrary to simple, basic moral laws revealed by God through Scripture? Jesus said His food was to do the will of His Father. Voting for a Democrat or doing anything that would put Democrats in power is totally contrary to what it means to be a Christian.

CONGRESSIONAL SCORECARDS: NATIONAL RIGHT TO LIFE

INTRODUCTION: National Right to Life produces "Vote Scorecards" similar to that of Family Research Council Action and Citizenlink (formerly Focus Action). They show how members of Congress voted on issues related to abortion, health care, etc. All voting results discussed within this chapter are from the National Right to Life Committee (NRLC) "Federal NRLC Scorecard" for 110th Congress and 112th Congress.[123] The author of this book calculated all percentages. Go to http://www.nrlc.org to view scorecards and see exactly how every member of Congress voted.

2008 SENATE SCORECARD: The 2008 National Right to Life scorecard for 110th Congress reveals amazing disparity between the voting records of Republicans and Democrats in the U.S. Senate. Senator Obama and Senator Biden scored 0%. Senate Republicans scored an average of 88%. Most Republicans scored 100% (63%; 32 of 51). Eleven Republicans (22%) scored 83-85%. Five Republicans (10%) scored 57-66%. Three Republicans (6%) scored only 14%. No Republican scored lower.[124]

In 2008 Senate Democrats scored an average of only 9%, about one-tenth the average score of Republicans. Most

---

[123] National Right to Life Committee, "Federal NRLC Scorecard - 110th Congress, Combined Sessions," http://www.nrlc.org (accessed July 7, 2008); National Right to Life Committee, "Federal NRLC Scorecard - 110th Congress, Combined Sessions," http://www.nrlc.org (accessed July 21, 2012).

[124] National Right to Life Committee, "Federal NRLC Scorecard - 110th Congress, Combined Sessions," http://www.nrlc.org (accessed July 7, 2008).

Democrats scored 0% (71%; 35 of 49). They voted against the position of NRLC, against Christian values, on all 7 issues. Six Democrats (12%) scored 14%. Five Democrats (10%) scored 28-33%. Two Democrats (4%) scored 57-66%. One Democrat (2%) scored 85% (Senator Nelson of Nebraska). No Democrat scored 100%.[125]

Senators were evaluated on 7 critical "pro-family" issues. The legislation included:

Issue 1: Regulation of "grassroots lobbying" groups. Amendment (No. 20) to 2007 Lobby Reform Act (S.1) This amendment "infringed on rights protected by the First Amendment, and would inhibit groups from providing timely motivating information to members of the public about matters under consideration in Congress." It would "require registration and reporting by certain activists and groups who spend money to encourage members of the general public to communicate with members of Congress or other federal officials about legislative and policy matters." Violations would were punishable by fines of up to $200,000 and prison terms of up to 10 years.[126]

Issue 2: Stem Cell Research Enhancement Act (S. 5). This bill "would mandate federal funding of the type of stem cell research that requires the killing of human embryos."[127]

Issue 3: Medicare prescription drug price controls (Senate Bill 3). This bill would prevent "older people from being allowed to spend their own money…to save their own lives through access to unrationed prescription drugs under Medicare. Under the guise of allowing "government negotiation" the bill would authorize the imposition of price controls that would limit access to and discourage the development of innovative life-saving medicines."[128]

---

[125] Ibid.
[126] Ibid.
[127] Ibid.
[128] Ibid.

Issue 4: Health Insurance for Unborn Child. Amendment (No. 2535) to H.R. 976, a bill to reauthorize the State Children's Health Insurance Program (SCHIP). "The State Children's Health Insurance (SCHIP) program is a federal program that provides funds to states primarily to provide health services to children of low-income families. The Amendment states that a covered child "includes, at the option of a State, an unborn child."[129]

Issue 5: Banning Funding of Organizations that Support Coercive Abortion Programs. Amendment (No. 2707) to the Senate State, Foreign Operations and Related Programs Appropriations Act 2008 (H.R. 2764). The Kemp-Kasten Anti-Coercion law has been in effect since 1985. It prohibits U.S. "population assistance" funds from going to any organization that "supports or participates in the management of a program of coercive abortion or involuntary sterilization." "However, in crafting the Fiscal Year 2008 State-Foreign Operations Appropriations Bill (H.R. 2764), the Senate Appropriations Committee removed the traditional Kemp-Kasten language.... Senator Sam Brownback (R-Ks.) offered an NRLC-backed amendment...to restore the...Kemp-Kasten anti-coercion language."[130]

Issue 6: Funding International Abortion Groups. Amendment (No. 2719) to the Senate State, Foreign Operations and Related Programs Appropriations Act 2008 (H.R. 2764). "Known as the "Boxer Amendment to overturn pro-life "Mexico City Policy"... Under the pro-life "Mexico City Policy," private overseas organizations that "perform or actively promote abortion as a method of family planning" are not eligible to receive funds for "population assistance." Pro-abortion Senator Boxer (D-Ca.) offered an amendment to prohibit enforcement of any pro-life policy.[131]

Issue 7: Prohibition on Abortion Services in Indian

---

[129] Ibid.
[130] Ibid.
[131] Ibid.

Health Programs. Vitter amendment to Senate Bill 1200. The federal government funds health programs for American Indians. During the 1970s, it paid for abortions. Funding of abortions was stopped in the 1980s, but this policy depended on annual renewal of the Hyde Amendment. On February 26, 2008, , Senator Vitter (R-La.) offered an NRLC-backed amendment to permanently prohibit coverage of abortion (except to save the life of the mother, or in cases of rape or incest)."[132]

Note the types of legislation supported by Republicans and Democrats in the Senate. Most Republicans opposed: (1) laws regulating lobbying that would inhibit Christian organizations from providing information to the public on matters before Congress (Senate issue 1); (2) federal funds for embryonic stem cell research that require the destruction of human embryos (Senate issue 2); (3) laws that would impose "price controls that would limit access to and discourage the development of innovative life-saving medicines" for elderly Americans using Medicare (Senate Issue 3); (4) federal funds for international groups that support abortion or involuntary sterilization (Senate issue 5,6);and (5) federal funds for abortions by American Indians (Senate issue7). Most Republicans supported: (1) laws that permit states to have health insurance for unborn children (Senate issue 4). Most Senate Democrats supported all anti-Christian legislation opposed by Republicans and opposed all pro-Christian values legislation supported by Republicans.

2008 HOUSE OF REPRESENTATIVES SCORECARD: The 2008 National Right to Life Committee (NRLC) Scorecard also reveals great disparity between the voting records of Republicans and Democrats in the U.S. House of Representatives. House Republicans scored an average of 88%. A large majority of Republicans scored 100% (71%; 143 of 201). They voted on all 7 pro-family issues, and they always

---

[132] Ibid.

voted with the recommendation of NRLC. 20 Republicans (10%) scored 76-99%. 19 Republicans (9.5%) scored 51-75%. 11 Republicans (5.5%) scored 26-50%. Five Republicans (2.5%) scored 1-25%). Three Republicans (0.5 %) scored 0%.[133]

In 2008 House Democrats scored an average of only 7%, less than one-tenth the average score of Republicans. A very large majority of Democrats scored 0% (85%; 199 of 233). They always voted against the position of NRLC, against Christian values, on all issues. 10 Democrats (4%) scored 1-25%. 8 Democrats (3%) scored 26-50%. 8 Democrats (3%) scored 51-75%. 8 Democrats (3%) scored 76-99%. No Democrat scored 100%.[134]

Representatives were evaluated on 7 critical "pro-family" issues. The legislation included:
Issue 1: Prohibition on Funding of Human Cloning. Stem Cell Research Enhancement Act" (H.R. 3) Anti-Cloning Amendment. "On January 11, 2007, the House of Representatives debated H.R. 3, authored by Rep. Diana DeGette (D-Co.) and Mike Castle (R-De.), a bill that would mandate federal funding of the type of stem cell research that requires the killing of human embryos in order to harvest their stem cells. The embryos would be those "donated from in vitro fertilization clinics, [and that] were created for the purposes of fertility treatment," after authorization by the parents. The bill, which NRLC strongly opposed, is intended to overturn the pro-life policy that President Bush announced on August 9, 2001, under which federal funds do not support research that requires the killing of human embryos. The House Democratic leadership brought the bill to the floor under a "closed rule," which allowed the pro-life side to offer only a single proposed modification to the bill. This amendment (technically called a "motion to recommit with instructions") would have added language to the

[133] Ibid.
[134] Ibid.

bill to prohibit any of the funds authorized by the bill from being given to labs or other entities that do research on stem cells obtained from human embryos created by cloning. NRLC is opposed to human cloning, so NRLC supported this anti-human-cloning motion/amendment."[135]

Issue 2: Stem Cell Research. Embryonic Stem Cell Research Enhancement Act (H.R. 3). H.R. 3 was "a bill that would mandate federal funding of the type of stem cell research that requires the killing of human embryos in order to harvest their stem cells."[136]

Issue 3: Medicare Prescription Drug Price Negotiation Act (H.R. 4). This bill "would effectively prevent older people from being allowed to spend their own money, if they choose, to save their own lives through access to unrationed prescription drugs under Medicare. Under the guise of "government negotiation" the bill would result in the imposition of price controls that would limit access to and discourage the development of innovative life-saving medicines."[137]

Issue 4: Phony Ban on Human Cloning. Human Cloning Protection Act (H.R. 2560). This bill (H.R. 2560) is "deceptively titled "The Human Cloning Prohibition Act." But in reality H.R. 2560 does not ban any human cloning at all. H.R. 2560 would allow the creation of any number of cloned human embryos, for the specific purpose of harvesting their stem cells or using them in other research that will kill them. H.R. 2560 actually bans only allowing a human clone to live, by implanting her or him "into a uterus or the functional equivalent of a uterus," or "to ship, mail, transport, or receive" such an embryo. NRLC strongly opposes this "clone-and-kill bill."[138]

Issue 5: Embryonic Stem Cell Research Enhancement Act of 2007 (S. 5). This bill "would mandate federal funding of the type of stem cell research that requires the killing of human

---

[135] Ibid.
[136] Ibid.
[137] Ibid.
[138] Ibid.

embryos. This bill would <u>overturn President Bush's policy</u> that prohibits such funding."[139]

Issue 6: International Abortion Funding. Amendment (H.AMDT. 368) to the State, Foreign Operations and Related Programs Appropriations Act, 2008 (H.R. 2764). This amendment was known as the "Smith-Stupak Amendment" to protect the pro-life "Mexico City Policy." "Under President Bush's pro-life "Mexico City Policy," <u>private overseas organizations that "perform or actively promote abortion</u> as a method of family planning" are not eligible to receive <u>funds under the U.S. foreign aid program for "population assistance</u>." The Fiscal Year 2008 State-Foreign Operations Appropriations Bill (H.R. 2764) contained language, authored by pro-abortion Rep. Nita Lowey (D-NY), designed to undermine the "Mexico City Policy" by requiring the U.S. Agency for International Development (USAID) to provide such pro-abortion organizations with certain U.S.-funded contraceptive supplies. Pro-life Representatives Chris Smith (R-NJ) and Bart Stupak (D-Mi.) offered an <u>amendment</u>, which was <u>strongly supported by NRLC, to remove the pro-abortion language from the bill</u>."[140]

Issue 7: Restrict Funding to Planned Parenthood. Amendment (H.AMDT. 594) to the Labor, Health and Human Services, and Education Appropriations Act, 2008 (H.R. 3043). <u>This amendment would deny federal "family-planning" funds to Planned Parenthood</u>. "Title X ("Title 10") of the Public Health Service Act provides more than $300 million annually for grants to state and private entities for "family planning" programs. Although federal law does not permit such funds to be used to pay for abortions, large amounts of Title X funds go to organizations that operate abortion clinics, including affiliates of the Planned Parenthood Federation of America (PPFA), the <u>nation's largest abortion provider</u>. On July 19, 2007, during consideration of the Fiscal Year 2008 appropriations bill for the federal Department of Health and Human Services, pro-life

---

[139] Ibid.
[140] Ibid.

Congressman Mike Pence (R-In.) offered an amendment to prohibit any Title X funds from going to any arm of Planned Parenthood."[141]

Note that most Republicans in the House, like Republicans in the Senate, opposed: (1) federal funds for embryonic stem cell research that requires the destruction of human embryos (House issues 2,4,5); (2) laws that would impose "price controls that would limit access to and discourage the development of innovative life-saving medicines" for elderly Americans using Medicare (House Issue 3); (3) federal funds for international groups that support abortion or involuntary sterilization (House issue 6). House Republicans also opposed: (1) taxpayer funds for cloning human embryos for destructive research (House issue 1) and (2) federal funds for Planned Parenthood, the nation's largest abortion provider (House issue 7). Most Democrats in the House supported all anti-Christian values legislation supported by Republicans and opposed all pro-Christian values legislation supported by Republicans. No Democrat sponsored any pro-Christian, pro-life legislation, but they did sponsor all bills and amendments contrary to Christian values. Republicans sponsored all bills and amendments that support Christian values.

2012 SENATE SCORECARD: The 2012 National Right to Life Committee (NRLC) Scorecard reveals great disparity between the voting records of Republicans and Democrats in the U.S. Senate. Senators were evaluated on 5 issues. Senate Republicans scored an average of 97%. Most Republicans scored 100% (90%; 43 of 48). Only five Republicans (10%; 5 of 48) scored less than 100%. Senate Democrats scored an average of only 1%. Most Democrats scored 0% (94%; 48 of 51). They voted against the position of NRLC, against Christian values, on all issues. Only 3 Democrats (6%) scored higher than 0%.[142]

---

[141] Ibid.
[142] National Right to Life Committee, "Federal NRLC Scorecard - 110th

Senators were evaluated on 5 critical "pro-family" issues. The legislation included:

Issue 1: Repeal Obamacare health care law. This was an amendment to completely repeal Obamacare, the Patient Protection and Affordable Care Act, the "massive health care restructuring law enacted March 2010. The PPACA contained many provisions that would implement government –imposed rationing of life-saving health care and included federal funding of abortion.[143]

Issue 2: Block funding of Obamacare health care law. This bill was an attempt to block funding of Obamacare, the Patient Protection and Affordable Care Act discussed above.[144]

Issue 3: Cut federal funding of Planned Parenthood. This was a bill to cut all federal funding to Planned Parenthood Federation of American (PPFA), the nation's number one provider of abortions.[145]

Issue 4: Prevent Obama abortion mandates. This bill, the Respect for Rights of Conscience Act, would amend the Obamacare law to permit employers and health insurers to refuse to cover services to which they had a moral or religious objection, services such as abortion.[146]

Issue 5: "Disclose Act" to restrict political free speech. This bill, opposed by NRLC, was designed to restrict freedom of "political speech about members of Congress, candidates for Congress, and ongoing developments in Congress."[147]

2012 HOUSE OF REPRESENTATIVES SCORECARD: The 2012 National Right to Life Committee

---

Congress, Combined Sessions," http://www.nrlc.org (accessed July 21, 2012).

[143] Ibid.
[144] Ibid.
[145] Ibid.
[146] Ibid.
[147] Ibid.

(NRLC) Scorecard reveals great disparity between the voting records of Republicans and Democrats in the House of Representatives. Members of the House of Representatives were evaluated on 5 issues. House Republicans scored an average of 98%. Most Republicans scored 100% (94%; 229 of 243). Only 14 Republicans (6%; 14 of 243) scored less than 100%. House Democrats scored an average of only 5%. Most Democrats scored 0% (88%; 171 of 194). They voted against the position of NRLC, against Christian values, on all issues. Only 23 Democrats (12%) scored higher than 0% (23 of 243).[148]

Representatives were evaluated on 9 critical "pro-family" issues. The legislation included:

Issue 1: H.R.2 to repeal Obamacare health care law. This was an amendment to completely repeal Obamacare, the Patient Protection and Affordable Care Act, the "massive health care restructuring law enacted March 2010. The PPACA contained many provisions that would implement government –imposed rationing of life-saving health care and included federal funding of abortion.[149]

Issue 2: Cut federal funding of Planned Parenthood. This was a bill to cut all federal funding to Planned Parenthood Federation of American (PPFA), the nation's number one provider of abortions.[150]

Issue 3: Block funding of Obamacare health care law. This was an amendment to block funding of the Patient Protection and Affordable Care Act, the "massive health care restructuring law enacted March 2010. The PPACA contained many provisions that would implement government –imposed rationing of life-saving health care and included federal funding of abortion.[151]

Issue 4: Cut federal funding of Planned Parenthood. This

---

[148] Ibid.
[149] Ibid.
[150] Ibid.
[151] Ibid.

was a bill to cut all federal funding to Planned Parenthood Federation of American (PPFA), the nation's number one provider of abortions.[152]

Issue 5: The No Taxpayer Funding of Abortion Act (H.R.3) would permanently block the use of federal funds for abortion and health insurance coverage of abortions by federal programs.[153]

Issue 6: This amendment would block the use of federal funds to train abortionists. It would also establish conscience protections that would prohibit any medical facility to discriminate against any doctor, nurse, or medial provider who refused to "provide, pay for, provide coverage of, or refer for abortions"[154]

Issue 7: The Protect Life Act would "repeal and/or correct all of the pro-abortion components" of Obamacare, the Patient Protection and Affordable Care Act, the "massive health care restructuring law.[155]

Issue 8: The Prenatal Nondiscrimination Act is a ban on sex-selection abortions. This law would make it illegal to knowingly: (1) perform an abortion based upon sex of child, (2) to use force or threats to coerce sex-based abortion, (3) to "solicit or accept funds" for sex-based abortions, and (4) to transport a woman across state lines or into the nation for sex-based abortion.[156]

Issue 9: Repeal of Obamacare health care law. This was an amendment to completely repeal Obamacare, the Patient Protection and Affordable Care Act, the "massive health care restructuring law enacted March 2010. The PPACA contained many provisions that would implement government –imposed rationing of life-saving health care and included federal funding of abortion.[157]

---

[152] Ibid.
[153] Ibid.
[154] Ibid.
[155] Ibid.
[156] Ibid.
[157] Ibid.

CONCLUSION: The 2008 National Right to Life Committee (NRLC) "Vote Scorecard", like the Focus Action and Family Research Council Action "Vote Scorecard", reveals extreme differences between the voting records of Republicans and Democrats. Senator Obama scored 0%. Senator McCain scored 66%. In the U.S. Senate, Republicans scored an average of 88%. Most Republicans scored 100% (63%; 32 of 51), voting Christian values every time that they voted on the right to life issues selected by NRLC. Democrats scored an average of only 9%, about one-tenth the average score of Republicans. Most Democrats scored 0% (71%; 35 of 49), always voting against Christian values. In the U.S. House of Representatives, Republicans scored an average of 88%. Most Republicans scored 100% (71%; 143 of 201), always voting for Christian values. Democrats scored an average of only 7%, less than one-tenth the average score of Republicans. Most Democrats scored 0% (85%; 199 of 233), voting against Christian values every time that they voted.

The 2012 National Right to Life Committee (NRLC) Scorecard reveals the same great disparity between the voting records of Republicans and Democrats. Senate Republicans scored an average of 97%. Most Republicans scored 100% (90%; 43 of 48). Only five Republicans (10%; 5 of 48) scored less than 100%. Senate Democrats scored an average of only 1%. Most Democrats scored 0% (94%; 48 of 51). They voted against Christian values on all issues. Only 3 Democrats (6%) scored higher than 0%.[158] House Republicans scored an average of 98%. Most Republicans scored 100% (94%; 229 of 243). Only 14 Republicans (6%; 14 of 243) scored less than 100%. House Democrats scored an average of only 5%. Most Democrats scored 0% (88%; 171 of 194). They voted against

---

[158] National Right to Life Committee, "Federal NRLC Scorecard - 110th Congress, Combined Sessions," http://www.nrlc.org (accessed July 21, 2012).

Christian values on all issues. Only 23 Democrats (12%) scored higher than 0% (23 of 243).[159]

Knowing these facts raises the same questions raised by the "Vote Scorecard" developed by Focus Action and Family Research Council Action. How can any Christian vote for any Democrat knowing that Democrats are so united in voting against Christian values? How can any Christian do anything that would help put Democrats in power, knowing that they would govern totally contrary to simple, basic moral laws revealed by God through Scripture? Voting for most Democrats or doing anything that would put Democrats is totally contrary to what it means to be a Christian.

---

[159] Ibid.

PRESIDENTIAL CANDIDATES

SECTION REVIEW: This section reviews Christian voter guidance on the 2012 presidential candidates. The first chapter provides a overview of many subject areas. The second chapter tackles homosexuality and same-sex marriage. The third chapter summarizes guidance on abortion. The fourth chapter discusses the Supreme Court. The fifth chapter shows how President Obama buys votes with government benefits. The sixth chapter answers the question: Is President Obama a Christian? The answer will surprise many readers.

CHAPTERS: Chapters in this section include the following:

PRESIDENTIAL CANDIDATES: OVERVIEW

INTRODUCTION: The best way to evaluate a presidential candidate, especially President Obama, is not to look at what he said or promised when trying to get elected, but how he actually voted and what actions he took as President. Christian websites provide excellent voter guidance regarding presidential candidates. Three of the best are Family Research Council Action (FRC Action), Citizenlink, an affiliate of Focus on the Family, and National Right to Life Committee (NRLC).[160] They compare positions of candidates on many topics. The Heritage Foundation does not compare candidates, but provides very detailed briefs on many public policy subjects.[161] These briefs enable one to make informed choices between candidates.

2008 FRC ACTION AND FOCUS ACTION CONGRESSIONAL SCORECARD: The 2008 Family Research Council Action/Focus on the Family Action (now Citizenlink) congressional scorecard reveals extreme differences between the voting records of the presidential candidates. Like most Democrats, President Obama and Senator Biden scored 0%, in total contrast to most Republicans, who scored 100%. They voted against Christian values (against the position of FRC Action and Focus Action) every time they voted. Senator McCain, the 2008 Republican presidential candidate, scored 42%, lower than most Republicans, but infinitely greater than 0% scores of President Obama and Senator Biden.[162]

---

[160] Family Research Council Action (FRC Action), http://www.frcaction.org; Citizenlink, an affiliate of Focus on the Family, http://www.citizenlink.com; and National Right to Life Committee (NRLC), http://www.nrlc.org.
[161] The Heritage Foundation, http://www.heritage.org.
[162] FRC Action and Focus on the Family Action, "Vote Scorecard, 110th Congress, 1st Session," http://www.frcaction.org (accessed July 9, 2008).

<u>2008 NATIONAL RIGHT TO LIFE</u>
<u>CONGRESSIONAL SCORECARD</u>: The 2008 National Right
to Life Scorecard also reveals extreme differences between the
voting records of presidential candidates. Again, like most
Democrats, President Obama and Senator Biden both scored
0%, in total contrast to most Republicans, who scored 100%.
Senator McCain scored 66%, lower than most Republicans, but
infinitely greater than 0% scores of President Obama and
Senator Biden.[163]

    <u>2012 CONGRESSIONAL SCORECARDS</u>: The 2012
scorecards do not show the 2012 presidential candidates because
neither President Obama nor Governor Romney were members
of Congress (2009-2012). However, other documents show
where they stand on all the issues reviewed in this chapter.

    <u>JOBS AND THE ECONOMY</u>: President Obama
promised to solve the national economic crisis and put
Americans back to work. He failed miserably. His actions reflect
lack of understanding of the business world and what is required
to improve jobs and the economy. Governor Romney is a very
successful businessman who has infinitely greater understanding
of what is required to put Americans back to work and improve
the economy. He chose as his Vice Presidential candidate a
Congressman with a degree in economics and greater
understanding of economics than any other member of
Congress.

    <u>ROLE OF GOVERNMENT</u>: One of the reasons that
President Obama and Democrats do not have the right solutions
for America's problems because they have a totally wrong,
unbiblical and unconstitutional understanding of the role of
government. Their position is totally contrary to the biblical and

---

[163] National Right to Life Committee, "Federal NRLC Scorecard - 110th
Congress, Combined Sessions," http://www.nrlc.org (accessed July 7, 2008).

constitutional ideal embraced by the Founding Fathers and most Republicans of smaller government, lower taxes, and greater personal freedom and responsibility for all citizens. They want legislation that favors the poor and cares for the people. This requires a tremendous increase in the size and cost of government, a cost that must be passed on to taxpayers.

FEDERAL SPENDING AND DEFICIT: President Obama greatly increased federal spending. He failed to produce any budget that can bring the totally runaway federal spending under control and reduce the national deficit and national debt. He wants even more government spending to take better care of more Americans with Obamacare, welfare, food stamps, educational benefits, etc. That means higher taxes, greater deficits, and greater national debt. Governor Romney is a businessman and former governor who balanced his state budget every year. Congressman Ryan's budget will help bring federal spending under control. It is not enough, but it is a giant step in the right direction. See http://www.heritage.org for detailed discussion of budget developed by Congressman Ryan for Congress.

NATIONAL DEBT: President Obama promised to reduce the national debt. He did just the opposite; he greatly increased it. National debt led to economic collapse in Greece. The United States is heading in the same direction, much faster thanks to President Obama, who lives to spend more taxpayer dollars to take better care of more Americans. Governor Romney and Congressman Ryan have a budget that will reduce the national debt.

HOMOSEXUALITY AND SAME-SEX MARRIAGE: Homosexuality and same-sex marriage are abominations to God, extreme perversions of His design for man, woman, and marriage. See chapter on "Biblical Law: Homosexuality and Same-Sex Marriage." Absolutely no American who calls himself a Christian should vote for any candidate who so strongly opposes God and his laws. Homosexuality and same-sex marriage are even more important to God and the future of our nation than abortion, more important than life and death.

No president in the history of the United States has been a stronger supporter of homosexuality and same-sex marriage than President Obama. See chapter that follows on "Presidential Candidates: Homosexuality and Same-Sex Marriage." Americans pay higher taxes to fund health care for same-sex partners when civil unions or same-sex marriage are legalized. American companies charge more for products and services. Airlines, for example, charge higher airfares to fund civil unions.

ABORTION: In the eyes of God, abortion is murder. See chapter on "Biblical Law: Abortion." Every American who votes for any candidate who supports abortion has blood on his hands, the blood of millions of American children. No president in the history of the United States has been a stronger supporter of abortion, partial-birth abortion, and the killing of aborted children born alive than President Obama. See chapter that follows on "Presidential Candidates: Abortion." All Americans are paying for abortions, because President Obama has diverted millions of taxpayer dollars to national and international groups that perform or support abortions.

SUPREME COURT APPOINTMENTS: One of the greatest and most important powers of a President of the United States is the ability to appoint Supreme Court justices. They serve for life, and continue to have a major impact on the nation countless years after the President is no longer in office. See chapter that follows on "Presidential Candidates: Supreme Court" for more information on this vitally important topic.[164]

---

[164] National Right to Life, "The Presidential Record on Life: President Barack Obama 2009-present," http://www.nrlc.org.

APPOINTMENT OF FEDERAL JUDGES: Governor Romney and President Obama differ sharply on judicial appointments. President Obama would appoint judges who interpret the law in accordance with their personal beliefs. What does this mean? He would appoint judges who would legislate from the bench and create laws which would legalize same-sex marriage, mandate taxpayer and private company funds for health care and other benefits for same-sex partners, mandate taxpayer funds for abortion and partial birth abortion by national and international organizations, and other laws totally contrary to laws enacted by Congress.[165]

Governor Romney, in total contrast to President Obama, supports the appointment of federal judges and Supreme Court Justices who do not try to make federal policy or legislate from the bench but simply interpret and apply the law to the facts of each case.[166] Legislation, making law, is the duty of elected members of the legislature, which at the federal level is Congress (Senate and House of Representatives).

OTHER APPOINTMENTS: President Obama appointed Kathleen Sebelius, a long-time opponent of curbs on abortion (including late abortions) as Secretary of Health and Human Services. President Obama has appointed many other pro-abortion advocates to high government offices.[167]

OBAMACARE HEALTH CARE LAW: Obamacare is discussed in greater detail in another chapter. On March 23, 2010, President Obama "signed the Patient Protection and Affordable Care Act (Obamacare) into law, which will provide federal funding for health plans that pay for abortion on demand

---

[165] OK FRC Action, "Values Voter Guide for 2008 Presidential Candidates," http://www.frcaction.org (accessed July 9, 2008).
[166] FRC Action, "2012 Values Voter Presidential Voter Guide," http://www.frcaction.org (accessed August 3, 2012).
[167] National Right to Life, "The Presidential Record on Life: President Barack Obama 2009-present," http://www.nrlc.org.

and lead to large-scale rationing of lifesaving medical treatments."[168] Obamacare will probably result in a greater abortion rate and greatly increased U.S. taxpayer funding of abortions, contraceptives, etc. Governor Romney believes that the Obama health care law should be repealed.[169] See chapter on "Obamacare" for further discussion.

RELIGIOUS FREEDOM: In February 2011, the Obama Administration rescinded a regulation issued by the Bush Administration, which protected health-care providers from being penalized for refusing to provide abortions.[170] It "issued a 'final rule' mandating that groups, including religious schools and hospitals, provide health insurance plans that cover certain drugs or procedures, even if it violates the groups "religious and moral convictions."[171] See chapters on "Obamacare" and "Hate Crimes and Freedom of Religion" for further discussion

Governor Romney, totally contrary to President Obama, supports legal protections for individuals, organizations, and institutions from government forcing them to violate their moral or religious beliefs.[172] He said, "On day one I will eliminate the Obama Administration rule that compels religious institutions to violate the tenants of their own faith. Such rules don't belong in the America that I believe in."[173]

---

[168] National Right to Life, "National Right to Life Endorses Governor Mitt Romney," "Where Do the Candidates Stand on Life: Mitt Romney, Barack Obama," Carol Tobias, "Statement by Carol Tobias, National Right to Life President," April 12, 2012, State Senate," http://www.nrlc.org.
[169] National Right to Life, "National Right to Life Endorses Governor Mitt Romney," Carol Tobias, "Statement by Carol Tobias, National Right to Life President," April 12, 2012, State Senate," http://www.nrlc.org.
[170] National Right to Life, "The Presidential Record on Life: President Barack Obama 2009-present," Carol Tobias, "Statement by Carol Tobias, National Right to Life President," April 12, 2012, State Senate," http://www.nrlc.org.
[171] National Right to Life, "Where Do the Candidates Stand on Life: Mitt Romney, Barack Obama," http://www.nrlc.org.
[172] FRC Action, "2012 Values Voter Presidential Voter Guide," http://www.frcaction.org (accessed August 3, 2012).

HATE CRIMES LAW: Federal hate crimes laws punish hateful thoughts as crimes, totally contrary to biblical principles and the U.S. Constitution. In the United States we still have freedoms of thought, speech, and religion, but many Democrats are trying to restrict those freedoms. President Obama said that he would sign a "federal hate crimes law that included protections based upon sexual orientation and 'gender identity'.[174] See chapter on "Hate Crimes and Freedom of Religion" for further discussion.

EDUCATION: God has given parents, not government, responsibility for the education of their children. President Obama does not support parental choice in education. Governor Romney supports parental rights and choice in education.[175]

GUN RIGHTS: The Constitution of the United States grants Americans the right to own weapons. Careful reading of the U.S. Constitution helps one more clearly understand the types of weapons allowed. The Second Amendment states: "A well regulated Militia, being necessary to the security of a free State, the right of the people to keep and bear Arms, shall not be infringed."[176] Note that the primary reason for the right to bear arms is not hunting or protecting or providing for self or family. The primary reason is "the security of a free State." Thus the types of weapons allowed should be the type needed for the defense of a state. Also, it was the right to bear arms that enabled the Founding Fathers of the United States to write and publish the Declaration of Independence from Great Britain and

---

[173] National Right to Life, "Where Do the Candidates Stand on Life: Mitt Romney, Barack Obama," http://www.nrlc.org.
[174] OK FRC Action, "Values Voter Guide for 2008 Presidential Candidates," http://www.frcaction.org (accessed July 9, 2008).
[175] FRC Action, "2012 Values Voter Presidential Voter Guide," http://www.frcaction.org (accessed August 3, 2012).
[176] "Bill of Rights," U.S. National Archives & Records Administration, http://www.archives.gov/exhibits/charters/constitution.html.

to fight the Revolutionary War that gave Americans their freedom and independence. The Declaration of Independence makes it perfectly clear that it is the right of the people to bear arms and to overthrow any government that denies the God-given inalienable rights to life, liberty, and the pursuit of happiness. President Obama supports greater restrictions on gun ownership. He opposed President Bush's decision to not renew the federal ban on assault weapons.[177]

FEDERAL ESTATE TAX (DEATH TAX): The federal estate tax taxes individuals after death, thereby reducing the inheritance of their children and anyone else entitled to their inheritance. President Obama supports the federal estate tax (death tax)..[178] Governor Romney supports complete repeal of the federal estate tax.[179]

CONCLUSION: Christian voter guidance reveals extreme differences between Governor Romney and President Obama on virtually all issues: jobs and the economy, federal spending, federal debt, religious freedom, same-sex marriage, abortion, appointment of federal judges and Supreme Court justices, education, gun rights, estate tax (death tax), etc.

Consider the extreme consequences of re-electing Obama as President. In violation of the U.S. Constitution and the God-given inalienable rights of liberty and freedom of religion, he will continue to force Americans and American organizations who believe that abortion is murder to fund countless abortions in the United States and other nations. He will, in violation of the U.S. Constitution and the same God-given inalienable rights, force Americans who understand that

---

[177] OK FRC Action, "Values Voter Guide for 2008 Presidential Candidates," http://www.frcaction.org (accessed July 9, 2008).
[178] FRC Action, "Values Voter Guide for 2008 Presidential Candidates," http://www.frcaction.org (accessed July 9, 2008).
[179] FRC Action, "2012 Values Voter Presidential Voter Guide," http://www.frcaction.org (accessed August 3, 2012).

homosexuality and same-sex marriage are abominations to God to pay higher taxes to support civil unions and same-sex marriages. He would support repeal of the Federal Defense of Marriage Act (1996) which "declares marriage to be the union of one man and one woman…and declares that states do not have to recognize same-sex 'marriages' from other states."[180] He would legalize same-sex marriage.

President Obama has taken positions on all issues totally opposed to God and His laws revealed through Scripture. He will continue with failed economic policies that hurt jobs and the economy. He will continue to greatly expand federal spending and the national debt, increasing the speed of America toward an economic collapse like that of Greece. Today, about one third of Americans receive government support; they live off other Americans. He will increase that number and force Americans to pay higher taxes to fund more benefits for more Americans i.e. healthcare, welfare, education and other benefits.

Governor Romney supports Christian values. His positions on all issues are in line with laws of God revealed through Scripture. He will implement totally different policies in all areas, policies in line with God's laws revealed through Scripture. Obedience to God's laws will restore God's blessings to America.

---

[180] FRC Action, "Values Voter Guide for 2008 Presidential Candidates," http://www.frcaction.org (accessed July 9, 2008).

PRESIDENTIAL CANDIDATES: HOMOSEXUALITY AND SAME-SEX MARRIAGE

INTRODUCTION: No President in the history of the United States has been a stronger supporter of homosexuality and same-sex marriage than President Obama. He directed the Department of Justice to not enforce DOMA, the Federal Defense of Marriage Act (1996), which "declares marriage to be the union of one man and one woman…and declares that states do not have to recognize same-sex 'marriages' from other states."[181] He is opposed to any amendment to the U.S. Constitution or state constitutions that would define marriage as the union of one man and one woman.[182] In 2012 he finally officially announced that he supports same-sex marriage.

Governor Mitt Romney believes that marriage is defined as the union of one man and one woman. He fully supports DOMA and would support any amendments to the U.S. Constitution or state constitutions that define marriage as the union of one man and one woman.[183]

PRESIDENTIAL ELECTIONS: During the 2008 and 2012 presidential elections, President Obama's campaign websites had sections for the Lesbian, Bisexual, Gay, and Transvestite (LBGT) movement, one of his strongest and most enthusiastic supporters. During the 2008 election, President Obama said that he would sign a bill "to give federal civil rights

---

[181] OK FRC Action, "Values Voter Guide for 2008 Presidential Candidates," http://www.frcaction.org (accessed July 9, 2008).
[182] FRC Action, "2012 Values Voter Presidential Voter Guide," http://www.frcaction.org (accessed August 3, 2012).
[183] FRC Action, "2012 Values Voter Presidential Voter Guide," http://www.frcaction.org (accessed August 3, 2012).

protection based upon sexual orientation and 'gender identity'."[184] President Obama supports the federal Employment Non-Discrimination Act, which grants "special employment rights based upon sexual behavior."[185] Governor Romney is opposed to legislation that grants special rights based upon sexual orientation. [186]

INAUGURATION: January 2009 President Obama chose Gene Robinson, a gay bishop, to give the opening prayer at his inauguration.[187] The announcement came "after weeks of outcry from the gay community over Obama's choice of evangelical, anti-gay pastor Rick Warren to deliver the inaugural invocation."[188] Robinson told the *Seattle Post-Intelligencer.* "I believe in my heart that the church got it wrong about homosexuality. There is great excitement in my heart to be living in a time when the church is starting to get it right."[189] President Obama chose Robinson to maintain support from the LGBT movement, which fought hard to get him elected.

SUPREME COURT: On May 11, 2010, President Obama appointed Elena Kagan, a strongly pro-gay rights woman who never served as a judge, to the Supreme Court. As Dean of Harvard Law School, Kagan barred Armed Forces recruiters from the Law School's Office of Career Services to protest a government policy against homosexuals serving openly in the military.[190]

---

[184] OK FRC Action, "Values Voter Guide for 2008 Presidential Candidates," http://www.frcaction.org (accessed July 9, 2008).
[185] FRC Action, "2012 Values Voter Presidential Voter Guide," http://www.frcaction.org (accessed August 3, 2012).
[186] FRC Action, "2012 Values Voter Presidential Voter Guide," http://www.frcaction.org (accessed August 3, 2012).
[187] Rachel Weiner, Gene Robinson: Gay Bishop Giving Obama Inauguration Prayer, The Huffington Post, February 12, 2009, http://www.huffingtonpost.com/2009/01/12/gene-robinson-gay-bishop_n_157076.html.
[188] Ibid.
[189] Ibid.

MILITARY POLICY: On December 22, 2010, President Obama abolished the "Don't Ask, Don't tell" policy regarding homosexuals in the military. The White House Blog stated:

> With his signature today, the President put in motion the end of a policy that has hurt our military as a whole, that has forced thousands of those who serve to do so under a cloud of anxiety and isolation, and that has stood as a symbol of the barriers to unity and equality in our country. As the President put it, "For we are not a nation that says, 'don't ask, don't tell.' We are a nation that says, 'Out of many, we are one.'"[191]

DOMA—DEFENSE OF MARRIAGE ACT: President Obama has always been strongly opposed to DOMA, the Federal Defense of Marriage Act (1996), which "declares marriage to be the union of one man and one woman…and declares that states do not have to recognize same-sex 'marriages' from other states."[192] During the 2008 Presidential campaign, he promised to "support repeal of the provision of DOMA that defines marriage as the union of one man and one woman…thus freeing the federal government to give marital benefits to same-sex couples" and repeal of "the provision…that declares states do not have to recognize same-sex 'marriages' from other states, thus leaving courts free to require such

---

[190] Jonathan Blakely, "One Top GOP Line of Attack: Kagan's Opposition to Military Recruitment at Harvard Law School's Office of Career Services," ABC News, http://abcnews.go.com/blogs/politics/2010/05/one-top-gop-line-of-attack-kagans-opposition-to-military-recruitment-at-harvard-law-schools-office-of-career-services/
[191] Jesse Lee, The President Signs Repeal of "Don't Ask Don't Tell": "Out of Many, We Are One," The White House Blog, December 22, 2010, http://www.whitehouse.gov/blog/2010/12/22/president-signs-repeal-dont-ask-dont-tell-out-many-we-are-one.
[192] OK FRC Action, "Values Voter Guide for 2008 Presidential Candidates," http://www.frcaction.org (accessed July 9, 2008).

recognition under the Constitution's 'full faith and credit' clause."[193]

On February 23, 2011, President Obama ordered the Department of Justice to not enforce the Defense of Marriage Act because it did not permit same-sex marriage. He "instructed the Justice Department to no longer defend the constitutionality of the Defense of Marriage Act, or DOMA, the legal prohibition on federal recognition of same-sex marriages."[194] Attorney General Eric Holder said that the Justice Department would "stop defending the policy because it has now been challenged in the Second Circuit."[195] He said,

> After careful consideration, including a review of my recommendation, the President has concluded that given a number of factors, including a documented history of discrimination, classifications based on sexual orientation should be subject to a more heightened standard of scrutiny…. The <u>President has also concluded</u> that Section 3 of <u>DOMA, as applied to legally married same-sex couples,</u> fails to meet that standard and <u>is therefore unconstitutional</u>. Given that conclusion, the President has instructed the Department not to defend the statute in such cases. I fully concur with the President's determination.[196]

<u>SAME-SEX MARRIAGE</u>: On May 6, 2012, on national television, Vice-President Biden made it clear that he strongly

---

[193] OK FRC Action, "Values Voter Guide for 2008 Presidential Candidates," http://www.frcaction.org (accessed July 9, 2008).
[194] Brian Montopoli, "Obama Administration Will No Longer Defend DOMA," Political Hotsheet, February 23, 2011, http://www.cbsnews.com/8301-503544_162-20035398-503544.html.
[195] Ibid.
[196] Ibid.

supported same-sex marriage. Later the same day the White House issued a statement that Biden's comments did not indicate a change in administration policy. A few days later President Obama, contrary to what he had publicly stated beforehand, said that he now supports same-sex marriage. The President's view is totally contrary to God's laws revealed through Scripture and his design for man, woman, and marriage.

A White House Talking Points on Same-Sex Marriage memo stated:

(1) The President was "personally" in favor of same-sex marriage.[197]

(2) "The President's personal view is that it's wrong to prevent couples who are in loving, committed relationships, and want to marry, from doing so."[198]

(3) "We make it absolutely clear that we are talking about civil marriages and civil laws."[199]

(4) "We must be respectful of religious liberty, that churches and other faith institutions are still going to be able to make determinations about what their sacraments are, what they recognize." [200]

(5) "We need to recognize that people are going to have differing views on marriage and those views, even if we disagree strongly, should be respected." [201]

(6) "The President has long supported a legislative repeal of DOMA." [202]

(7) "If a couple is married under state law, whether they are gay or straight, they're entitled to exactly the same legal rights as any other couple, and the federal government has no business invalidating those marriages." [203]

---

[197] Citizenlink, "White House Talking Points on Same-Sex Marriage: Some Questions," May 17, 2012, http://www.citizenlink.com.

[198] Ibid.

[199] Ibid.

[200] Ibid.

[201] Ibid.

[202] Ibid.

HATE CRIMES LAW: Federal hate crimes laws punish hateful thoughts as crimes, totally contrary to biblical principles and the U.S. Constitution. In Sweden a minister was placed in prison for giving a sermon that discussed Scripture regarding homosexuality. In the United States we still have freedoms of thought, speech, and religion, but many Democrats are trying to restrict those freedoms. President Obama said that he would sign a "federal hate crimes law that included protections based upon sexual orientation and 'gender identity'.[204]

CONCLUSION: President Obama, more than any other President in the history of the United States, stands firmly in total opposition to God and His laws regarding homosexuality and same-sex marriage. Governor Romney stands firmly in total harmony with God and His laws regarding homosexuality and same-sex marriage. Homosexuality and same-sex marriage are abominations to God, extreme perversions of His design for man, woman, marriage, and family (see chapter on Scripture on Homosexuality and Same-Sex Marriage). Anyone who votes for President Obama stands in total opposition to God and his laws revealed through Scripture.

Reelection of President Obama and other Democrats does not simply mean laws that promote homosexuality and same-sex marriage, which are abominations to God in part because they are so destructive to his design for the two sexes, marriage, and family, the most basic, fundamental unit of society, the backbone of the nation. It means that Christians will be forced to pay higher federal and state taxes to fund Obamacare to pay for the healthcare bills of same-sex marriages. It means that Christians will have less freedom of speech and freedom of religion, and less freedom to live out their Christians

---

[203] Ibid.
[204] OK FRC Action, "Values Voter Guide for 2008 Presidential Candidates," http://www.frcaction.org (accessed July 9, 2008).

values, as is already true in European nations with laws that grant protections based upon sexual orientation (see chapter with examples of religious persecution in Europe).

PRESIDENTIAL CANDIDATE: ABORTION

INTRODUCTION: Why is a separate chapter dedicated to presidential candidates and abortion? First, abortion should be a deciding factor in voting for President because it reveals so much about the heart and mind of the candidate and how he stands in relation to the heart and mind of God and God's laws. Second, because abortion has been one of the most important subjects to President Obama, and he has worked so hard and fought so many hard battles not just to ensure "a woman's right to abortion," but to ensure funding of abortion. Most of his battles have been about U.S. taxpayer funding of abortion.

Take a moment to think about it. President Obama said, "I am pro-choice."[205] He knows that millions of Americans consider abortion to be murder, but he wants to force these Americans, against their will and against their firm moral and religious convictions, to pay for what they clearly understand to be the totally wrongful and totally unjustified killing of unborn or partially born children.

ABORTION—OVERALL RECORD: In the over 230 years of the history of the United States, there has never been a more pro-abortion president than President Obama. Carol Tobias, President of National Right to Life, describes President Obama as the "country's most pro-abortion president."[206] He has a 0% voting record on pro-life issues with the National Right to Life, and a 100% rating from NARAL Pro-Choice America.[207]

---

[205] National Right to Life, "Where Do the Candidates Stand on Life: Mitt Romney, Barack Obama," http://www.nrlc.org.
[206] Carol Tobias, "Statement by Carol Tobias, National Right to Life President," April 12, 2012, State Senate," http://www.nrlc.org.
[207] National Right to Life, "Where Do the Candidates Stand on Life: John

Obama said, "I have consistently advocated for reproductive choice and will make preserving women's rights under Roe v. Wade a priority as President."[208] He further clarified his position on abortion by saying:

> "Thirty-five years after the Supreme Court decided Roe v. Wade, it's never been more important to protect a woman's right to choose. Throughout my career, I've been a consistent and strong supporter of reproductive justice, and have consistently had a 100% pro-choice rating with Planned Parenthood and NARAL Pro-Choice America."[209]

President Tobias describes President Obama's "abysmal record on life:"[210]

> On his second day in office, January 22, 2009, President Obama issued a statement reaffirming his commitment to defend the Rowe v. Wade ruling, which gave us abortion on demand. On his third day in office, he overturned the "Mexico

---

McCain, Barack Obama," "Senator John McCain Record on Abortion in the United States Senate," and "Senator Barack Obama Record on Abortion, United States Senate, Illinois State Senate," http://www.nrlc.org (accessed August 28, 2008).

[208] National Right to Life, "Where Do the Candidates Stand on Life: John McCain, Barack Obama," "Senator John McCain Record on Abortion in the United States Senate," and "Senator Barack Obama Record on Abortion, United States Senate, Illinois State Senate," http://www.nrlc.org (accessed August 28, 2008).

[209] National Right to Life, "Where Do the Candidates Stand on Life: John McCain, Barack Obama," "Senator John McCain Record on Abortion in the United States Senate," and "Senator Barack Obama Record on Abortion, United States Senate, Illinois State Senate," http://www.nrlc.org (accessed August 28, 2008).

[210] Carol Tobias, "Statement by Carol Tobias, National Right to Life President," April 12, 2012, State Senate," http://www.nrlc.org.

City Policy" so that hundreds of millions of our tax dollars would be given to organizations that perform and promote abortion overseas [and]... to lobby against the current pro-life laws in those countries.... Another of his early acts was to release $50 million to the United Nations Population Fund—an agency...[that supports] China's one-child population-control program, which relies heavily upon forced abortion.... Forced abortions...are commonplace and...up to nine months of pregnancy...so violent that the women die along with their full term babies.[211]

After discussing Obama's record, President Tobias strongly endorsed Romney for President. "While some would like to call into question Mitt Romney's pro-life position, let me state clearly and emphatically, 'Mitt Romney IS pro-life."[212] National Right to Life issued a strong endorsement of Romney for President:

Determined to secure a pro-life victory in the November election, which will decide the fate of unborn children for decades to come, the National Right to Life Committee (NRLC), the federation of 50 state right-to-life affiliates and more than 3,000 local chapters, today endorsed Mitt Romney for President of the United States.[213]

The National Right to Life website states: "Mitt Romney has taken a strong pro-life position and is committed to implementing policies to protect the unborn, the medically

---

[211] Carol Tobias, "Statement by Carol Tobias, National Right to Life President," April 12, 2012, State Senate," http://www.nrlc.org.
[212] Carol Tobias, "Statement by Carol Tobias, National Right to Life President," April 12, 2012, State Senate," http://www.nrlc.org.
[213] National Right to Life, "National Right to Life Endorses Governor Mitt Romney," http://www.nrlc.org (accessed July 22, 2012).

dependent and disabled, and the elderly."[214] President Tobias said, "It is now time for pro-life Americans to unite behind Mitt Romney. For the sake of unborn children, the disabled, and the elderly, we must win."[215]

PARTIAL BIRTH ABORTION: How candidates stand on the absolutely horrific procedure called partial-birth abortion, where a child is killed after being partially born, reveals the extreme morally depravity of some politicians. Partial birth abortion is described by NRLC as follows: "The partial-birth abortion procedure—used from the fifth month on—involves pulling a living baby feet-first out of the womb, except for the head, puncturing the skull and suctioning out the brain. The great majority of partial-birth abortions are performed on healthy babies of healthy mothers."[216] No one who votes for one of these politicians should consider himself or herself a Christian.

Governor Romney is strongly opposed to partial birth abortion. President Obama, taking a totally opposite position, sharply criticized the Supreme Court ruling in Gonzales v. Carhart upholding the Partial-Birth Abortion Ban Act by stating, "I strongly disagree with today's Supreme Court ruling...I am extremely concerned that this ruling will embolden state legislatures to enact further measures to restrict a woman's right to choose, and that the conservative Supreme Court justices will look for other opportunities to erode Roe v. Wade, which is established federal law and a matter of equal rights for women."[217]

---

[214] National Right to Life, "National Right to Life Endorses Governor Mitt Romney," http://www.nrlc.org (accessed July 22, 2012).
[215] Carol Tobias, "Statement by Carol Tobias, National Right to Life President," April 12, 2012, State Senate," http://www.nrlc.org.
[216] National Right to Life, "Where Do the Candidates Stand on Life: John McCain, Barack Obama," "Senator John McCain Record on Abortion in the United States Senate," and "Senator Barack Obama Record on Abortion, United States Senate, Illinois State Senate," http://www.nrlc.org (accessed August 28, 2008).

ABORTION—INFANTS BORN ALIVE: How candidates stand on the killing of infants born alive is even more revealing about the extreme morally depravity of some politicians. Governor Romney strongly opposes the killing of infants born alive. As an Illinois State Senator, Obama voted three times and spoke twice on the Senate floor against the Illinois "Born-Alive Infants Protection Act" (BAIPA), which was similar to the federal BAIPA signed into law by President Bush in 2002. This bill would have given babies who survive abortions the same protection as babies who are born prematurely.[218] Senator Obama strongly opposed it.

ABORTION—ROW V. WADE: Roe v. Wade is the 1973 Supreme Court decision that legalizes abortion in all 50 states. President Obama said, "I am pro-choice. I believe in Roe v. Wade."[219] Governor Romney opposes abortion and has called the Supreme Court's Roe v. Wade decision "a big mistake."[220] He said, "I support the reversal of Roe v. Wade, because it is bad law and bad medicine. Roe was a misguided ruling that was a result of a small group of activist federal judges legislating from the bench."[221] He believes that Roe v. Wade should be overturned.[222]

---

[217] National Right to Life, "Where Do the Candidates Stand on Life: John McCain, Barack Obama," "Senator John McCain Record on Abortion in the United States Senate," and "Senator Barack Obama Record on Abortion, United States Senate, Illinois State Senate," http://www.nrlc.org (accessed August 28, 2008).

[218] National Right to Life, "Where Do the Candidates Stand on Life: John McCain, Barack Obama," "Senator John McCain Record on Abortion in the United States Senate," and "Senator Barack Obama Record on Abortion, United States Senate, Illinois State Senate," http://www.nrlc.org (accessed August 28, 2008).

[219] National Right to Life, "Where Do the Candidates Stand on Life: Mitt Romney, Barack Obama," http://www.nrlc.org.

[220] National Right to Life, "National Right to Life Endorses Governor Mitt Romney," http://www.nrlc.org (accessed July 22, 2012).

[221] National Right to Life, "Where Do the Candidates Stand on Life: Mitt

ABORTION—FREEDOM OF CHOICE ACT: The "Freedom of Choice Act" was a bill that would "make partial-birth abortion legal again, provide for taxpayer funding of abortion, and invalidate virtually all state and federal limitations on abortion" to include limitations now permitted by the Supreme Court, such as waiting periods and parent notification laws.[223] President Obama was a co-sponsor of the act.[224] Governor Romney opposes all abortion and all taxpayer funding of abortion.[225]

ABORTION—PROTECT LIFE ACT: In 2011, the Obama White House issued formal veto threats against the Protect Life Act, a bill that would repeal the abortion-expanding provisions of the 2010 Obamacare law.[226]

ABORTION—UNBORN VICTIMS OF VIOLENCE:

Romney, Barack Obama," http://www.nrlc.org.

[222] National Right to Life, "Where Do the Candidates Stand on Life: Mitt Romney, Barack Obama," "The Presidential Record on Life: President Barack Obama 2009-present," Carol Tobias, "Statement by Carol Tobias, National Right to Life President," April 12, 2012, State Senate," http://www.nrlc.org.

[223] National Right to Life, "Where Do the Candidates Stand on Life: John McCain, Barack Obama," "Senator John McCain Record on Abortion in the United States Senate," and "Senator Barack Obama Record on Abortion, United States Senate, Illinois State Senate," http://www.nrlc.org (accessed August 28, 2008).

[224] National Right to Life, "Where Do the Candidates Stand on Life: John McCain, Barack Obama," "Senator John McCain Record on Abortion in the United States Senate," and "Senator Barack Obama Record on Abortion, United States Senate, Illinois State Senate," http://www.nrlc.org (accessed August 28, 2008).

[225] National Right to Life, "National Right to Life Endorses Governor Mitt Romney," "Where Do the Candidates Stand on Life: Mitt Romney, Barack Obama," Carol Tobias, "Statement by Carol Tobias, National Right to Life President," April 12, 2012, State Senate," http://www.nrlc.org.

[226] National Right to Life, "The Presidential Record on Life: President Barack Obama 2009-present," http://www.nrlc.org.

McCain: Senator McCain voted for the Unborn Victims of Violence Act ("Laci and Conner's Law"), a bill that stated that when an unborn child was killed or injured during commission of a violent federal crime, the accused could also be charged with an offense against the killed or injured unborn child.[227]

ABORTION—PARENTAL NOTIFICATION LAWS: President Obama voted against a bill that would require an abortionist "to notify at least one parent before performing an abortion on a minor girl from another state."[228]

ABORTION—ULTRASOUND IMAGE: President Obama opposes a law requiring abortion clinics to show women an ultrasound image of their baby.[229]

STEM CELL RESEARCH: President Obama refused to support "President Bush's ban on the use of federal funds for research on human embryonic stem cell lines created after August 2001."[230] In March 2009, he issued an executive order to allow federal funding of research that requires the killing of human embryos.[231] Governor Romney opposes use of federal funds for stem cell research.[232]

---

[227] National Right to Life, "Where Do the Candidates Stand on Life: John McCain, Barack Obama," "Senator John McCain Record on Abortion in the United States Senate," and "Senator Barack Obama Record on Abortion, United States Senate, Illinois State Senate," http://www.nrlc.org (accessed August 28, 2008).

[228] National Right to Life, "Where Do the Candidates Stand on Life: John McCain, Barack Obama," "Senator John McCain Record on Abortion in the United States Senate," and "Senator Barack Obama Record on Abortion, United States Senate, Illinois State Senate," http://www.nrlc.org (accessed August 28, 2008).

[229] FRC Action, "Values Voter Guide for 2008 Presidential Candidates," http://www.frcaction.org (accessed July 9, 2008).

[230] FRC Action, "Values Voter Guide for 2008 Presidential Candidates," http://www.frcaction.org (accessed July 9, 2008).

[231] National Right to Life, "The Presidential Record on Life: President Barack

ABORTION FUNDING: It is absolutely amazing how many times President Obama fought hard battles for legislation to force U.S. taxpayers to pay for abortion or to block legislation that would prevent taxpayer funding of abortion. Carol Tobias, President of National Right to Life, correctly stated that President Obama "wants our hard-earned tax dollars to pay for the killing of unborn children."[233] Governor Romney opposes any use of U.S. taxpayer dollars to support abortion.[234]

ABORTION FUNDING—PLANNED PARENTHOOD: President Obama threatened to veto the entire federal spending bill, thereby forcing a government shutdown, rather than cut federal funds to Planned Parenthood, the nation's number one abortion provider.[235] The Obama Administration blocked efforts by several states to cut off government funds to Planned Parenthood.[236] After the North Carolina legislature redirected $343,000 in taxpayer dollars from Planned Parenthood, President Obama stepped in and had the Department of Health and Human Services (HHS) given $426,000 in U.S. taxpayer dollars to Planned Parenthood in North Carolina.[237] President Dannenfelser of the Susan B. Anthony said,

---

Obama 2009-present," http://www.nrlc.org.

[232] FRC Action, "2012 Values Voter Presidential Voter Guide," http://www.frcaction.org (accessed August 3, 2012).

[233] Carol Tobias, "Statement by Carol Tobias, National Right to Life President," April 12, 2012, State Senate," http://www.nrlc.org.

[234] FRC Action, "2012 Values Voter Presidential Voter Guide," http://www.frcaction.org (accessed August 3, 2012); Carol Tobias, "Statement by Carol Tobias, National Right to Life President," April 12, 2012, State Senate," http://www.nrlc.org.

[235] National Right to Life, "Where Do the Candidates Stand on Life: Mitt Romney, Barack Obama," "The Presidential Record on Life: President Barack Obama 2009-present," Carol Tobias, "Statement by Carol Tobias, National Right to Life President," April 12, 2012, State Senate," http://www.nrlc.org.

[236] National Right to Life, "The Presidential Record on Life: President Barack Obama 2009-present," http://www.nrlc.org.

[237] Bethany Monk, "Obama Administration Funds Planned Parenthood—

President Obama's decision to overrule the North Carolina Legislature today marks the…fifth time in the last year – that he has stepped in to contract directly with the nation's largest abortion provider. [238]

In New Jersey, when Governor Chris Christie vetoed a bill funding Planned Parenthood and its affiliates, President Obama stepped in and gave an amazing $3.2 million in U.S. taxpayer dollars to fund the groups. When the Tennessee legislature cut funding to Planned Parenthood, the Obama Administration stepped in again, funding Planned Parenthood and its affiliates with U.S. taxpayer dollars. [239]

Governor Romney opposes giving any taxpayer dollars to Planned Parenthood.[240] He said, "I will support efforts to prohibit federal funding for any organization like Planned Parenthood, which primarily performs abortions or offers abortion-related services."[241]

ABORTION FUNDING—NO TAXPAYER FUNDING FOR ABORTION ACT: The No Taxpayer Funding for Abortion Act (H.R.3), a bill to permanently prohibit any federal program from funding elective abortions,[242] was passed by the House of Representatives during 2011.[243] President Obama's

Again," July 26, 2012, http://www.citizenlink.com.

[238] Bethany Monk, "Obama Administration Funds Planned Parenthood—Again," July 26, 2012, http://www.citizenlink.com.

[239] Bethany Monk, "Obama Administration Funds Planned Parenthood—Again," July 26, 2012, http://www.citizenlink.com.

[240] FRC Action, "2012 Values Voter Presidential Voter Guide," http://www.frcaction.org (accessed August 3, 2012).

[241] National Right to Life, "Where Do the Candidates Stand on Life: Mitt Romney, Barack Obama," http://www.nrlc.org.

[242] National Right to Life, "The Presidential Record on Life: President Barack Obama 2009-present," http://www.nrlc.org.

[243] National Right to Life, "Where Do the Candidates Stand on Life: Mitt

Administration strongly opposed it, issuing formal veto threats against it.[244] The White House issued a statement saying, "If the President is presented with H.R.3, his senior advisors would recommend that he veto the bill."[245]

ABORTION FUNDING—D.C. ABORTIONS:
President Obama succeeded, for 16 months, in removing a ban on government funded abortion on demand in the District of Columbia.[246]

ABORTION FUNDING—HYDE AMENDMENT (MEDICAID): The Hyde Amendment prevents the use of federal dollars from being used to pay for abortions through Medicaid programs. President Obama opposes the Hyde Amendment[247] and supports Medicaid funded abortions.[248] Governor Romney opposes Medicaid funded abortions.[249] He

Romney, Barack Obama," "The Presidential Record on Life: President Barack Obama 2009-present," Carol Tobias, "Statement by Carol Tobias, National Right to Life President," April 12, 2012, State Senate," http://www.nrlc.org.

[244] National Right to Life, "Where Do the Candidates Stand on Life: Mitt Romney, Barack Obama," "The Presidential Record on Life: President Barack Obama 2009-present," Carol Tobias, "Statement by Carol Tobias, National Right to Life President," April 12, 2012, State Senate," http://www.nrlc.org.

[245] National Right to Life, "Where Do the Candidates Stand on Life: Mitt Romney, Barack Obama," http://www.nrlc.org.

[246] National Right to Life, "The Presidential Record on Life: President Barack Obama 2009-present," http://www.nrlc.org.

[247] National Right to Life, "Where Do the Candidates Stand on Life: John McCain, Barack Obama," "Senator John McCain Record on Abortion in the United States Senate," and "Senator Barack Obama Record on Abortion, United States Senate, Illinois State Senate," http://www.nrlc.org (accessed August 28, 2008).

[248] FRC Action, "Values Voter Guide for 2008 Presidential Candidates," http://www.frcaction.org (accessed July 9, 2008).

[249] National Right to Life, "Where Do the Candidates Stand on Life: Mitt Romney, Barack Obama," "The Presidential Record on Life: President Barack Obama 2009-present," Carol Tobias, "Statement by Carol Tobias, National Right to Life President," April 12, 2012, State Senate,"

said, "I support the Hyde Amendment, which broadly bars the use of federal funds for abortions."[250]

ABORTION FUNDING—INTERNATIONAL GROUPS: "On his third day in office, President Obama nullified the pro-life "Mexico City Policy," making organizations that perform and promote abortion as a method of family planning overseas eligible for U.S. foreign aid funds."[251] In 2009, President Obama issued an order to fund private organizations that perform and promote abortion overseas. His choice as Secretary of State, Hillary Clinton, later told Congress that the Administration would advocate world-wide that "reproductive health includes access to abortion."[252]Governor Romney said he would reinstate the Reagan-era Mexico City Policy that prevents federal dollars from going to organizations that perform or promote abortion overseas.[253]

ABORTION FUNDING--OBAMACARE: On March 23, 2010, President Obama "signed the Patient Protection and Affordable Care Act (Obamacare) into law, which will provide federal funding for health plans that pay for abortion on demand."[254] Obamacare will increase abortions by greatly increasing access and funding for abortions. Americans will be forced to pay higher federal and state taxes to pay for

---

http://www.nrlc.org.

[250] National Right to Life, "Where Do the Candidates Stand on Life: Mitt Romney, Barack Obama," http://www.nrlc.org.

[251] National Right to Life, "Where Do the Candidates Stand on Life: Mitt Romney, Barack Obama," http://www.nrlc.org.

[252] National Right to Life, "The Presidential Record on Life: President Barack Obama 2009-present," http://www.nrlc.org.

[253] National Right to Life, "National Right to Life Endorses Governor Mitt Romney," Carol Tobias, "Statement by Carol Tobias, National Right to Life President," April 12, 2012, State Senate," http://www.nrlc.org.

[254] National Right to Life, "National Right to Life Endorses Governor Mitt Romney," "Where Do the Candidates Stand on Life: Mitt Romney, Barack Obama," Carol Tobias, "Statement by Carol Tobias, National Right to Life President," April 12, 2012, State Senate," http://www.nrlc.org.

Obamacare, which will fund abortions and abortive drugs. Christian organizations will be forced to provide and/or support abortions and abortive drugs, or face steep fines that force them out of business. Governor Romney "believes the Obama health care law, which would open the door to federal subsidies for abortion...should be repealed.[255] See chapter on Obamacare for more details.

SUPREME COURT APPOINTMENTS: President Obama appointed Elena Kagan (2010) and Sonia Sotomayor (2009) to the U.S. Supreme Court. As a key political aide to President Clinton, Kagan helped direct a political strategy preventing enactment of a ban on partial-birth abortions during the Clinton Administration. Sotomayor had previously helped direct the litigation projects of a private organization that filed multiple pro-abortion lawsuits, including challenges to parental notification requirements.[256]

OTHER APPOINTMENTS: President Obama appointed Kathleen Sebelius, a long-time opponent of curbs on abortion, to include late abortions, as Secretary of Health and Human Services. President Obama has appointed many other pro-abortion advocates to high government offices.[257]

CONCLUSION: President Obama, more than any other President in the history of the United States, stands firmly in total opposition to God and His laws regarding abortion. President Obama has an absolute zero percent voting record on

---

[255] National Right to Life, "National Right to Life Endorses Governor Mitt Romney," Carol Tobias, "Statement by Carol Tobias, National Right to Life President," April 12, 2012, State Senate," http://www.nrlc.org; FRC Action, "2012 Values Voter Presidential Voter Guide," http://www.frcaction.org (accessed August 3, 2012).

[256] National Right to Life, "The Presidential Record on Life: President Barack Obama 2009-present," http://www.nrlc.org.

[257] National Right to Life, "The Presidential Record on Life: President Barack Obama 2009-present," http://www.nrlc.org.

pro-life issues scored by the National Right to Life, but a 100% rating from NARAL Pro-Choice America. [258] Governor Romney is firmly pro-life and has the strong endorsement of National Right to Life. In the eyes of God, abortion is murder (see chapter on Scripture on Abortion). Any American who voted for President Obama and other Democrats who support abortion has blood on his hands, the blood of thousands of unborn or partially born children.

Reelection of President Obama and other Democrats does not simply mean the death of more American children. It means that Christians will be forced to pay higher federal and state taxes to fund Obamacare to fund the killing of millions of unborn or partially born American children. It means that Christian organizations will be forced, against their deeply held moral and religious beliefs, to perform or support abortions, abortive drugs, sterilization, contraceptives, etc. Organizations that fail to comply may be fined and forced into bankruptcy. It means that countless millions of U.S. taxpayer dollars will go to national and international organizations that support or perform abortions.

---

[258] National Right to Life, "Where Do the Candidates Stand on Life: John McCain, Barack Obama," "Senator John McCain Record on Abortion in the United States Senate," and "Senator Barack Obama Record on Abortion, United States Senate, Illinois State Senate," http://www.nrlc.org (accessed August 28, 2008).

PRESIDENTIAL CANDIDATES: SUPREME COURT

INTRODUCTION: One of the greatest and most important powers of the President of the United States is the ability to appoint Supreme Court justices who serve for life. They continue to have a major impact on the nation countless years after the President is no longer in office.

In May 2012, President Obama complimented Supreme Court Justice Stevens when awarding the nation's highest civilian medal by saying that his decisions were always "pragmatic" and not "ideological." President Obama has boasted that he is not "constrained by ideology." In other words, he is not constrained by God's laws, which are fixed, uniform, and universal. They do not change because they are rooted in God's unchanging character. President Obama takes pride in doing whatever works best, whatever is most pragmatic. In other words, the end justifies the means, totally contrary to God's law.

Governor Romney, in total contrast to President Obama, supports the appointment of federal judges and Supreme Court Justices who do not try to make federal policy or legislate from the bench but simply interpret and apply the law to the facts of each case.[259] Legislation, making law, is the duty of elected members of the legislature, which at the federal level is Congress (Senate and House of Representatives).

On January 22, 2008, Senator Obama said, "With one more vacancy on the court, we could be looking at a majority

---

[259] "2012 Values Voter Presidential Voter Guide," Family Research Council Action, http://www.frcaction.org (accessed August 3, 2012).

hostile to a woman's right to choose for the first time since Roe v. Wade, and that is what is at stake in this election."[260] In other words, Obama used talk about the Supreme Court and abortion to win votes and become President.

During his first two years in office, President Obama replaced 2 of the 9 Supreme Court Justices, as many as President George W. Bush replaced in 8 years. Obama's advisors were "preparing for the possibility of a third vacancy, which could make his imprint even more indelible."[261]

APPOINTMENT OF SONIA SOTOMAYER TO SUPREME COURT: In 2009 President Obama appointed Sonia Sotomayor to the U.S. Supreme Court. Sotomayor helped direct litigation of a private organization that filed many pro-abortion lawsuits, to include challenges to parental notification requirements.[262] Tony Perkins, President of Family Research Council, said:

> President Obama has chosen a nominee with a compelling personal story over a judicial pick with a solid judicial philosophy…. Judge Sotomayor's failure to premise her decisions on the text of the Constitution has resulted in an extremely high rate of reversal before the high court to which she has been nominated…. Judge Sotomayor appears to subscribe to a very liberal judicial philosophy that considers it appropriate for judges to impose their personal views from the bench. President Obama promised us a jurist committed to the "rule of law," but, instead, he appears to have nominated a legislator to the

---

[260] "Where Do the Candidates Stand on Life: Mitt Romney, Barack Obama," National Right to Life, http://www.nrlc.org.
[261] "Where Do the Candidates Stand on Life: Mitt Romney, Barack Obama."
[262] "The Presidential Record on Life: President Barack Obama 2009-present," National Right to Life, http://www.nrlc.org.

Supreme Court.... In a 2005 panel discussion at the Duke University Law School...the judge stated that the U.S. Court of Appeals is "where policy is made".... Our constitution states otherwise and public surveys indicate that the American public understands this constitutional principle and wants judges who interpret the law and do not act as life-tenured judicially empowered social workers. [263]

In other words, Judge Sotomayor is an extremely liberal judge who believes in making policy and legislating from the bench, totally contrary to her duty to interpret and apply the law to the facts of each case. Legislation, making law, is the duty of elected members of the legislature, which at the federal level is Congress i.e. the Senate and House of Representatives.

APPOINTMENT OF ELANA KAGAN TO SUPREME COURT: On May 11, 2010, the Washington Post announced President Obama's appointment of Elena Kagan, a woman who never served as a judge at any level and only short time as Solicitor General, to the Supreme Court. As former Dean of Harvard Law School, Kagan barred Armed Forces recruiters from the Law School's Office of Career Services in protest of the "Don't ask, don't tell" policy regarding homosexuals serving in the Armed Forces.[264] As a key political aide to President Clinton, Kagan helped direct a political strategy that would nullify a ban on partial-birth abortions during the Clinton Administration.[265]

---

[263] "Sotomayor: A Policy Maker or a Jurist?", Family Research Council Action, May 26, 2009, http://www.frcaction.org.

[264] Jonathan Blakely, "One Top GOP Line of Attack: Kagan's Opposition to Military Recruitment at Harvard Law School's Office of Career Services," ABC News, http://abcnews.go.com/blogs/politics/2010/05/one-top-gop-line-of-attack-kagans-opposition-to-military-recruitment-at-harvard-law-schools-office-of-career-services/.

[265] "The Presidential Record on Life: President Barack Obama 2009-present,"

Tony Perkins, President of Family Research Council, said:

> Throughout her career, Ms. Kagan has supported
> the promotion of abortion, even if it includes
> funding with American tax dollars. She publicly
> disagreed with the decision in Rust v. Sullivan
> that gave the government the right to deny
> taxpayer funds to groups that perform or promote
> abortions. A large majority of Americans
> disagree with her on that point, as did the
> Supreme Court.... Ms. Kagan's memo to
> President Bill Clinton in 1997…advised the
> President to support a "compromise" allowing for
> "health exceptions" to the ban on the gruesome
> and cruel procedure of partial birth abortion… a
> blatant attempt to create a giant loophole
> rendering the bill meaningless.[266]

In other words, Elena Kagan is a woman who never served as a judge and is a very strong supporter of partial birth abortion, taxpayer funding of abortion, and the homosexual lifestyle. She is absolutely, without any question whatsoever, the Supreme Court Justice who is least qualified to be on the U.S. Supreme Court.

A Washington Post article discussing the significance of the Kagan appointment stated:

> With his second Supreme Court nomination in as
> many years, President Obama has laid down clear

National Right to Life, http://www.nrlc.org.
[266] "FRC Action: Elena Kagan's Pro-Abortion Record is Far Outside the Mainstream", Family Research Council Action, May 19, 2010, http://www.frcaction.org.

markers of his vision for the court, one that could prove to be among his most enduring legacies. Together with Justice Sonia Sotomayor, Elena Kagan's confirmation would represent a shift toward a younger, changing court, one that values experiences outside the courtroom and emphasizes personal interactions as much as deep knowledge of the law. Kagan, 50, the solicitor general named to replace outgoing liberal Justice John Paul Stevens, would…almost certainly provide a lasting, liberal presence, and administration officials hope she would, in the words of one, "start to move the court into a different posture and profile."[267]

Advisers said that President Obama believed that "although Kagan has never been a judge, she would be able to play an "outsize role" on the bench by swaying her colleagues when opinion is divided."[268] Richard Garnett, law professor and associate dean of the University of Notre Dame Law School and former law clerk for Chief Justice William H. Rehnquist, said Obama was "poised to make a lasting impact on the court."

The notion that he is just replacing one member of the so-called liberal wing with another, I think, is superficial…President Obama has a chance to entrench his view of the Constitution for many years to come.[269]

Why would President Obama appoint someone who never served as a judge on any court at any level to the highest

---

[267] Anne E. Kornblut and Robert Barnes, "Kagan Would Emphasize Supreme Court Moving in New Direction," The Washington Post, May 11, 2010, http://www.washingtonpost.com/wp-dyn/content/article/2010/05/10/AR2010051001116.html.

[268] Anne E. Kornblut and Robert Barnes.

[269] Anne E. Kornblut and Robert Barnes.

court in the nation? Simply put, his objective was not to pick someone who would simply do the job of a judge, to interpret and apply the law to the facts of each case. His goal was to choose someone who could influence others to legislate from the bench and implement his policies.

CONCLUSION: The President of the United States appoints Supreme Court justices who serve for life.. President Obama has appointed two extremely liberal justices who will continue to greatly influence the direction of our nation for many years after he is no longer in office. If reelected he may appoint one or two more Supreme Court Justices..

What are the consequences of appointment of extremely liberal justices to the Supreme Court? Why should Christians care? First, liberal Supreme Court Justices will rule constitutional many totally unconstitutional decisions of the President, Congress, state legislatures, and federal, state, and local courts. These decisions will greatly increase federal and state taxes and greatly reduce the freedom of religion and freedom of speech of Christians. Christians will be forced to pay greater taxes used to pay the health care bills of other Americans. Christians and Christian organizations will be forced to pay for abortions, abortive drugs, sterilization, contraceptives, and support homosexual couples by paying for their healthcare. Christian organizations that refuse will be fined and may be forced into bankruptcy.

In other words, reelecting President Obama may enable him to appoint one or two additional liberal Supreme Court Justices who will make decisions that increase taxes and reduce the freedoms of Christians. When Democrats have a majority in the Senate, they chair the Senate Judiciary Committee, and block the nomination of pro-life conservative Christian justices.

PRESIDENT OBAMA: BUYING VOTES

INTRODUCTION: Democrats have a great advantage over Republicans. They can buy votes with taxpayer dollars. Promises and gifts are a major way that Democrats win votes. President Obama is the perfect example.

ALL AMERICANS: No President has offered a greater gift to more Americans than President Obama's totally unconstitutional gift of healthcare to all Americans. He probably bought more votes with healthcare than with any other gift. See chapter on Obamacare.

OLDER AMERICANS: Both presidential candidates have promised to save Medicare, which is headed for bankruptcy. No part of the Constitution authorizes Medicare, but the federal government has taken money from Americans for it and therefore has a moral obligation to provide the benefits.

WOMEN: No President has offered more totally unconstitutional and totally unethical taxpayer funding of women's healthcare than President Obama. This healthcare included contraceptives paid for by Catholics who believe their use to be unethical and abortions paid for by Americans who know that abortion is murder. See chapters on abortion and Obamacare.

ILLEGAL IMMIGRANTS: In the midst of a presidential election, President Obama has offered a greatly coveted path to citizenship for young illegal immigrants, who have come forward by the thousands to take advantage of this generous gift. All Americans will pay the very high cost for education, healthcare, and other benefits for these illegal immigrants.

183

STUDENTS: In the midst of a presidential election, President Obama has offered the totally unconstitutional gift of lower interest rates on college loans, a much-needed gift for college students and college graduates. He secured the votes of millions of young Americans with this gift.

AFRICAN-AMERICANS: During 2008 about 95% of black Americans voted for President Obama, the greatest example of racial voting in American history. During 2012, polls indicate that virtually all blacks favor Obama. Nevertheless, to secure their votes, he has offered prejudice in their favor. "He could have been my son," said President Obama, commenting on the death of a young black man. Can the man who killed him in self-defense expect a fair trial from the government when the head of the United States government and chief law enforcement officer of the United States expresses prejudice before the trial?

LGBT (LESBIAN, GAY, BI-SEXUAL, TRANSVESTITE): No President has offered more totally unconstitutional and totally ungodly federal government support for the LGBT movement and same-sex marriage than President Obama. He has thereby secured the support of virtually all of these voters and their supporters. See chapters on homosexuality and same-sex marriage.

CONCLUSION: President Obama knows that most Americans vote for whoever will best serve them, not whoever will best serve God or the nation. No President in the history of the United States has offered more benefits to more Americans to win their votes than President Obama. No President has acted more contrary to the Constitution and incurred more national debt than President Obama. He promised to decrease the national debt, but greatly increased it, in part to buy the votes of Americans. This makes it very difficult to defeat him, in spite of his terrible record in office. It's a wonder that any Americans

184

vote for Republicans, who can never compete with all the promises and gifts offered by Democrats.

PRESIDENT OBAMA: IS HE A CHRISTIAN?

Why does Senator Obama, an intelligent man who has a Harvard law degree and has attended church for over 20 years, take so many positions totally contrary to biblical law? Is he really a Christian? More specifically, does he meet Christ's definition of a Christian? First, consider his own words about how he was raised.

> I was not raised in a particularly religious household, as undoubtedly many in the audience were. My father, who returned to Kenya when I was just two, was born Muslim but as an adult became an atheist. My mother, whose parents were non-practicing Baptists and Methodists, was probably one of the most spiritual and kindest people I've ever known, but grew up with a healthy skepticism of organized religion herself. As a consequence, so did I. It wasn't until after college, when I went to Chicago to work as a community organizer for a group of Christian churches, that I confronted my own spiritual dilemma.[270]

Obama states that: (1) he was "not raised in a particularly religious household," (2) his father was a Muslim who became an atheist, (3) his father abandoned him when he was two years old, (4) his mother's parents were "non-practicing Baptists and Methodists," (5) his mother and he grew up with "a healthy skepticism of organized religion," (6) he did not confront his

---

[270] Barack Obama, "Call to Renewal Keynote Address," June 28, 2006, http://www.Barackobama.com/speech/060628-call_to_renewal/print.php.

"own spiritual dilemma" until after college. In other words, his parents and grandparents did not even know what it means to be a Christian, a follower of Christ. They did not really believe or live the Christian faith. They raised him with a negative attitude toward Christians and complete misunderstanding of what it means to be a Christian. He never received a proper Christian education as a child or even as a college student. Like most Americans, he did not even understand what it means to be a Christian, a follower of Christ.

Working "as a community organizer for a group of Christian churches" after college made him realize that he was missing something in his life.

> I was working with churches, and the Christians who I worked with recognized themselves in me. They saw that I knew their Book and that I shared their values and sang their songs. But they sensed that a part of me that remained removed, detached, that I was an observer in their midst. And in time, I came to realize that something was missing as well -- that without a vessel for my beliefs, without a commitment to a particular community of faith, at some level I would always remain apart, and alone.[271]

In his book "The Faith of Barack Obama," Stephen Mansfield explains that Obama "was seeking a 'vessel' for his values, a 'community of shared traditions in which to ground my most deeply held beliefs'."[272] In other words, Obama was beginning to see that the Christian faith might be something useful to him, as "a vessel for my beliefs" and something that

---

[271] Ibid.
[272] Stephen Mansfield, The Faith of Barack Obama, (Nashville, Dallas: Thomas Nelson, 2008), p. 52-53.

would solve his problem of feeling "apart, and alone" by allowing him to be part of this "particular community of faith."

Senator Obama then makes a statement essential to understanding his faith and his understanding of what it means to be a Christian.

> And if it weren't for the particular attributes of the historically black church, I may have accepted this fate. But as the months passed in Chicago, I found myself drawn - not just to work with the church, but to be in the church.[273]

Senator Obama states that he may have remained "without a vessel for my beliefs, without a commitment to a particular community of faith…apart, and alone" if he had not been "drawn…to be in the church" by the "particular attributes of the historically black church."   In other words, he was not drawn to the church by awareness of his sinful state, repentance for his sins, need for a Savior, the feeling for the need to change anything about the way that he was living his life, or anything else that is part of the gospel message which is also present in non-black Christian churches. He was attracted by "particular attribute" that were unique to the "black church."

Then he explains what he means by these "particular attributes" of the "black church."

> For one thing, I believed and still believe in the power of the African-American religious tradition to spur social change, a power made real by some of the leaders here today. Because of its past, the black church understands in an intimate way the Biblical call to feed the hungry and cloth

---

[273] Ibid.

the naked and challenge the powers and principalities.[274]

The attributes of the black church that attracted Obama included: "power…to spur social change" and understanding of the Biblical calls to: (1) "feed the hungry," (2) "cloth the naked," and (3) "challenge the powers and principalities." The black church should be greatly respected and highly commended for its strong desire and all its efforts to do all these things. All are part of obedience to God's commandment: "Thou shalt love thy neighbour as thyself" (Matthew 22:39, KJV). It is a sad commentary on other churches if they do not do all these things as well as the black church. However, there is nothing all this that indicates that he was attracted to the church by awareness of his sinful state, repentance for his sins, or the need to change anything about the way that he was living his life.

Obama then states how these "particular attributes" of the "black church" led him to understanding of two key points that led him to publicly affirm his faith. The first point is:

> In its historical struggles for freedom and the
> rights of man, I was able to see faith as more than
> just a comfort to the weary or a hedge against
> death, but rather as an active, palpable agent in
> the world. As a source of hope.[275]

The first point that led Obama to publicly affirm his faith was understanding that faith was "more than just a comfort…or a hedge against death" but an (1) "active, palpable agent in the world" and (2) "source of hope." In other words, he affirmed his faith in part because he realized the usefulness of faith as a "source of hope" and "agent" for bringing needed change.

---

[274] Ibid.
[275] Ibid.

Then Obama explains the second point that let him to publicly affirm his faith.

> And perhaps it was out of this intimate
> knowledge of hardship -- the grounding of faith
> in struggle -- that the church offered me a second
> insight, one that I think is important to emphasize
> today. Faith doesn't mean that you don't have
> doubts. You need to come to church in the first
> place precisely because you are first of this
> world, not apart from it. You need to embrace
> Christ precisely because you have sins to wash
> away - because you are human and need an ally
> in this difficult journey.[276]

Note that he does not express any remorsefulness for sin or any need to change anything about the way that he was living. He simply realized the usefulness of Christ to (1) cleanse him from sin and (2) be his ally in life's "difficult journey." Note that he does not refer to Christ as Lord, but simply his "ally."

Then Obama states, "It was because of these newfound understandings that I was finally able to walk down the aisle of Trinity United Church of Christ on 95th Street in the Southside of Chicago one day and affirm my Christian faith."[277]

In his book "The Faith of Barack Obama," Stephen Mansfield tries to explain the true meaning and significance of what Barack Obama experienced and understood.

> Exactly what Barack Obama experienced and
> what he understood is hard to discern. He does
> not use the language of the traditional convert to
> Christianity. He is the product of a new, post-

---

[276] Ibid.
[277] Ibid.

modern generation that picks and chooses its own truth from traditional faith, much as a man customizes his meal at a buffet. Obama does <u>not recount that he felt an emptiness in his soul, was burdened by the weight of his sins,</u> and so responded to the love of Jesus, who promised to save him and remake him in the image of God. This is the language of evangelicalism.[278]

In other words, Stephen Mansfield seems to agree that it appears that Obama's profession of faith was not motivated by true remorsefulness or repentance for sin, but by a decision that faith was useful to him. It was useful to him because it was a (1) "source of hope" and (2) "agent" for bringing needed change and because it (3) cleansed him of sin and (4) made Christ is his "ally" in life's "difficult journey."

Obama continues his own explanation of the nature and meaning of his profession of faith.

It came about as a choice, and not an epiphany. I didn't fall out in church. The questions I had didn't magically disappear. But kneeling beneath that cross on the South Side, I felt that I heard God's spirit beckoning me. I <u>submitted myself to His will, and dedicated myself to discovering His truth.</u> That's <u>a path that has been shared by millions upon millions of Americans - evangelicals, Catholics, Protestants, Jews and Muslims alike</u>....[279]

Note that although he now understood the two key points which led to his profession of faith, his questions did not "magically disappear" because his understanding was

---

[278] Stephen Mansfield, p. 52-53.
[279] Ibid.

incomplete and so he "dedicated [himself] to discovering [God's] truth." However, although he dedicated himself to "discovering His truth" over 20 years ago, there is no evidence to indicate that he gained true biblical understanding on any major issue. Although he states, "I submitted myself to His will," there is no evidence to indicate any change in behavior. Totally to the contrary, his voting record seems to be the perfect illustration of the principle that faith without works is dead. It proves that he completely failed to discover truths clearly revealed through Scripture and continued to vote totally contrary to God's will over 20 years after his supposed conversion.

Also note that he describes his conversion as "a path that has been shared by millions upon millions of Americans - evangelicals, Catholics, Protestants, Jews and Muslims alike....[280] Becoming a convert to a non-Christian religion does not require awareness of one's sinful state, repentance for sins, the need for a Savior, or any knowledge of Christ. His words do not seem to make much sense until you realize that he is a politician wanting the votes of Americans of all faiths. Also, note that most of the biblical law cited in Scripture and this book is from the Old Testament, from Scripture that Jews call the "Torah" or "the law and the prophets," from Moses, Jeremiah, King David, and others. Senator Obama's voting record proves complete lack of understanding and compliance with biblical law, an essential part of being a Christian or Jew.

Again, in his book "The Faith of Barack Obama," Stephen Mansfield tries to explain the true meaning and significance of what Barack Obama experienced and understood.

> He says, instead, that he was seeking a "vessel" for his values, a "community of shared traditions in which to ground my most deeply held beliefs."

---

[280] Ibid.

Rather than yield his mind without reserve to Scripture and its revelation of God, Obama was relieved that a "religious commitment did not require me to suspend critical thinking." Rather than "renounce the world and its ways"— standard Christian language for breaking with the sinful ways of society—he was pleased that his faith would not require "retreat from the world that I knew and loved."[281]

How does any of this explain why Obama, an extremely intelligent man who has a Harvard law degree and attended church for over 20 years, is so ignorant about biblical law? First, the fact that he made a public profession of his faith, committed his life to doing God's will, and dedicated himself to discovering God's truth did not mean that he suddenly had a complete understanding of biblical law and how it should be applied to his life, the church, and government. His voting record proves just the opposite, that he never discovered truths clearly revealed through Scripture and continued to vote totally contrary to God's will.

Second, Obama and the "black church" clearly understand the need for individuals and the church to strive for obedience to God's commandment to love one's neighbor as oneself by striving to: (1) "spur social change," (2) "feed the hungry," (2) "cloth the naked," and (3) "challenge the powers and principalities." However, it appears that they do not understand that government does not have any God-given command, responsibility, authority, or jurisdiction to force any citizen to obey this commandment. Love is by its very nature an act of the will. No government can force any individual to love his neighbor. Also, no government has the right to take by force money from one person who lawfully earned that money and give it to another person just because he has less money. That is

---

[281] Stephen Mansfield, p. 52-53.

theft, a violation of a commandment which government has a duty to enforce.

Failure to understand these principles explains why, when running for president, Obama implied in public statements that it was that "fundament concept that I am my brother's keeper" that motivated him to want to serve as president. It also explains why the list of what he wants to accomplish as president includes a very long list of extremely costly social programs that would greatly increase the size and cost of government and greatly increase, on a permanent basis, the tax burden on Americans.

This may also explain why Obama's pastor shouted from the pulpit, "Not God bless American, but God [curse] America!" He seemed to express great anger and hatred for America not because he hated America, but because he blamed the American government for failure to properly care for African-Americans. Later, after videotapes of him saying these words were played many times on national television, he seemed totally unrepentant. In fact, he justified his conduct by saying that he was doing what he had to do as a pastor, and Obama was doing what he had to do as a politician.

All this may also explain why Obama stayed in the same church, "Trinity United Church of Christ…in the Southside of Chicago,"[282] for 20 years. Rev. Wright did not suddenly change his heart, mind, and message during the presidential race. As a matter of fact, one of the things that probably attracted Obama to this church was the strong drive of the pastor "to spur social change" and "challenge the powers and principalities" (government) to do a better job of fulfilling its duty to care for African-Americans, to give them their fair share of the American pie. That is why Obama remained a faithful friend to his pastor for 20 years, even after Rev. Wright had an affair with

---

[282] Ibid.

a church worker, until that friendship threatened his chances of becoming president.

So is Barack Obama a Christian? Answering this question requires careful review of Christ's words.

> Not every one that saith unto me, Lord, Lord, shall enter into the kingdom of heaven; but he that doeth the will of my Father which is in heaven. Many will say to me in that day, Lord, Lord, have we not prophesied in thy name? and in thy name have cast out devils? and in thy name done many wonderful works? And then will I profess unto them, I never knew you: depart from me, ye that work iniquity (Matthew 7:21-23, KJV).

Believing in Christ as Lord and Savior and doing great miracles in His name does not make one a Christian. A Christian is one who does "the will of my Father."

Alan Keyes is a brilliant, deeply committed African-American Christian who ran against Barack Obama during the 2004 U.S. Senate election. Barack Obama admitted, in his "Call to Renewal" speech given on June 28, 2006 and later posted on his campaign website, that Alan Keys said:

> Jesus Christ would not vote for Barack Obama. Christ would not vote for Barack Obama because Barack Obama has behaved in a way that is inconceivable for Christ to have behaved…. Mr. Obama says he's a Christian…and yet he supports a lifestyle that the Bible calls an abomination…Mr. Obama says he's a Christian, but supports the destruction of innocent sacred life.[283]

Alan Keyes clearly understood that Barack Obama's policies were in complete opposition to biblical laws given by God. He understood that Barack Obama rejected God and God's law.

Consider the positions of Senator Obama, and how they conflict with Scripture. He would repeal the Federal Defense of Marriage Act (1996), which "declares marriage to be the union of one man and one woman…and declares that states do not have to recognize same-sex 'marriages' from other states."[284] He would sign bills "to give federal civil rights protection based upon sexual orientation and 'gender identity'" and "to overturn the statutory ban on homosexuals serving in the military."[285] He would support mandated taxpayer and private company funds for health care and other benefits for same-sex partners, greater restrictions on gun rights, and taxation of individuals after death (reducing inheritance of children and others). He also supports a massive increase in the size and cost of government, which seems totally contrary to the Biblical ideal of smaller government established by the founding fathers.

He has an absolute zero percent voting record on pro-life issues scored by the National Right to Life Committee, but a 100% rating from NARAL Pro-Choice America. [286] He supports partial birth abortion, the killing of aborted children born alive, and U.S. taxpayer funds for abortion by national and international organizations. "The partial-birth abortion

---

[283] Barack Obama, "Call to Renewal Keynote Address," June 28, 2006, http://www.Barackobama.com/speech/060628-call_to_renewal/print.php.
[284] "Values Voter Guide for 2008 Presidential Candidates," Family Research Council Action, http://www.frcaction.org (accessed July 9, 2008).
[285] Ibid.
[286] "Where Do the Candidates Stand on Life: John McCain, Barack Obama," "Senator John McCain Record on Abortion in the United States Senate," and "Senator Barack Obama Record on Abortion, United States Senate, Illinois State Senate," National Right to Life Committee, http://www.nrlc.org (accessed August 28, 2008).

procedure — used from the fifth month on — involves pulling a living baby feet-first out of the womb, except for the head, puncturing the skull and suctioning out the brain. The great majority of partial-birth abortions are performed on healthy babies of healthy mothers."[287]

Even more critical than all of the preceding, Senator Obama is an extreme liberal who would appoint liberal judges who would legislate from the bench and create laws which would legalize same-sex marriage, mandate taxpayer and private company funds for health care and other benefits for same-sex partners, mandate taxpayer funds for abortion, partial birth abortion, and the killing of aborted children born alive by national and international organizations, and other laws totally contrary to biblical law.[288] Those judges and justices would, contrary to the U.S. Constitution, legislate from the bench many years after the president is no longer in office. Some would do their best to legalize same-sex marriage and partial birth abortion. Some have already tried. Obama would make it more likely that they would succeed.

Barack Obama is not like someone throwing darts, trying to hit the bull's-eye, who occasionally misses. He continually and consistently misses the entire target. He has many very firm beliefs, many strong moral convictions that are totally contrary to Scripture. His moral compass is broken and continually points him in the wrong direction.

On Judgment Day many people who "prophesied" and "cast out demons" and did "many wonderful works" in His name will be rejected by Christ because they did not do "the will of my Father which is in heaven." Christ will say, "I never knew you: depart from me, ye that work iniquity (Matthew 7:23,

---

[287] Ibid.
[288] "Values Voter Guide for 2008 Presidential Candidates," Family Research Council Action, http://www.frcaction.org (accessed July 9, 2008).

KJV). The key words in this passage are "the will of my Father." That is the deciding factor for Christ. If "many" people who believe they are doing such a great job of being Christians and serving Christ by doing great miracles in His name will be rejected by Christ on Judgment Day, then what will happen to someone like Barack Obama? I do not believe that after 20 years of attending church he is so completely ignorant of the teachings of Scripture. He deliberately and continually rejected clear teachings of Scripture and chose to not do "the will of the Father." Therefore he does not meet Christ's definition of a Christian. The same is true for many Americans who do exactly the same, rejecting clear teachings of Scripture and choosing to not do "the will of the Father."

Although I considered all factors discussed in this chapter, the real deciding factor for me is what Christ said will be His deciding factor on Judgment Day: whether someone did "the will of the Father." That is not to say that one is saved by doing "the will of the Father." No one is saved by what they do because God is holy, His standard is perfection, and no one can meet that standard except Christ. He was the Lamb of God, the perfect Holy One who was fully God and fully man, the only one who could make payment for our sins by His death on a cross. Everyone is saved by faith, not works, but faith without works is dead. That is why Obama and most Democrats who vote contrary to biblical principles and anyone who votes for them should not consider themselves to be Christians. That is not to say that all Republicans are Christians. Some may not even believe in God or Christ. God's standards are higher than those of Republicans and Democrats. However, any person who fails to vote Christian values fails to meet one of the minimum standards for being a Christian. They prove by their voting that they do not do "the will of the Father" and that they do not meet Christ's clearly stated standard for being a Christian. A Christian is not someone who believes in Christ and accepts Christ as Lord and Savior, but someone who takes up their cross and follows Christ.

It is vitally important to understand what is best for African-Americans is the exact same thing that is best for all Americans. God is no respecter of persons. He does not favor one race over another. He creates all men equal, meaning that he forms every man and woman within the womb and all have equal value in His eyes. Races are like colors of the rainbow. Each is just a precious as the other. Each reveals the glory of God in a very special way. Every life is very precious to God, and should be to us.

What all Americans need are citizens and government officials who act and govern in obedience to God's commandments. That seems like common sense, but it is not. What seems right to the most intelligent of men is often not right in the eyes of God. His ways are higher than man's ways, His thoughts are higher than man's thoughts, and He has revealed His heart, mind, thoughts, and laws through Scripture. The founding fathers were Christians who had a much better understanding of Scripture and God's law than most Americans today. Acutely aware of the abuses of power of the British king and government, they declared independence from England, and designed a Constitution that granted limited authority to three branches of government and checks and balances to keep each branch from abusing its authority. They created a federal government with very limited powers to maximize individual freedom and responsibility for all Americans. What is best for all Americans is a smaller federal government which does not try to care for all of its citizens, but which protects the rights of all Americans to life, liberty, and the pursuit of happiness. These rights are not rights to handouts of any kind from the federal government, but rights that mean protection of every man's right to work and enjoy the fruits of his labor, without having them wrongfully taken from him by any other man.

LIES AND DECEPTION

SECTION REVIEW: This section addresses deception employed by Democrats during the 2008 and 2012 presidential campaigns. The first chapter reviews deception during the 2012 presidential campaign. The second chapter addresses deception during the 2008 presidential campaign.

CHAPTERS: Chapters in this section include the following:

LIES AND DECEPTION: 2012 ELECTION

INTRODUCTION: If lies and deception are primary tools of Satan, and if life and the political realm are spiritual battlefields between forces of good and evil, then one can expect to see lies and deception used extensively by those who are not on God's side. It is amazing how much this is true in politics. It appears to be truer with President Obama than any other President in the history of the United States. What is even more amazing is how well they work, how much they are believed by Americans, how much they turn the hearts and minds of Americans against political opponents. Many Americans reward lying politicians with their support. They make lying profitable.

How can you tell when a Democrat is telling a lie? Republicans might be tempted to say, "When their lips are moving." However, it would probably be more accurate to say that they normally are not being truthful when: (1) they are talking about their political opponent or (2) they are promising government benefits to voters that do not have to be paid for by those voters.

As an Army officer, the author of this book helped plan and write operations orders for a division commander. Part of the staff writing the order would develop a deception plan. That is what President Obama's campaign staff has done, and that presents a major moral problem. It is morally right and totally proper to deceive one's enemy in combat. No commander wants the enemy to know his mission, concept of operations, or the location of all friendly forces. However, it is morally wrong and totally improper for a presidential candidate to use lies and deception to win the support of American voters. President Obama cannot run on his record, so he will use lies and deception to turn the hearts and minds of Americans against his political opponents.

LIES ABOUT POLITICAL OPPONENTS: President Obama cannot run on his record on jobs and the economy or anything else. Therefore his primary strategy is to destroy his political opponents with lies and false allegations. This section presents just a few examples. Many more will come after this book is published, as the election draws closer.

1. LIES ABOUT HILLARY CLINTON: During the 2008 presidential primary, Hillary Clinton angrily accused Senator Obama of using lies to gain political support. "He continues to spend millions perpetuating falsehoods...so shame on you, Barack Obama.".[289]

2. LIES ABOUT ROMNEY BEING AN "EXTREMIST": One of first lies voiced by President Obama during the 2012 presidential election was that Governor Romney is an extremist. As continually restated by Rush Limbaugh and presidential candidates, Romney is not a conservative. He is a moderate. Romney won the Republican nomination in part because conservatives divided their votes among conservative candidates, so the conservatives lost. On April 10, 2012, President Obama said that voters face the "biggest contrast" in candidates seen since the 1964 race between Lyndon Johnson and Barry Goldwater.[290] President Obama's statement is true not because Romney is an extremist, but because Obama is a left-

---

[289] Quote from Romney political advertisement broadcast on NBC during August 2012.

[290] "'This election will probably have the biggest contrast that we've seen maybe since the Johnson-Goldwater election - maybe before that,' the president said at an off-camera fundraiser.... Johnson won the 1964 race by 61 percent of the popular vote, making it the largest Democratic landslide since 1820." Mary Bruce, "Obama: Voters Face Starkest Contrast Since Johnson-Goldwater," ABC OTUS News, April 10, 2012.

wing extremist, the most liberal President in the history of the United States.

3. LIES ABOUT ROMNEY KILLING A WOMAN:
During August 2012, a pro-Obama organization falsely but very clearly implied that Governor Romney was responsible for the death of a woman who died from cancer because she was allegedly denied health insurance by Bain Capital, Romney's company. First, the allegation is false because the woman died about 10 years after Romney left Bain Capital. Second, the allegation is false because the woman had her own insurance, not with Bain Capital.[291]

4. LIES ABOUT ROMNEY NOT PAYING TAXES:
During August, 2012, Senator Harry Reid, Senate Majority Leader, the highest ranking Democrat in Congress, repeatedly accused Governor Romney of not paying any taxes for 10 years. First, he said that he was told this by an "investor" in Bain Capital, but refused to name his source. Think about it. Any American could invest in Bain Capital, and investing in Bain Capital would not in any way give someone access to information about what taxes were paid by Romney. So why would Senator Reid make such blatantly false accusations on the floor of the Senate, and not even try to offer any proof of the false accusations? The answer is simple. He knows that some Americans will believe the lies, turn their hearts and minds against Romney, and vote for Obama. In other words, he knows there can be great profit in telling lies about his political opponent, so he does it for the political gain.[292] Later, Governor Romney announced that during this period he never paid less than 13% in taxes, and said that figure would always be over 20% if you added donations.

---

[291] Comments broadcast live on Fox News, August 9, 2012.
[292] Comments broadcast live on CNN on August 10, 2012.

Another reason Democrats are willing to tell blatant lies about Governor Romney not paying taxes is because they want to force him to release more tax returns. Why do they want more tax returns? First, they want to turn Americans against Romney by showing that he is, unlike most Americans, a very wealthy man. President Obama and other Democrats have continually tried to portray Romney as a rich man who is out of touch with most Americans. Second, they have continually stated or implied that "rich" Americans are somehow immoral or unethical because they did not really earn their wealth and they do not pay their fair share of taxes. Third, they want more evidence to prove that Romney has not paid he "fair share" of taxes. Americans should ask themselves whether Abraham, Job, and King Solomon, all extremely wealthy men, were wealthy because they were dishonest or evil or because they found favor with God, were obedient to his will and his laws, and were, as a result, richly blessed by God.

President Obama and other Democrats have repeatedly stated that Romney only paid 14% in federal income tax. They have repeatedly falsely implied that he did not pay his "fair share" of taxes, and is therefore probably guilty of a the very serious crime of tax evasion. In other words, they have falsely accused Romney of being dishonest and a criminal and have completely failed to offer any evidence to prove their lies. Americans should be aware of some of the reasons that Romney paid only 14% in taxes. First, he most certainly, like all other Americans, took full advantage of all possible tax deductions, tax credits, and tax shelters. Second, most of his income probably comes from investments, which are taxed at a lower rate. Third, he was extremely generous in his giving (another tax deduction). Americans should also understand that God's "tax rate" for both the rich and the poor is 10%, and Romney paid more than that in taxes and gave much more than that to charities.

JOBS, ECONOMY, AND TAXES: President Obama promised to solve the national economic crisis and put Americans back to work. He failed miserably. He promised change that Americans could believe in. He delivered the opposite. Therefore he has resorted to lies and deception to detract from his poor job performance.

1. LIES ABOUT JOBS AND THE ECONOMY: In April 2012 Obama claimed unemployment went down. The announcement was intended to deceive Americans, because although the officially published unemployment rate did go down slightly, the actual unemployment rate went up because more Americans gave up looking for work and were not counted in the official numbers.

2. LIES ABOUT ECNONOMIC POLICIES OF BUSH ADMINISTRATION: Many Democrats have claimed that President Romney would return to the failed economic policies of Bush Administration that led to the economic crash in 2008. The economic crash was not caused by the economic policies of the Bush Administration, but by banks and mortgage companies approving loans for Americans who could not afford homes, and by the financial institutions that pooled these risky investments and gave them a much higher quality rating than they deserved. The regulations that may have contributed to the crash originated during the Clinton Administration, not the Bush Administration.

3. LIES ABOUT BUSH TAX CUTS: Democrats accuse Republicans of wanting to keep the "Bush tax cuts" which they say favor the rich and discriminate against the "middle class." First, there are no "Bush tax cuts." They are tax cuts enacted by Congress during the 8 years that President Bush was in office. President Bush has questioned why Democrats call them "Bush tax cuts." The reason is simple—Democrats are using lies and deception to vilify Republicans turn the hearts of Americans against them and their tax cuts.

4. LIES ABOUT TAXING THE RICH: One of the primary themes of President Obama's 2012 campaign is fairness in taxation. Obama claims that "rich" Americans are not paying their fair share of taxes, and that they should therefore be taxed a "little more" to support the overtaxed "middle class." His statements are false. First, about 49% of Americans, mostly middle and lower class, do not pay any federal taxes. They are not paying their fair share. Second, God's "tax rate" is exactly the same rate for the rich and the poor: 10%. See chapter on Taxing the Rich for further discussion.

5. NATIONAL DEBT: President Obama promised to reduce the national debt. He did just the opposite; he greatly increased it. Why should Americans care about the national debt, federal spending, and the deficit? Look at the economic collapse in Greece. Thousands of Greeks rioted to protest extreme austerity measures imposed by other European nations who at very great cost to themselves bailed them out. Look at all the cities in California and other states forced into bankruptcy by spending far more than they had, going far into debt. The United States is heading in the same direction, much faster thanks to President Obama and other Democrats who live to spend more taxpayer dollars to take better care of more Americans. No one can or will bail out the United States.

6. FEDERAL SPENDING AND DEFICIT: The biggest lie being told to Americans by President Obama and other Democrats is that the United States can continue to spend more money than it takes in, continue to greatly increase the national debt, without facing an economic collapse like Greece and like the cities in California and other states forced into bankruptcy. President Obama and Democrats are like an American with totally out of control credit card spending who incurs insurmountable debt and is forced into bankruptcy.

7. WELFARE STATE: The United States is not headed toward becoming a welfare state. The United States already is a welfare state. About one third of Americans receive government assistance. That number will grow considerably as more baby boomers retire and start living off social security, Medicare, and other government benefits. What is so amazing is that President Obama and Democrats want even more, much more, government spending to take better care of more Americans with healthcare, welfare, food stamps, educational benefits, etc. That means higher taxes, greater deficits, greater national debt, and eventually an economic collapse similar to that of Greece.

8. VICE PRESIDENT RYAN'S BUDGET: Vice President Ryan's budget will help bring some of the completely runaway federal spending under control. It is not enough, but it is a step in the right direction. See www.heritage.org for further discussion of Ryan's budget. President Obama and the Democrats have failed to produce any budget that can bring the totally runaway federal spending under control and reduce the national deficit and national debt.

MORAL ISSUES: President Obama has used lies and deception about moral issues to turn voters against Republicans. He has taken strong actions to impose his ungodly values upon Americans. His actions mean that Christians, in violation of the Constitution and their rights of liberty and freedom of religion, are forced to pay the healthcare bills of other Americans, bills that include abortions, contraceptives, etc. If President Obama is reelected and gets his way, Christians will also be forced to pay the healthcare bills of same-sex partners of civil unions and same-sex marriages.

1. WAR AGAINST WOMEN: On April 15, 2012, NBC's Meet the Press announced that 57% of women voters supported Obama but only 38% supported Romney. On the same program, Michelle Backman pointed out that women lost 92% of the jobs lost under President Obama (858,000 jobs).

Question: If women have suffered so much under President Obama, why do most support him? Answer: President Obama and Democrats deceived women. First, totally contrary to simple ethics and the U.S. Constitution, they used legislation by Congress (Obamacare) to order U.S. taxpayer to fund abortions, abortive drugs, contraceptives, etc. Then President Obama issued an executive order forcing Catholic and other organizations, contrary to their firmly held moral and religious beliefs, to provide these services. When Republicans and others objected, Democrats accused Republicans of declaring war on women by refusing to provide women's healthcare.

2. LIES ABOUT CONTRACEPTIVES: In 2012 Democrats falsely accused Republicans of wanting to deny a woman's rights to contraception. No Republican tried to deny any woman the right to contraceptives. The real issues are: (1) who pays for the contraceptives, (2) freedom of religion and (3) jurisdiction of the federal government. First, President Obama ordered Catholic organizations to provide "free" contraceptives (paid for by Catholics) contrary to their firmly held religious beliefs. Second, Democrats wanted to provide "free" contraceptives (paid for by taxpayers) to "middle class" women. The Constitution gives absolutely no authority for any branch of the federal government to force any American to pay for any healthcare benefits of another American.

3. LIES ABOUT ABORTION: Americans who oppose abortion call themselves pro-life. Americans who support a "woman's right" to abortion are called pro-choice. Which side is being truthful? Which side is being deceptive? Clue: In 2012 Mississippi voters voted that life does not begin at conception. Why would voters deny a simple, scientific fact? Answer: Because it is an inconvenient truth. Another clue: When asked in 2008 about when life begins, Senator Obama responded that the answer was "above his pay grade." The real issue is life, not choice. If choice was the real issue, a woman would have the right to terminate the life of a child before and after birth.

Indeed, after birth, after living with the child for a period of time, the woman would have even more information about the child to enable a more informed decision on whether or not to terminate the life of the child.

4. PRO-CHOICE HYPOCRITES: Why do pro-choice Americans like President Obama and other Democrats so desperately want to force other Americans who believe that abortion is murder to pay for abortions? Why do they want to force Catholic organizations, against their deeply held moral and religious beliefs, to provide and pay for contraceptives and abortions? In the name of freedom to choose whatever is right in their own eyes, a totally morally corrupt philosophy, they demand respect for their immoral choices, and totally disrespect and deny the ethical choices of anyone who disagrees with them. They are absolute hypocrites!

5. LIES ABOUT HOMOSEXUALITY AND SAME-SEX MARRIAGE: Homosexuals and President Obama and other Democrats who support them and their ungodly lifestyle falsely claim or imply that homosexuality and same-sex marriage are morally acceptable behavior that should be tolerated and accepted. Scripture clearly teaches that they are abominations to God, extreme perversions of His creation of sex and marriage, deserving of the death in the eyes of God and at the hands of God.

6. LIES ABOUT ANTI-HOMOSEXUALS: Homosexuals call those who oppose them "homophobes." "Homo" refers to homosexuals. "Phobe" means fear. A homophobe is someone who "fears" homosexuals. In other words, homosexuals falsely accuse those who do not approve of their extremely sexual perversion as being the ones who have the problem, and falsely state that their problem is fear.

CONCLUSION: The author apologizes for the incompleteness of this chapter. It is difficult to properly address all the lies, deception, and false promises of President Obama and Democrats. There will be many more after this book is published. This chapter presents a few examples, enough to give the readers some understanding regarding the morality of President Obama and Democrats.

Why are so many Americans so gullible? Why do they believe the countless lies of President Obama and Democrats and reward their dishonesty with their support? Why do most Americans vote for whoever promises them the greatest personal benefits, and not vote whoever will best serve God and our beloved nation?

LIES AND DECEPTION: 2008 ELECTION

INTRODUCTION: Most Americans are more concerned about the economy and their finances than Christian values. They vote for whoever promises them the greatest financial benefit. During the 2008 election, Senator Obama promised more government assistance and financial aid to more Americans than any other presidential candidate in U.S. history. This gave him great political advantage during a national financial crisis. The challenge for Christians was to see through all the lies and false promises and vote Christian values.

QUALIFICATIONS/EXPERIENCE: One of the major themes of the Democrats during the 2008 election was the lie that Senator Obama was more qualified to be President of the United States and Commander in Chief than Senator McCain. Senator Obama's resume included 7 years in the Illinois Senate (1997-2003) and 4 years in the U.S. Senate (2005-2008). In other words, he was a state senator less than 4 years before the election. He started his run for president after only 143 days in the U.S. Senate. He was one of the most junior Senators in the U.S. Senate. He had virtually no experience in national or international affairs.

Senator McCain had over 50 years of federal service that included over 23 years of military service, 5 years as Naval Liaison to the U.S. Senate, 4 years as a member of the U.S. House of Representatives, and 22 years as U.S. Senator. His 26 years in Congress gave him extensive experience dealing with military, national, and international affairs. His 5 years of service as Naval Liaison to the U.S. Senate gave him special insight into the working relationship and all the dealings between the military and the U.S. Senate. His over 50 years of federal service included: 4 years at the U.S. Naval Academy (1954-1958); 23 years as a U.S. Navy Officer (1958-1981); 4 years as a member of the U.S. House of Representatives (1983-1986); and 22 years in the U.S. Senate (1987-2008). The 23 years as a U.S. Naval Officer included several years a Navy Fighter Pilot, 23 combat missions, over 5 years as a tortured Prisoner of War, and over 5 years as the Naval Liaison Officer to the U.S. Senate (1976-1981). Senator McCain was infinitely more qualified to be President of the United States and Commander in Chief than Senator Obama.

FOREIGN AFFAIRS EXPERIENCE: One insane, absurd, misleading argument vigorously advanced by the liberal press even more than the Obama campaign was that Senator Obama should be President because Senator Biden had more foreign affairs experience than Governor Palin. It is the President who meets with foreign heads of state, travels to foreign nations to meet their leaders, and who makes decisions regarding international affairs, not the Vice President. Senator Obama had less than 4 years of experience in international affairs as a U.S. Senator. Senator McCain had 26 years. The difference could not have been greater.

LIBERAL MEDIA: Some of the greatest distortion of truth comes from the liberal media. During 2008, extreme media bias was reflected through discussions of candidates that only solicited opinions from liberal commentators, biased interviews aimed at degrading Republican candidates, broadcast of documentaries and movies critical of former Republican Presidents, late night comedy programs which continually mocked Republican Presidents and candidates, and reporting of mistakes by Republicans but not Democrats. Most Americans have seen the biased discussions, interviews, and late talk shows. A movie that ridiculed President Bush was released October 17, 2008, just a couple weeks before the November 4, 2008 election.

Governor Palin was questioned about her lack of experience regarding international affairs, an area in which no governors have any significant expertise. She was ridiculed for any minor mistakes she made, but nothing was said when Senator Biden said that Vice President Cheney should read Article I of the U.S. Constitution regarding the duties of the Executive Branch. Article I, which is the first and by far the largest part of the U.S. Constitution, deals with the Legislative Branch, which Senator Biden was part of for 36 years. See U.S. Constitution in Appendixes. Senator Biden did not even know what part of the U.S. Constitution described the duties that he had performed for 36 years.

LIES ABOUT SENATOR McCAIN: Senator Obama and Senator Biden told many lies about Senator McCain. Senator Biden falsely accused Senator McCain of signing a bill when Senator McCain was campaigning in another state and did not even vote on the bill. Senator Obama accused Senator McCain of planning to tax the health care benefits of all Americans but deliberately failed to mention that Senator McCain would give a tax credit ($2,500/individual; $5,000/family) which would result in a net savings not loss for most Americans. Another blatant lie promulgated by Senator Obama during debates and by television advertisements was that Senator McCain supported more government spending than Senator Obama. The opposite was true. These are just a couple of the countless incorrect comments made during debates, corrected later by experts interviewed by television news commentators.

FALSE PROMISES OF SENATOR OBAMA: One of the greatest lies put forth by Senator Obama during debates and by television advertisements was that Americans could enjoy about $1 trillion in additional government benefits, to include health care, without paying for it, because 95% of Americans would receive tax cuts. Exactly how would Senator Obama, during a major national economic crisis, pay for: (1) $1 trillion increased federal spending, (2) $84 billion bailout of AIG, (3) $700 billion bailout of other financial institutions, (4) tax cuts for 95% of all Americans, and (5) sending more troops to Afghanistan, which he agreed was necessary. The national economic crisis, which included a mortgage crisis with countless homeowners facing foreclosure and a financial institution crisis with the failure of major financial institutions invested in these mortgages, meant greatly reduced income for the federal government due to reduced income and investment losses for so many Americans. Also, how could Senator Obama do all the things that he promised without the largest permanent tax increase in American history? How much more of each year would taxpayers have to work just to pay their taxes? <u>Do we want our nation to make a giant leap from the individual freedom and responsibility that made it such a great nation to less personal freedom and responsibility, greater taxes, more socialism, and more redistribution of wealth?</u>

BLAMING PRESIDENT BUSH: Another lie, the main theme of the Democrats during the 2008 election, repeated countless times by every Democratic presidential candidate and in countless television advertisements, was that President George W. Bush was to blame for every major problem faced by the nation, to include sharply rising oil prices, the mortgage crisis, the financial institution crisis, everything that ailed the United States economy, the health care crisis, the war on terror, the September 11, 2001 attacks on New York City and Washington, D.C., and all other major problems facing Americans. President Bush was not to blame, and his name was not on the ballot. Sharply rising world oil prices were caused by rising global demand, especially from China, and speculation by investors. The mortgage crisis was caused by borrowers, lenders, and investors assuming far too much risk. Borrowers sought, lenders granted, and investors backed mortgages that were too large for the budget of the borrowers or had flexible interest rates that increased the cost beyond what the borrower could pay. The failure of financial institutions was caused by investors and financial institutions that put too much money into these mortgages and other risky investments.

The health care crisis was caused by misuse of benefits and overcharging by doctors, hospitals, and health care institutions for supplies and services. The failure to predict the September 11, 2001 attacks was due to failures by many individuals at many levels in customs, law enforcement, and intelligence organizations. Like the attack on Pearl Harbor on December 7, 1941, the September 11, 2001 attacks were a surprise and shock to all Americans, to include the President. No American knew that the terrorists were planning to use airplanes to bring down the World Trade Center buildings until after the airplanes hit the buildings. President Clinton had Osama Bin Laden and other Alcaida leaders in the crosshairs of a Predator unmanned aircraft armed with Hellfire missiles and failed to fire. That decision left the leadership of Alcaida intact and cost many American lives.

Democrats falsely accused President Bush of lying about weapons of mass destruction in Iraq. Saddam Hussein used weapons of mass destruction to kill thousands of Iraqis. He failed to cooperate with weapons inspectors, obstructing their efforts to search for weapons. He did not want the world and Iran, with which he fought a costly war, to know that he no longer had the weapons. American, British and other intelligence organizations did not have good on-the-ground human intelligence, and all believed that he was doing his best to hide the fact that he still had the weapons. After the invasion of Iraq, U.S. military personnel searched for the weapons. Democrats exploited the situation, falsely accusing the President of lying about the weapons.

Many Democrats falsely accused President Bush of not caring for victims of September 11, 2001 and Hurricane Katrina. Nothing could be further from the truth. The President,

215

Republicans, and even Democrats all cared deeply about their fellow Americans. The President immediately went into action to find and target the leadership of the terrorists who attacked the United States. He sent military forces into Afghanistan and Iraq because he cared about all Americans and wanted to do his best to protect them from another attack. If Democrats implied otherwise they were being dishonest.

The United States never suffered hurricane damage as bad as that of Hurricane Katrina, and local, state, and federal agencies were not prepared to face a disaster of that magnitude. Most deaths were the result of the failure of local authorities to evacuate many citizens. Today, thanks to the leadership of President Bush, federal, state, and local agencies are all better trained, equipped, and prepared to work together to properly react to a major disaster. The author's brother, an Air Force Flight Surgeon, was on call during another hurricane (Ike). He has been a part of the comprehensive federal disaster training instituted by President Bush. During Hurricane Ike, local, state, and federal agencies all worked together better than ever before to evacuate and care for Americans in the path of the hurricane.

What is it that made so many Americans want to blame President Bush for so many problems and to look to the new president to solve all those problems? What filled their hearts and minds with so much hatred for their political opponents? President Bush worked more diligently than most presidents to serve Americans to the very best of his ability. Americans need to return to the idea of personal responsibility that made this nation so great, giving credit and blame to every person as it is due.

Senator Obama and other Democrats accused Senator McCain of voting with President Bush most of the time, and thereby being part of the problem that demands change. However, although few Americans realize it now, that is a great compliment. President Bush was a wonderful Christian man of great moral integrity who promoted and/or signed pro-Christian values legislation strongly opposed by most Democrats. Related to this is the totally false implication that Senator Obama and the Democrats had the right solutions for all the problems they blamed on President Bush.

CHRISTIAN VALUES: Part of the false impression given by Senator Obama and other Democrats was that they supported Christian values and that Americans would have greater blessings if they placed their hope in them. This whole book proves that to be a lie. Senator Obama and Senator Biden did not even meet Christ's definition of a Christian. They did not do "the will of the Father." They strongly opposed biblical laws given by God to Moses. They were consistently and continually driven to make wrong decisions by a completely wrong, false, unbiblical understanding of God, man, law, and what God requires of man. They were morally deficient leaders with broken moral compasses that continually pointed them in the wrong direction, as proven by their scoring absolute zero on voting Christian values. Senator Obama supported special rights for homosexuals and lesbians, partial birth abortion, and the killing of aborted children born alive. See voting scorecards and campaign website of Senator Obama. These are major moral issues that prove the extreme degree to which his moral compass is broken. Senator McCain supported Christian values on issues.

CONCLUSION: The 2008 presidential campaign of Senator Obama was marked by countless lies and false promises. Most of the lies were blatantly false and the promises were ridiculous. Why then did so many Americans believe the lies and false promises and vote for Senator Obama? How could they expect God's blessings if they ignored his laws and voted for whoever promised them the greatest benefit?

RELATED TOPICS

SECTION REVIEW: This section reviews several additional vitally important topics related to living and voting Christian values. The first chapter addresses the failure of Christian leaders to provide guidance to Christians on hot political topics. The second chapter discusses God's judgment on America. The third chapter explores what God really wants from Christians.

CHAPTERS: Chapters in this section include the following:
9.1 Failure of Christian Leaders
9.2 Judgment on America
9.3 What God Desires

FAILURE OF CHRISTIAN LEADERS

INTRODUCTION: "All that is needed for evil to triumph is for good men to do nothing."[293] Why are so many Christian leaders such absolute failures at providing moral guidance to Christians in the area of politics and government? Do they fear man more than God, or are they simply blind to reality and how Scripture applies to the political realm? They are like Emperor Nero, playing his fiddle as Rome was burning, as our beloved nation, founded as one nation under God, embraces abominations to God deserving of death.

REASONS FOR FAILURE: So why are so many Christian leaders failures at providing moral guidance regarding politics and government? Part of the answer lies in a sermon that I heard. Without saying a word, the pastor started throwing brightly colored tennis balls into the congregation. Then he added words to give meaning to the balls: "abortion, same-sex marriage." Finally he explained: "Some Christians tend to be

---

[293] "All that is necessary for the triumph of evil is that good men do nothing." "This is probably the most quoted statement attributed to Burke, and an extraordinary number of variants of it exist, but all without any definite original source. These very extensively used remarks may be based on a paraphrase of some of Burke's ideas, but he is not *known* to have ever declared them in so succinct a manner in any of his writings. They may have been adapted from these lines of Burke's in his Thoughts on the Cause of Present Discontents (1770): "When bad men combine, the good must associate; else they will fall one by one, an unpitied sacrifice in a contemptible struggle." This purported quote bears a resemblance to the narrated theme of Sergei Bondarchuk's Soviet film adaptation of Leo Tolstoy's book War and Peace, in which the narrator declares "All that is necessary for evil to triumph is for good men to do nothing", although since the original is in Russian various translations to English are possible." Edmund Burke, "Edmund Burke," Wikiquote, http://en.wikiquote.org/wiki/Edmund_Burke.

incendiary," raising issues like abortion and same-sex marriage; Christians "should be invitational, not incendiary."

GREAT COMMISSION: Why do Christian leaders want to be invitational, not offensive? First and foremost, they want to be obedient to the Great Commission and reach lost souls for Christ. They understand that the stakes are far more important than life and death—they are a matter of eternal life with God or eternal condemnation, punishment and separation from God. They also understand that life on this earth is a totally meaningless shadow of what God created life to be without salvation and living for Christ.

Many Christians and Christian leaders mistakenly believe that their primary duty is to be obedient to the Great Commission, given by Christ to his disciples before His ascension:

> "Go ye therefore, and make disciples of all the nations, baptizing them into the name of the Father and of the Son and of the Holy Spirit: teaching them to observe all things whatsoever I commanded you: and lo, I am with you always, even unto the end of the world." (Matt. 28:19-20, ASV).

However, God created man's life to be God-centered, not man-centered. Making saving souls the top priority makes life man-centered, not God-centered. Also, Christian leaders concentrate on the first part of the Great Commission, saving souls, but give less emphasis to the second part: "teaching them to observe all things whatsoever I commanded you" (Matt. 28: 19-20, ASV).

GREATEST COMMANDMENT: The primary duty of all men is not to be obedient to the Great Commission, but to be obedient to the Greatest Commandment: "Thou shalt love the

Lord thy God with all thy heart, and with all thy soul, and with all thy might" (Deut. 6:5, KJV). The foundation of all other laws, it is the one law that should govern every thought and action. That is why the first four of the ten commandments concentrate on God, not man.

> I am the LORD thy God, which brought thee out of the land of Egypt, from the house of bondage.
> [First Commandment] Thou shalt have none other gods before me.
> [Second Commandment] Thou shalt not make thee any graven …for I the LORD thy God am a jealous God, visiting the iniquity of the fathers upon the children unto the third and fourth generation of them that hate me, And shewing mercy unto thousands of them that love me and keep my commandments.
> [Third Commandment] Thou shalt not take the name of the LORD thy God in vain: for the LORD will not hold him guiltless that taketh his name in vain.
> [Fourth Commandment] Keep the sabbath day to sanctify it… (Deut. 5:6-15, KJV).

BIBLICAL LAW: Loving God requires obedience to God's commandments. However, most clergy never have a course in biblical law. They may not consider biblical law to be very important. They may view the law as part of the old covenant with Israel, and point to Paul's words about not living under the law. They may consider primary purpose of the law to make men aware of how much they fall short of God's holy standard and how much they need salvation through Christ. "So that the law is become our tutor to bring us unto Christ, that we might be justified by faith. But now faith that is come, we are no longer under a tutor" (Gal. 3:24-25, ASV).

God has a very different attitude about His laws than most clergy. He knows that His people desperately need the guidance that His laws provide. He knows if they do what is right in their own eyes, they will live totally contrary to His laws. "There is a way that seems right to a man, but its end is the way of death" (Proverbs 14:12; 16:25. Lev. 27:8; Isaiah 55:9.). God knows that freedom cannot be found in defiance of his laws, but through submission to them. King David said, "And I will walk at liberty: for I seek thy precepts" (Psalm 119:44-46). Also, God wants His people to have the blessings that come only from obedience to His commandments. See Chapter on Biblical Law for further discussion.

PEACE AND HARMONY: Another reason Christian leaders want to avoid divisive issues is simply because they want to maintain peace and harmony within their congregation, something which can often be a major challenge to a pastor. Contrary to popular opinion among many non-Christians, church members are never all like-minded right-wing extremists. All church members are very different individuals who may have very different priorities and very different opinions regarding right and wrong and what best serves God and the church. Also, a pastor who talks too much about divisive issues may lose part or all of his congregation, and all the money they give to the church, money needed for vital ministries, church maintenance, etc. So what could possibly be wrong with Christian leaders trying to maintain peace and harmony by avoiding divisive issues? They sacrifice teaching right and wrong to maintain peace and harmony. They sacrifice serving God for serving man.

SEPARATION OF CHURCH AND STATE: Many Christian leaders have an incorrect understanding of separation of church and state. They believe that the church is only called to deal with "spiritual matters." They may quote Christ. "My kingdom is not of this world." "Render unto Caesar what is Caesar's, and unto God what is God's." They may believe that something is wrong with Christians who talk too much about or demonstrate too much concern for "politics." They fail to fully realize politics is faith in action, that God wants to be God in all areas of life, that government officials are truly "ministers of

God," that "righteousness exalts a nation," and that our nation can only enjoy God's blessings if its laws are in harmony with God's higher laws revealed through Scripture.

UNDERSTANDING GOD: There is an even more basic, more fundamental reason that Christian leaders avoid politics: they fail to fully understand the heart and mind of God. They are very much in tune with the love of God clearly reflected through the death of Christ on the cross. They fail to give much attention to the holiness and righteousness of God, which required the death of Christ. Without meaning to do so, they cheapen the love of God and the full meaning of the death of Christ by not giving proper emphasis to the holiness and righteousness of God. Also, they fail to demonstrate proper fear and respect for a holy God who does not in any way, shape or form tolerate sin.

DEFINITION CHRISTIAN: Some Christian leaders fail to fully understand what it means to be a Christian. They repeatedly emphasize that man is saved by faith not works, but rarely mention that faith without works is dead. They fail to fully realize that on Judgment Day Christ will reject many Americans who claim to be Christians and attend church faithfully every Sunday because they failed to do the will of the Father. They fail to follow Paul's counsel: "work out your own salvation with fear and trembling" (Phil. 2:11-13). "I press toward the mark for the prize of the high calling of God in Christ Jesus" (Phil. 3:14). "Know ye not that they which run in a race run all, but one [receives] the prize? So run, that ye may obtain" (1 Cor. 9:23-25).

DICTATING MORALITY: "YOU CANNOT DICTATE MORALITY." Some Christian leaders believe the lie embodied in this statement. They may believe, for example, that abortion and same-sex marriage are wrong, but that neither they nor the government have the right to dictate the moral behavior of others. They fail to understand the jurisdiction and the primary purpose of government. See chapter on Jurisdiction of Federal Government.

JUDGING CHRISTIANS: Christian leaders rarely teach the duty of Christians to judge and correct their fellow Christians. "Judge not, that ye be not judged" (Matthew 7:1-3). "Judge not, and ye shall not be judged: condemn not, and ye shall not be condemned: forgive, and ye shall be forgiven" (Luke 6:37). Many Christians misinterpret these words of Christ to mean that it is wrong to judge anyone, to include their fellow Christians.

Christians, for example, have about the same divorce rate as non-Christians, in part because Christians rarely confront a Christian who wrongfully divorces his or her spouse. They do not understand the clear teaching of Scripture, that two Christians must not separate and must not divorce (1 Cor. 7). They do not understand that two people who claim that Christ is Lord have absolutely no excuse for divorce, and that a Christian must not divorce a non-Christian who wants to remain faithful to the marriage.

"A cadet will not lie, cheat, steal, or tolerate those who do." As a West Point Cadet, the author of this book had a duty to report any violation of the honor code. Failure to report was a violation that could result in expulsion. The same principle applies to all Christians. Jesus said,

> "If thy brother shall trespass against thee, go and tell him his fault between thee and him alone: if he shall hear thee, thou hast gained thy brother. But if he will not hear thee, then take with thee one or two more, that in the mouth of two or three witnesses every word may be established. And if he shall neglect to hear them, tell it unto the church: but if he neglect to hear the church, let him be unto thee as an heathen

man and a publican" (Matt. 18:15-17).

Paul ordered the church in Corinth to excommunicate a church member involved in sexual sin, "to deliver such an one unto Satan for the destruction of the flesh, that the spirit may be saved in the day of the Lord Jesus" (1 Cor. 5:5). All Christians have a duty to judge and take appropriate action to correct wrongdoing by other Christians. Christians should also confront elected officials who claim to be Christian.

CONCLUSION: Today Christians are sharply divided on hot political issues. Many Christians vote for candidates who support the murder of unborn and partially born children and a lifestyle that is an abomination to God deserving of death. Many Christian leaders stand silently on the sidelines, detached and irrelevant, not wanting to raise hot issues that divide Christians.

Christians need to fear God, not man. They need to demonstrate greater love for God through study, teaching, and obedience to His laws. Christians leaders should speak out with a united bold voice on hot political topics. They should challenge all Americans who call themselves Christians to greater understanding and obedience of God's laws revealed though Scripture.

JUDGMENT ON AMERICA

REASON FOR CHAPTER: Most Americans regard anyone who talks about God's judgment on American as a fruitcake. They completely fail to realize how much our beloved has already suffered the natural and immediate consequences of rejection of God. On Judgment Day Christ will judge every man, woman, and child, showing perfect justice and absolutely no mercy to toward anyone who is not "saved" by the "blood of the Lamb." Today God brings judgment upon nations, as He did countless times throughout biblical history.

The first and immediate consequence of rejection of God is that life becomes a totally meaningless shadow of what God created it to be. Jesus said, "I am the way, the truth, and the life: no man cometh unto the Father, but by me" (John 14:5-7). Paul said, "For to me to live is Christ, and to die is gain" (Phil. 1:20-22). Paul said,

> If I speak with the tongues of men and of angels, but have not love, I am become sounding brass, or a clanging cymbal. And if I have the gift of prophecy, and know all mysteries and all knowledge; and if I have all faith, so as to remove mountains, but have not love, I am nothing. And if I bestow all my goods to feed the poor, and if I give my body to be burned, but have not love, it profit[s] me nothing (1 Cor. 13:1-3, ASV).

Life without Christ is totally meaningless, and shadow of what it was meant to be.

In the eyes of God, abortion is murder. Americans are very foolish if they believe that they can murder thousands of unborn or partially born children without suffering immediately consequences of such serious violation of God's laws and the principles upon which this nation was founded and without suffering the present and future judgment of God. Homosexuality is an abomination to God, an extreme perversion of his design for man, woman, marriage, and family. Americans are absolute fools if they believe that can tolerate as morally acceptable and reward such extreme moral depravity without suffering immediately consequences of such serious violations of God's laws and the principles upon which our nation was founded and without suffering the present and future judgment of God.

Neither God's laws revealed through Scripture nor the U.S. Constitution, the highest law of the land, support the vision of President Obama and Democrats of a government that cares for and provides for its people. Again, Americans are fools to believe that they can somehow profit from violation of God's laws, the U.S. Constitution, and the principles upon which this nation was founded. The United States has already become a welfare state that rewards its citizens for not working and robs the rich to support the poor and middle class. Our nation began with the God-given inalienable rights to life, liberty, and the pursuit of happiness. Now many Americans believe that they have a right to food, shelter, education, and healthcare paid for by other Americans. And the national debt soars as the nation tries to pay for all these rights and benefits.

The first chapter of Paul's letter to the Romans explains the consequences of rejection of God. The same basic principles apply to nations.

> For I am not ashamed of the gospel of Christ: for
> it is the power of God unto salvation to every one
> that believeth; to the Jew first, and also to the

Greek. For therein is the righteousness of God revealed from faith to faith: as it is written, the just shall live by faith. For the wrath of God is revealed from heaven against all ungodliness and unrighteousness of men, who hold the truth in unrighteousness; because that which may be known of God is manifest in them; for God hath shewed it unto them. For the invisible things of him from the creation of the world are clearly seen, being understood by the things that are made, even his eternal power and Godhead; so that they are without excuse: because that, when they knew God, they glorified him not as God, neither were thankful; but became vain in their imaginations, and their foolish heart was darkened. Professing themselves to be wise, they became fools, and changed the glory of the [incorruptible] God into an image made like to corruptible man, and to birds, and fourfooted beasts, and creeping things. Wherefore God also gave them up to uncleanness through the lusts of their own hearts, to [dishonor] their own bodies between themselves: who changed the truth of God into a lie, and worshipped and served the creature more than the Creator, who is blessed for ever. Amen. For this cause God gave them up unto vile affections: for even their women did change the natural use into that which is against nature: and likewise also the men, leaving the natural use of the woman, burned in their lust one toward another; men with men working that which is unseemly, and receiving in themselves that [recompense] of their error which was meet. And even as they did not like to retain God in their knowledge, God gave them over to a reprobate mind, to do those things which are not convenient; being filled with all unrighteousness,

228

fornication, wickedness, covetousness,
maliciousness; full of envy, murder, debate,
deceit, malignity; whisperers, backbiters, haters
of God, despiteful, proud, boasters, inventors of
evil things, disobedient to parents, without
understanding, covenantbreakers, without natural
affection, implacable, unmerciful: who knowing
the judgment of God, that they which commit
such things are worthy of death, not only do the
same, but have pleasure in them that do them"
(Rom. 1:16-32, KJV).

God has revealed the "invisible things" about Himself, including His "eternal power and Godhead," through creation to all Americans so "they are without excuse." Therefore the "wrath of God is revealed from heaven against all" Americans guilty of "ungodliness and unrighteousness" because "when they knew God, they glorified him not as God, neither were thankful; but became vain in their imaginations, and their foolish heart was darkened. Professing themselves to be wise, they became fools." In other words, rejecting God by not properly acknowledging Him, glorifying Him as God, and thanking Him for His countless blessings results in "vain...imaginations" and "foolish heart[s]." "God also gave them up to uncleanness through the lusts of their own hearts"...and to "vile affections," including the homosexuality discussed in the chapter on homosexuality.

Scripture is clear. There is a judgment of God upon all those who fail to properly acknowledge Him. The Founding Fathers of our nation properly acknowledged Him. They knew the God. They glorified God. They were thankful for their God-given freedoms, and for the many blessings of God upon our nation. Today we see the judgment of God upon many Americans who refuse to properly acknowledge God. We see extreme foolishness deeply embedded in the hearts and minds of our teachers, professors, lawyers, judges, elected officials, and all other Americans who refuse to properly acknowledge God.

There is also a judgment of God against all "ungodliness and unrighteousness." Americans who believe that they can profit from disobedience to God's laws are even more foolish than a man trying to defy God's law of gravity by jumping off a tall building without a parachute. He will only prove God's laws. Freedom and blessings only come from obedience to God's laws. That is why King David said, "And I will walk at liberty: for I seek thy precepts" (Psalm 119:44-46). See Chapter on Biblical Law.

CHAPTER 9.3

GOD'S DESIRE FOR MAN

If you have enjoyed this book, allow me to share a personal story with a lesson from God. The story begins on a rainy day in February 2008, with me driving our 1985 BMW 318 home from a hardware store, with equipment needed to fix a flooding basement. I thought that God had given me more than enough problems for the day. I was wrong. Suddenly hot, steaming radiator fluid was pouring into the car near my gas pedal, fogging all windows. It was raining very hard, so I could not roll down the windows. I had the wipers going fast and was continually wiping the fogged windows with a towel, so I could see where I was going. I was only able to travel about one mile at a time, before the engine overheated and I was forced to stop and refill the radiator with water from rain puddles.

As I was waiting for the engine to cool before refilling the radiator, I was listening to a sermon on the radio. It was about King David and his sin with Bathsheba. I was asking God what I had done wrong, how I had failed Him, what I had done to deserve His "loving" correction, and what He was trying to say to me. I had not been unfaithful to my wife. The pastor was describing how David was bold to come before God, to repent of his sin, ask for forgiveness, turn from wrongdoing, restore a right relationship with God, and boldly move forward in obedience to God.

Then, when I stepped out of the car and had my back to the interstate, I heard a large truck hitting a very large puddle of water. I braced as out of the corner of my eye I saw a tall wall of water coming at and then over me, completely drenching me from head to foot. I had to laugh, because there was nothing else I could do. I knew God was having a little fun with me. I was already soaked; now I was totally drenched.

Now move the clock forward to August 2008. My family and I were visiting my brother Michael and his family in Virginia. Michael is a Lieutenant Colonel in the Air Force, a Flight Surgeon. On Sunday we attended services at Bethel Baptist Church. The sermon was on King David's sin with Bathsheba and her husband Uriah. Suddenly the light came on. God was giving me the rest of the message, a message for me and for anyone willing to listen. The pastor was talking about how God does not want sacrificial, reluctant obedience to His commandments. God looks upon the heart, and he wants our hearts. He wants our love, like that of King David, a man after God's heart.

David immediately repented of his sin and was forgiven by God, but he and Israel suffered severe consequences for the rest of his life, to include a divided kingdom and the death of two of his sons. A man who commits murder is forgiven by God at the moment of repentance, but he may pay for his crime with his life and be with the Lord sooner. To read the story of King David, Bathsheba and Uriah, see 2 Samuel 11-12. To read the Psalms that David wrote asking God for forgiveness see Psalms 6,32,38,39,40, and 51.

In Psalm 51 King David provides a good example of true repentance. Read carefully and understand what God wants from man and why King David is called a man after God's heart.

> Have mercy upon me, O God, according to thy
> lovingkindness: according unto the
> multitude of thy tender mercies blot out
> my transgressions.
> Wash me thoroughly from mine iniquity, and
> cleanse me from my sin.
> For I acknowledge my transgressions: and my sin
> is ever before me.

232

Against thee, thee only, have I sinned, and done
this evil in thy sight: that thou mightest be
justified when thou speakest, and be clear
when thou judgest.

Behold, I was shapen in iniquity; and in sin did
my mother conceive me.

Behold, thou desirest truth in the inward parts:
and in the hidden part thou shalt make me
to know wisdom.

Purge me with hyssop, and I shall be clean: wash
me, and I shall be whiter than snow.

Make me to hear joy and gladness; that the bones
which thou hast broken may rejoice.

Hide thy face from my sins, and blot out all mine
iniquities.

Create in me a clean heart, O God; and renew a
right spirit within me.

Cast me not away from thy presence; and take
not thy Holy Spirit from me.

Restore unto me the joy of thy salvation; and
uphold me with thy free spirit.

Then will I teach transgressors thy ways; and
sinners shall be converted unto thee.

Deliver me from bloodguiltiness, O God, thou
God of my salvation: and my tongue shall
sing aloud of thy righteousness.

O Lord, open thou my lips; and my mouth shall
shew forth thy praise.

For thou desirest not sacrifice; else would I give
it: thou delightest not in burnt offering.

The sacrifices of God are a broken spirit: a
broken and a contrite heart, O God, thou
wilt not despise.

Do good in thy good pleasure unto Zion: build
thou the walls of Jerusalem.

Then shalt thou be pleased with the sacrifices of
righteousness, with burnt offering and

233

whole burnt offering: then shall they offer bullocks upon thine altar. Psalm 51:1-19 (KJV).

Note that true repentance requires: (1) full acknowledgment of sin against God; (2) true regret for sin against God; (3) humble request for God's forgiveness. However, God wants more than repentance. He wants restoration of His relationship with man. Think about it. The God who created all the stars and planets in every universe wants a loving relationship with every man, woman, and child on earth. What a great and absolutely wonderful God He is!

Restoration of one's relationship with God requires more than repentance. God is holy. He requires payment in full for sin. God is love. "For God so loved the world, that he gave his only begotten Son, that whosoever believeth in him should not perish, but have everlasting life" (John 3:16, KJV). Only Christ, who was fully God and fully man and without sin could be the unblemished "Lamb of God" who could through His death on the cross make payment in full for man's sin. Restoration of one's relationship with God requires belief in Christ and acceptance of Christ as Savior though belief in His death as payment in full for one's sin.

Acceptance of Christ as Savior requires: (1) true repentance and turning from sin like King David in Psalm 51; (2) acceptance of Christ's death on the cross as payment in full for sin; (3) cleansing and full restoration of relationship with God; and (4) acceptance of Christ as Lord. Acceptance of Christ as the Lord of one's life means dying to self, taking up one's cross, and following Christ in obedience to the letter and spirit of God's laws, striving for the perfection that Christ commands.

If a man accepts Christ as Lord and Savior but does not follow Christ in obedience to God's laws, he is not a Christian. Lack of obedience is proof that he was never repentant. One cannot be a Christian, a follower of Christ, and live contrary to God's commandments. That is why Christ said,

> Not every one that saith unto me, "Lord, Lord," shall enter into the kingdom of heaven; but he that doeth the will of my Father which is in heaven. Many will say to me in that day, "Lord, Lord, have we not prophesied in thy name? and in thy name have cast out devils? and in thy name done many wonderful works?" And then will I profess unto them, I never knew you: depart from me, ye that work iniquity (Matt. 7:21-23, KJV).

When a man accepts Christ as Lord and Savior, God enters his heart and mind in the form of the Spirit. The Spirit empowers and provides guidance to the new believer. God has also given Scripture for guidance. The Spirit enables understanding of Scripture.

However, God wants more from man and for man than "getting saved." He wants more than acceptance of Christ as Lord and Savior and empowerment by the Holy Spirit. Jesus said, "My meat is to do the will of him that sent me, and to finish his work" (John 4:34, KJV). He said that anyone who did not love Him more than his mother was not worthy to follow Him. Paul said, "For me to live is Christ, and to die is gain" (Phil. 1:21). A man is not a Christian, a true follower of Christ, unless Christ is his reason for living.

If a man is a Christian, a true follower of Christ, then he will want to be obedient to the Greatest Commandments:

> "Thou shalt love the Lord thy God with all thy heart, and with all thy soul, and with all thy mind." This is the first and great commandment. And the second is like unto it, "Thou shalt love thy neighbour as thyself." On these two

commandments hang all the law and the prophets (Matt. 22:37-40, KJV).

Jesus said, "I am come that they might have life, and that they might have it more abundantly" (John 10:11, KJV). However, this abundant life is not possible unless one: (1) repents of sin and turns from wrongdoing; (2) accepts Christ as Lord and Savior; (3) dies to self and takes up one's cross and follows Christ, walking in obedience to the letter and spirit of God's laws. Only then can one have the peace that passes all understanding and the "joy of the Lord that is your strength" (Neh. 8:11). Only then can one have life and have it abundantly. Only then can one say with Paul, "For me to live is Christ, and to die is gain" (Phil. 1:21). Only then can one join Paul in striving to run for the first prize. Only then can one be obedient to the Greatest Commandment, fulfilling God's desire for man, the purpose for which man was created, loving God with all one's heart, mind, soul, and strength (Deut. 6:5; Matt. 22:37-40; Luke 10:27).

However, God wants more than all this from Christians and for Christians. He does not just want them to get "saved" and have the "abundant life." He wants them to accomplish something with their lives. God wants every man, woman, and child to be a leader who leads others from darkness to light and to greater understanding and obedience to His laws.

God wants all men to be Christian soldiers who do battle for Him. Life is a spiritual battle between forces of good and evil. God wants the Christian to be properly equipped for battle. That requires putting on the whole armor of God. Paul said,

> Finally, my brethren, be strong in the Lord, and in the power of his might.[11] Put on the whole [armor] of God, that ye may be able to stand against the wiles of the devil. For we wrestle not against flesh and blood, but against principalities,

236

against powers, against the rulers of the darkness of this world, against spiritual wickedness in high places. Wherefore take unto you the whole [armor] of God, that ye may be able to withstand in the evil day, and having done all, to stand. Stand therefore, having your loins girt about with truth, and having on the breastplate of righteousness; And your feet shod with the preparation of the gospel of peace; Above all, taking the shield of faith, wherewith ye shall be able to quench all the fiery darts of the wicked. And take the helmet of salvation, and the sword of the Spirit, which is the word of God: Praying always with all prayer and supplication in the Spirit, and watching thereunto with all perseverance and supplication for all saints (Ephesians 6:10-18, KJV).

There is so much more to becoming a Christian and leading a Christian life. God does not desire that the Christian try to do it all alone. That is why Paul said, "Forsake not the fellowship of believers." Every new Christian needs to join a church where he can enjoy the support of the fellowship of believers. There he can join others in loving, serving, praising, and doing battle for the Lord of Lords and King of Kings. Blessed be the name of the Lord!

SUMMARY AND CONCLUSION

INTRODUCTION: Every vote is a vote for or against God and His laws. It is absolutely amazing how much Democrats are united in voting against Christian values. They do not simply fail to do God's will on the moral issues they dismiss as "social issues" (same-sex marriage, abortion). They fail to do God's will in virtually all areas. On Judgment Day Christ will reject many Americans who call themselves Christians because they failed to do God's will. Christ said:

> Not every one that saith unto me, Lord, Lord,
> shall enter into the kingdom of heaven; but he
> that doeth the will of my Father which is in
> heaven. Many will say to me in that day, Lord,
> Lord, have we not prophesied in thy name? and
> in thy name have cast out devils? and in thy name
> done many wonderful works? And then will I
> profess unto them, I never knew you: depart from
> me, ye that work iniquity (Matthew 7:21-23,
> KJV).

During every national election, millions of Americans who call themselves Christians vote for candidates who score zero for voting Christian values because they do not understand what it means to be a Christian or the teachings of Scripture. A Christian is not simply someone who believes in Christ or attends church every Sunday. Christ made it very clear that a Christian is not simply someone who calls Him Lord or performs miracles in His name, but someone who does "the will of the Father" (Matt. 7:21-23). Christ also made it clear that every word of Old Testament law remains in full effect until

238

fulfilled (Matt. 5:17-18). President Obama and Vice President Biden do not meet Christ's definition of a Christian, because they live and vote contrary to God's commandments. A vote for Democrats who score zero for voting Christian values is a vote against God and His commandments.

Many Americans believe that God does not care how they vote. Nothing could be further from the truth. First, God cares because He is love. His love for us is perfect. He loves us more than we can love ourselves. Second, God cares because He is holy. There is absolutely no conflict between the love and holiness of God. However, no one can vote against God and His laws without suffering consequences. Rejection of God and His laws is rejection of Christ and proof that one is not a Christian. It means that one has failed to do the "will of the Father" and that on Judgment Day Christ will say, "I never knew you: depart from me, ye that work iniquity" (Matt. 7:21-23, KJV). God is God in all areas of our lives, and we answer to Him for all of our thoughts, words, and actions. However, what God really wants is not reluctant obedience to His commandments but a heart to heart loving relationship with each man, woman, and child. Life apart from God is devoid of meaning. In Him we live and move and have our being.

OBJECTIVES: The primary objective of this book is obedience to the greatest commandment: "Thou shalt love the Lord thy God with all thy heart, and with all thy soul, and with all thy might" (Deut. 6:5, KJV). The second objective is obedience to the second greatest commandment: "Thou shalt love thy neighbour as thyself" (Matt. 22:37-40, KJV). The third objective is to secure for our nation blessings that only result from obedience to God's commandments. "Blessed is the nation whose God is the LORD…." (Psalm 33:11, KJV). "Righteousness exalt[s] a nation: but sin is a reproach to any people" (Prov. 14:34, KJV). "If my people, which are called by my name, shall humble themselves, and pray, and seek my face, and turn from their wicked ways; then will I hear from heaven,

239

and will forgive their sin, and will heal their land" (2 Chron. 7:14, KJV).

The final but more immediate objective of this book is to influence the 2012 election by challenging Christians to vote Christian values by challenging the ignorance of Americans regarding laws that God created to govern men and governments, laws are embodied in Scripture and the U.S. Constitution. Christian values are God's values, which He has revealed through Moses, King David, King Solomon, the prophets, Christ, Paul, and other authors of Scripture.

FOUNDATION—SCRIPTURE: Scripture is the foundation upon which this book is written. Belief in Scripture is more important than belief in God or Christ because Scripture defines God, Christ, and what it means to be a Christian. Every judge reviews two key elements of every case: the facts and the law. God uses Scripture to give man the facts and law needed to live the Christian life. The facts include facts regarding God, Christ, and the history of God and His people. The law includes God's moral laws, rooted in His unchanging character.

Without Scripture even Christians have wrong and conflicting opinions of God, Christ, and what it means to be a Christian. Scripture provides the guidance that Christians desperately need for living and voting Christian values. Paul said, "All Scripture is given by inspiration of God, and is profitable for doctrine, for reproof, for correction, for instruction in righteousness" (2 Tim. 3:16, KJV).

1. SCRIPTURE REVEALS GOD: Scripture reveals the one true God, the God of Abraham, Isaac, and Jacob. He is the Alpha and the Omega, the beginning and end. He always was, is, and ever shall be. He is the same yesterday, today, and tomorrow. He never changes. He is the creator of all things seen and unseen, and all the laws that govern all things seen and unseen.

God is love. He defines love. God is holy. He is perfect and righteous in every way. He cannot accept, tolerate, or in any way condone anything or anyone who is unholy, unrighteous. That is why He gave His only begotten son, who was fully God and fully man, the only perfect, blameless sacrificial Lamb of God whose blood could be shed as payment for man's sins. No man can be made right with God without belief in and acceptance of the death of Christ as payment in full for his sins.

2. SCRIPTURE DEFINES CHRISTIAN: Scripture reveals what it means to be a Christian. Most Americans who call themselves Christians do not understand a biblical definition of "Christian." Belief in God or Christ does not make one a Christian. Satan believes in God and Christ. A Christian is someone who: (1) believes in a triune God: Father, Son, and Holy Spirit; (2) is a repentant sinner who accepts Christ as Savior; (3) accepts Christ as Lord of his life, (5) is empowered and guided by the Holy Spirit. Finally, a Christian is (6) someone whose reason for living is Christ, someone who joins the Apostle Paul in saying, "For me to live is Christ, and to die is gain." The New Testament was written after the death and resurrection of Christ.

3. SCRIPTURE REVEALS GOD'S LAWS: Scripture reveals God's moral laws, which are rooted in his unchanging character. What was right and wrong at the time of creation is right and wrong today. Obedience to the two greatest commandments, loving God and loving one's fellow man, requires obedience to God's laws revealed through Scripture. This includes Old Testament laws. Christ referred to Old Testament law when He said, "Think not that I am come to destroy the law, or the prophets: I am not come to destroy, but to fulfill. For verily I say unto you, till heaven and earth pass, one jot or one tittle shall in no wise pass from the law, till all be fulfilled" (Matt. 5:17-18, KJV). The New Testament was written after Christ's death and resurrection.

The words, "Every man did that which was right in his own eyes" (Judges 17:5-7; 21:24-25) describe a period of lawlessness in Israel (See Deut. 12:7-9; Prov. 12:15; 21:2). Proverbs states, "The way of a fool is right in his own eyes: but he that hearken[s] unto counsel is wise" (Prov.12:14-16) and "there is a way which seem[s] right unto a man, but the end thereof are the ways of death (Prov. 14:12; 16:25). Jesus said, "Ye do err, not knowing the Scriptures, nor the power of God" (Matt. 22:29, KJV). Scripture reveals the wisdom of God. God spoke through Isaiah, saying, "For my thoughts are not your thoughts, neither are your ways my ways, saith the LORD. For as the heavens are higher than the earth, so are my ways higher than your ways, and my thoughts than your thoughts (Isa. 55:8-10). Often what seems right to even the most intelligent of men is totally contrary to God's ways, because God's ways are higher than man's ways (Isa. 55:8-10). The perfect example is President Obama, a very intelligent man with the best of intentions who fights for policies totally contrary to God's laws revealed through Scripture.

JURISDICTION: Jurisdiction, one of the most important principles of law, is the power and authority of a court to hear a case. It also refers to the power and authority of a federal, state, or local government, a branch of government, the church, or any other entity.

1. JURISDICTION OF GOVERNMENT: The federal government of the United States is a government of enumerated powers. Each branch only has those powers granted to it by the Constitution. All other powers are reserved to the states. No part of the U.S. Constitution grants the federal government any responsibility or authority to care for the poor or the middle class. Today the interstate commerce clause is wrongfully used to justify federal government action in many areas, especially social programs designed to care for citizens. In 2012 Chief

Justice Roberts improperly interpreted the clause granting Congress authority to tax to justify ruling in favor of Obamacare.

2. JURISDICTION OF CHURCH AND STATE: Today most Americans, to include most lawyers and judges, have a totally wrong understanding of the jurisdiction of church and state and the self-evident common sense truths our nation was founded upon. They exclude God, creation, and God's laws from politics, government, schools, and the workplace. They fail to recognize that all Americans have an absolute duty to properly acknowledge God in politics, government, schools, and the workplace in the way that our nation's Founding Fathers acknowledged Him. They do not understand that failure to properly acknowledge, respect and fear God reduces one to vain thinking and absolute foolishness because darkened hearts cannot see the light of the truth (Romans 1).

BIBLICAL LAW: As stated, obedience to the two greatest commandments, loving God and loving one's fellow man, requires obedience to God's laws revealed through Scripture. Being a Christian, a follower of Christ, requires obedience to biblical law. This section applies biblical law to hot political topics.

1. HOMOSEXUALITY AND SAME-SEX MARRIAGE: A candidate's position on homosexuality and same-sex marriage should be a deciding factor for Christian voters. Scripture is clear. God created man male and female, and marriage to be a special "one flesh" union between man and woman (Genesis 2:18-24). Homosexual and lesbian relations are an "abomination" to God, an extreme perversion of His design for man, woman, sex, and marriage (Lev. 18:22-26; 20:13-16; 1 Tim. 1:9-10; 1 Cor. 6:9-10; Rom. 1:16-32). God's penalty for sexual relations with the same sex is the death penalty, and God punishes a nation defiled by this sin (Lev. 18:22-26; 20:13-16). This does not mean that Americans should

243

kill anyone guilty of this sin. That is God's jurisdiction. It does mean that our laws should not condone, approve, or encourage something that is an "abomination" to God and brings the judgment of God upon our nation.

2. ABORTION: A candidate's position on abortion should be a deciding factor for Christian voters. Scripture is clear. Children are a blessing from God that brings responsibility for proper care before and after birth. Scripture teaches that a child is a child before and after birth. In the Old Testament, the same Hebrew word is used to refer to a child before and after birth. In the New Testament, the same Greed word is used to refer to a child before and after birth. See Gen. 16:11; 17:10,12,14; 19:36; 38:24,25; Ex. 21:22-23; 22:22; Lev. 12:2,5; 1 Sam. 4:19; 2 Sam. 11:5; 2Kin. 8:12; 15:16; Isa. 26:17,18; 49:15; 54:1; Jer. 31:8; Hos. 13:16; Am. 1:13; Luke 2:12,16; 18:15-16. Every child is "formed" and "fearfully and wonderfully made" and "skillfully wrought" by God within the womb (Ps. 139:13-16; Job 31:15; Is. 44:2; 44:24: 49:5; Jer. 1:5). The penalty for the deliberate killing of an unborn child is the death penalty (Ex. 21:22-23). This does not mean that God wants Americans to kill anyone guilty of abortion. That is God's jurisdiction. It does mean we should change our laws regarding abortion.

3. ROLE OF GOVERNMENT: Scripture discusses the role of government. Romans 13:1-7 states that all "authorities that exist are appointed by God," and that anyone who resists the authorities resists God's law and brings "judgment on themselves." Rulers are "God's ministers" for good. They do "not bear the sword in vain" because they are God's "avenger to execute wrath" on evildoers. Citizens must pay taxes and give proper respect to government officials.

Exactly what part of Scripture gives government any responsibility or authority to care for the poor or the middle class or anyone else? Answer: Absolutely no part. In "Matthew

22:37-40 Christ gives the command to "love thy neighbor as thyself." This commandment is given to individuals; it does not grant any authority to government. Obedience requires a very personal act of the will of the individual who chooses to love his neighbor. The purpose of government is not to provide or care for citizens, but to protect life and liberty and thereby enable the pursuit of happiness.

In 1 Samuel 8:8-20 God told Samuel to warn the people that a king would take their sons, daughters, fields, vineyards, menservants, maidservants, best young men, and 10% in taxes, the same amount due in tithes to God. God clearly recommends the smallest possible government, which gives the people greater freedom to keep and spend their own earnings. The founding fathers of the United States understood God's ideal, embodied in the U.S. Constitution, of smaller government, lower taxes, and greater personal freedom and responsibility for all citizens. They were fiercely independent men who greatly treasured their freedom and would not trade it for government benefits.

4. TAXING THE RICH: God's "tax rate" for tithes is exactly the same rate for the rich and the poor: 10% (Lev. 27:30-32). See Deut. 12:5-11; 14:22-28; Num. 18:24-28; Mal. 3:8-10; Heb. 7:1-4. In 1 Sam. 8:8-20, God warned Israel that a king would charge exactly the same rate for the rich and the poor: 10%. Thus it would seem that in the eyes of God a flat tax rate that is the same for the rich and the poor would be the "fairest" rate. This presumes little or no tax deductions or tax credits.

Governments do not have authority to take by force lawfully earned income from one person and give it to another. That is theft by government. Exodus 23:3 and Leviticus 19:15 direct government to not make judgments in favor of the poor, to ensure equal justice for the rich and poor. Government should show impartiality not partiality toward the poor, because the government does not have authority, responsibility, or jurisdiction to favor the poor. Government has the duty to ensure equality of opportunity, not equality of results. Equality of results requires denial of equality of opportunity. The Founding Fathers established America as a land of opportunity. Democrats are working very hard to change it. They mean well, but the road to hell is paved with good intentions. In other words, good intentions are not enough.

CONGRESSIONAL SCORECARDS: Congressional scorecards developed by Family Research Council Action (FRC Action) and Citizenlink (formerly called Focus Action), an affiliate of Focus on the Family show how members of Congress voted on "the most clear-cut, pro-family votes." During 2011, the average score for Republicans in the Senate was about 73%. The average score for Democrats was less than 2% (1.65%). No Democrat scored above 14%. 88% of Democrats scored an absolute 0%. In the U.S. House of Representatives, the average score for Republicans was about 89%. The average score for Democrats was about 9%. 91% of Democrats scored 10% or less.[294]

Scores for 2008 show the same pattern i.e. very high for Republicans and extremely low for Democrats. Most Republicans in the U.S. Senate and U.S. House of Representatives scored 100% for voting Christian values, while most Democrats scored zero or just 6%. View scorecards on websites of Family Research Council Action (http://www.frcaction.org), Focus Action (http://www.citizenlink.org) and National Right to Life Committee (http://www.nrlc.org).[295]

---

[294] "Vote Scorecard," Family Research Council Action, http://www.frcaction.org (accessed February 17, 2012).
[295] "Vote Scorecard," Family Research Council Action, http://www.frcaction.org (accessed July 9, 2008). "Vote Scorecard," National Right to Life Committee, http://www.nrlc.org (accessed July 7, 2008).

PRESIDENTIAL CANDIDATES: This section compares the 2012 presidential candidates: President Barak Obama (Democrat) and Governor Mitt Romney (Republican).

1. CONGRESSIONAL SCORECARDS: President Obama was the most liberal Senator in the U.S. Senate. He chose Senator Biden, the third most liberal member of the Senate, as his Vice President. Consider how being liberal relates to Christian values. Senators Obama and Biden both scored absolute zeros for voting Christian values on the vote scorecards of Focus on the Family Action and Family Research Council Action and National Right to Life Committee. They voted against Christian values every time they voted on the family-related legislation evaluated by Family Research Council Action and Citizenlink. Senator McCain scored 42% and 66%.

2. CHRISTIAN VOTER GUIDANCE: Other Christian voter guidance available on the websites of FRC Action, Citizenlink, and National Right to Life Committee reveal extreme differences between Governor Romney and President Obama on virtually all issues: same-sex marriage, abortion, taxes, national spending, national debt, appointment of judges, estate tax (death tax), etc. President Obama has taken positions opposed to Christian values in all areas. Governor Romney supports Christian values on all issues. Sections that follow contain information from these sources.

3. HOMOSEXUALITY AND SAME-SEX MARRIAGE: Homosexuality and same-sex marriage are abominations to God, extreme perversions of His design for man, woman, marriage, and family. President Obama is the most pro-homosexual President in the history of the United States. He supports repeal of the Federal Defense of Marriage Act (1996), which "declares marriage to be the union of one man and one woman…and declares that states do not have to recognize same-sex 'marriages' from other states."[296] Governor Romney

declares marriage to be the union of one man and one woman. Anyone who votes for President Obama stands in opposition to God and his laws revealed through Scripture. Governor Romney stands firmly in harmony with God's laws regarding homosexuality and same-sex marriage.

Reelection of President Obama and other Democrats does not simply mean laws that promote homosexuality and same-sex marriage, which are abominations to God in part because they are so destructive to his design for the two sexes, marriage, and family, the most basic fundamental unit of society and the backbone of the nation. It means that Christians will be forced to pay higher federal and state taxes to fund Obamacare to pay for the healthcare bills of same-sex marriages.

4. ABORTION: In the eyes of God, abortion is murder. President Obama is the most pro-abortion President in the history of the United States. He has a zero per cent voting record on pro-life issues scored by the National Right to Life Committee, but a 100% rating from NARAL Pro-Choice America.[297] President Obama supports partial birth abortion. "The partial-birth abortion procedure—used from the fifth month on—involves pulling a living baby feet-first out of the womb, except for the head, puncturing the skull and suctioning out the brain. The great majority of partial-birth abortions are performed on healthy babies of healthy mothers."[298] Even more amazing, President Obama has supported the after-birth killing of a child who survives abortion. As a State Senator, Obama voted three times and spoke twice on the Senate floor against the

[296] "Values Voter Guide for 2008 Presidential Candidates," Family Research Council Action, http://www.frcaction.org (July 9, 2008).
[297] "Where Do the Candidates Stand on Life: John McCain, Barack Obama," "Senator John McCain Record on Abortion in the United States Senate," and "Senator Barack Obama Record on Abortion, United States Senate, Illinois State Senate," National Right to Life Committee, http://www.nrlc.org (accessed August 28, 2008).
[298] Ibid.

Illinois "Born-Alive Infants Protection Act" (BAIPA).[299]

<u>Most Americans fail to grasp the primary abortion issue, which is exactly who provides and exactly who pays for abortions</u>. The U.S. Constitution does not give the federal government any authority to order any American to pay for abortions of other Americans. It is an extreme violation of the freedom of religion clause to order Christians or Christian organizations to violate their deeply held religious beliefs by providing or paying for abortions. It is highly unethical for any American to try to force any other American to violate their deeply held moral or religious beliefs by paying for or providing abortions.

Nevertheless, thanks to President Obama, in violation of the Constitution and basic, fundamental moral values, all Americans who believe that abortion is murder are now forced to pay for abortions. President Obama used executive orders and legislation to divert funds to national and international pro-abortion groups. Faced with government shutdown, he refused to cut federal funds (taxpayer dollars) to Planned Parenthood, the nation's number one abortion provider. When several states cut state funds to Planned Parenthood, President Obama funded it with millions in U.S. taxpayer dollars. He even ordered Christian organizations to violate their deeply held religious beliefs by providing and/or paying for abortions.

If reelected, President Obama will continue to force Christians and Christian organizations to provide or pay for abortions. Any American who votes for President Obama has blood on his hands, the blood of millions of American children. Governor Romney is pro-life. He has the strong endorsement of National Right to Life. He opposes forcing Christians to pay for abortions.

---

[299] <u>Ibid</u>.

5. ROLE OF GOVERNMENT: President Obama is the most liberal, most socialist President in the history of the United States. During the 2008, Senator Obama often quoted the words "I am my brother's keeper" to explain what motivates him to government service. These are not words of Christ, but words used by Cain after killing his brother Abel (Gen. 4:9). They have nothing to do with government.

President Obama and other Democrats have a wrong, unbiblical, unconstitutional understanding of the role of government. The federal government is a government of enumerated powers; each branch only has those powers granted to it by the Constitution. No part of the Constitution grants the federal government any power to establish social programs to take care of citizens. Nevertheless, the government has a duty to provide Social Security and Medicare benefits because it has taken money from citizens to fund these programs and therefore must return the money in the form of benefits.

President Obama has promised more benefits to more Americans than any other president in American history. He cannot do all the things that he has promised without the largest permanent tax increase in American history. The tax burden on Americans would be greater than fighting a war forever. Taxpayers will have to work longer each year just to pay their taxes. Do we want our nation to make a giant leap from the smaller government, lower taxes, and greater individual freedom and responsibility that has made it such a great nation to larger government, more taxes, and less individual freedom and responsibility for all citizens?

During the 2008 election, Senator McCain warned that Senator Obama would greatly increase government spending and debt. He greatly increased the national debt. Senator Obama said the cost of health care would be $150 billion dollars per year. The actual cost was much greater, and the estimated cost doubled in 2 years (see section on Obamacare). The original estimate was greater than the annual cost of the war in Iraq, and the cost will go on indefinitely and continue to rise (5% annual increase per year, Nightly Business Report, 9/24/2008).

President Obama promised to decrease the national debt. He did just the opposite, greatly increasing it by an amazing 3 trillion dollars.[300] Irresponsible debt is the primary reason we got into the financial crisis. Overspending is what caused economic failures in Greece, Spain, Italy, and many California cities. The United States is moving fast toward a major economic crisis. Governor Romney believes in smaller government, lower taxes, and greater freedom for all Americans.

If reelected, President Obama and Democrats will continue to increase the size and cost of government, a cost which must be passed on to the taxpayers one way or another, through individual or corporate taxes. Taxes on corporations will be passed on to taxpayers in the form of higher costs for sales and services.

6. TAXING THE RICH: "Fairness" is one of the primary themes of President Obama and Democrats in the 2012 election. They want to raise taxes on the "rich" to force them to pay their "fair share" to relieve the unfair tax burden on the "middle class." Like most arguments from President Obama, it is an absolute lie. Official federal income tax rates range from 10% to 35% ("2011 Tax Rate Schedules," page 98, 2011 Form 1040 Instructions). Actual tax rates are very different due to tax deductions and credits that, contrary to the totally false impression given by President Obama, benefit the poor and middle classes more than the wealthy. The bottom 60% of Americans pay much less than their share of federal taxes (14%), and the greatly and vilified top 1% pay far more than

---

[300] Figure of $1 trillion is from television advertisement by Republican Party, October 8, 2008. President Obama did not refute claims by Senator McCain of $860 billion in October 7 debate. $1 trillion is probably more accurate.

their share (27%).[301] About 49% of Americans, mostly middle and lower class, pay absolutely no federal income tax. In other words, they do not pay their fair share, and the top 1% pay far more than their share. God's "tax rate" for tithes is exactly the same rate for the rich and the poor: 10%.

President Obama and Governor Romney (both highest income tax group) paid about 21% and14% respectively. Governor Romney pays a lower rate because investments are taxed at a lower rate and because he gives so much more of his income than President Obama.

7. OBAMACARE: No part of Scripture or the U.S. Constitution gives the federal government any authority to enact a national healthcare program. Nevertheless, on March 23, 2010, President Obama "signed the Patient Protection and Affordable Care Act (Obamacare) into law, which will provide federal funding for health plans that pay for abortion on demand and lead to large-scale rationing of lifesaving medical treatments."[302] On June 28, 2012 the United States Supreme Court ruled Obamacare constitutional. Chief Justice Roberts, a conservative, joined four liberal justices in wrongfully ruling Obamacare constitutional. See chapter on Obamacare.

What does Obamacare mean for Christians? First, it means they are forced to pay higher federal and state taxes to pay the healthcare bills of other Americans and to fund the killing of millions of unborn or partially born American

---

[301] Catherine Mulbrandon, "How Much Taxes Are Paid by the Poor, Middle Class and Rich," February 2, 2012, http://visualizingeconomics.com/2010/02/12/. Source is Congressional Budget Office most recent figures (2005), http://www.cbo.gov/ftpdocs/88xx/doc8885/EffectiveTaxRates.shtml.
[302] "National Right to Life Endorses Governor Mitt Romney," "Where Do the Candidates Stand on Life: Mitt Romney, Barack Obama," Carol Tobias, "Statement by Carol Tobias, National Right to Life President, April 12, 2012, State Senate," National Right to Life Committee, http://www.nrlc.org.

children. Second, it means they are forced to buy heath insurance or be fined. Third, Christian organizations are forced, against their deeply held moral and religious beliefs, to perform or support abortions, abortive drugs, sterilization, contraceptives, etc. Those that fail to comply may be fined and forced into bankruptcy. The incredibly high cost of Obamacare for U.S. taxpayers will continue to rise dramatically. In 2010 the Congressional Budget Office estimated the ten-year cost to be $944 billion. In 2011 it estimated $1,442 billion. In 2012 it estimated $1,856 billion.[303] In just two years, the estimated cost doubled.

Governor Romney believes the Obama health care law, which would open the door to federal subsidies for abortion coverage and rationing of lifesaving medical care, should be repealed.[304] He opposes any attempt to force Christians to provide or support abortions against their deeply held religious beliefs.

8. SUPREME COURT AND FEDERAL JUDGES: One of the greatest and most important powers of the President is the ability to appoint Supreme Court justices who serve for life. President Obama appointed two extremely liberal Supreme Court justices. If reelected, he will continue to appoint very liberal federal judges and Supreme Court justices who will, contrary to the U.S. Constitution, legislate from the bench and greatly influence the direction of our nation for many years after he is no longer in office. President Romney would appoint much more conservative justices.

Liberal Supreme Court Justices will rule constitutional many totally unconstitutional decisions of the President,

---

[303] Avik Roy, "CBO: Obamacare Will Spend More, Tax More, and Reduce the Deficit Less Than We Previously Thought," August 27, 2012, http://www.forbes.com.
[304] "National Right to Life Endorses Governor Mitt Romney," Carol Tobias, "Statement by Carol Tobias, National Right to Life President."

Congress, state legislatures, and federal, state, and local courts. This will greatly increase federal and state taxes and greatly reduce the freedom of religion and freedom of speech of Christians. Christians will be forced to pay higher taxes to pay the health care bills of other Americans. Christians and Christian organizations will be forced to pay for abortions, abortive drugs, sterilization, contraceptives, and support homosexual couples by paying for their healthcare. Christian organizations who refuse will be fined and may be forced into bankruptcy.

9. WAR ON WOMEN: To win the support of women during the 2012 presidential campaign, in violation of the powers granted to the President by the Constitution and in violation of the freedom of religion granted by the First Amendment, President Obama ordered Catholic and other health organizations, contrary to their deeply held moral and religious beliefs, to provide contraceptives, abortions, abortive drugs, sterilization, etc. When Republicans objected, thousands of angry women falsely accused them of denying healthcare to women, and Democrats falsely accused Republicans of waging war on women.

Most Americans fail to grasp the primary issue, which is not women's healthcare, but exactly who provides and exactly who pays for women's healthcare. No Republican was trying to deny healthcare to women. No Republican was trying to prevent any woman from paying for her own abortions, contraceptives, etc. The U.S. Constitution does not give any branch of the federal government any authority to order any American to pay any medical bills of any other American. It is extremely unethical for any American to try to force other Americans to pay her healthcare bills. It is even more unethical for any American to try to force Americans who believe that abortion is murder to pay for abortions.

If reelected, President Obama will continue to issue executive orders and fight for legislation that will force

254

Christians and Christian organizations to pay for the medical bills of other Americans and to violate their deeply held religious beliefs by forcing them to pay for or provide abortions, abortive drugs, contraceptives, sterilization, etc. President Romney would fully support Christian values by taking opposite positions on all issues discussed in this section.

10. FREEDOM SPEECH, FREEDOM OF RELIGION:

No President in the history of the United States has done more to rob Christians of freedom of religion than President Obama. In February 2011, the Obama Administration rescinded a regulation issued by the Bush Administration that protected health-care providers from being penalized for refusing to provide abortions.[305] It "issued a 'final rule' mandating that groups, including religious schools and hospitals, provide health insurance plans that cover certain drugs or procedures, even if it violates the groups "religious and moral convictions."[306] Ordering any Christian or Christian organization to violate deeply held religious beliefs by providing or paying for abortions is a violation of the freedom of religion granted by the First Amendment.

No group of Americans has more restrictions on its freedom of speech and freedom of religion than Christians. Democrats have tried to silence Christians, to eliminate their competition during elections. A law called the LBJ law, because President Lyndon Baines Johnson pushed it through to silence his critics, threatens a church with loss of tax-exempt status if it endorses a candidate. During 2008, Democrats tried to enact legislation to silence conservative talk shows. The U.S. Supreme Court approved the use of laws designed for the mob for use

---

[305] "The Presidential Record on Life: President Barack Obama 2009-present," Carol Tobias, "Statement by Carol Tobias, National Right to Life President," April 12, 2012, State Senate," National Right to Life Committee, http://www.nrlc.org.

[306] "Where Do the Candidates Stand on Life: Mitt Romney, Barack Obama," National Right to Life Committee, http://www.nrlc.org.

against anti-abortion protestors. These are all violations of the First Amendment rights of freedom of speech and freedom of religion. If President Obama is elected and Democrats have a majority in the House and Senate, there will be more laws to restrict the freedom of speech of Christians and conservatives.

Governor Romney supports legal protections for individuals, organizations, and institutions from government forcing them to violate their moral or religious beliefs.[307] He said, "On day one I will eliminate the Obama Administration rule that compels religious institutions to violate the tenants of their own faith. Such rules don't belong in the America that I believe in."[308] He opposes Obamacare and federal funding of abortion.

11. HATE CRIMES LAW: Hate crimes laws are wrong because they punish hateful thoughts as crimes, totally contrary to biblical law and the U.S. Constitution. Governments have authority to punish wrongful actions, not thoughts that they deem wrong. The punishment should not be greater or lesser based upon the race or sexual orientation of the victim. Being a racist or hating homosexuals are not crimes punishable by government.

A government that tries to exercise jurisdiction over the hearts and minds of men becomes an oppressor and wrongfully deprives men of their God given inalienable rights to freedom of speech and freedom of religion. Government officials are "minister of God" with a duty to punish evildoers. Hate crimes laws written to protect men from discrimination based upon sexual orientation empower government officials to protect evildoers and punish Christians with fines and prison for living Christian values.

---

[307] "2012 Values Voter Presidential Voter Guide," Family Research Council Action, http://www.frcaction.org (accessed August 3, 2012).
[308] "Where Do the Candidates Stand on Life: Mitt Romney, Barack Obama."

Consider the consequences for Christians. They may go to jail for repeating words God's words to Moses in Leviticus or Paul's words to the Romans. In Europe a pastor was imprisoned for preaching on homosexuality. An elderly couple was fined for not renting a room with one bed to two gay men. A bishop was fined for not hiring a gay man. Schools and employers are conducting diversity training that teaches that the homosexual lifestyle, which God calls an abomination, is a morally acceptable lifestyle. Criticism of the homosexual lifestyle can result in counseling, disciplinary action, legal action, or job termination. Churches may be required to hire homosexuals. Christians will increasingly be punished for living Christian values.

President Obama said that he would sign a "federal hate crimes law that included protections based upon sexual orientation and 'gender identity'."[309] He said, "I will place the weight of my administration behind enactment of the Matthew Sheppard Act to outlaw hate crimes and a fully inclusive Employment Nondiscrimination Act.[310] See LGBT (Lesbian Gay Bisexual Transvestite) link under "People" on the campaign website of President Obama.[311] Governor Romney supports Christian values on all of these issues.

LIES AND DECEPTION: Lies and deception are primary tools of Satan. Life and the political realm are spiritual battlefields between forces of good and evil. It is amazing how much lies and deception are used by Democrats. This appears to

---

[309] "Values Voter Guide for 2008 Presidential Candidates," Family Research Council Action, http://www.frcaction.org (accessed July 9, 2008).
[310] Michael Foust, "Obama: If Elected I Will Use the Bully Pulpit for Gay Causes," Baptist Press, Feb 28, 2008, http://www.bpnews.netbpnews.asp?id=27510 as quoted in October 2008 letter from James Dobson, Ph.D., Founder and Chairman of Focus on the Family. See full letter at http://www.citizenlink.com.
[311] Ibid.

be truer with President Obama than any other President in the history of the United States. Most Americans are more concerned about the economy and their finances than Christian values. They vote for whoever promises them the greatest financial benefit. One of biggest lies is that so many Americans can enjoy so many government benefits without paying for them (healthcare, welfare, education, Social Security, Medicare, abortions, contraceptives, etc.). President Obama and other Democrats buy votes by promising "free" benefits to Americans (paid for by other Americans). President Obama has promised more benefits than any other presidential candidate in U.S. history. This gives him great political advantage during a time of financial crisis.

Why do so many Americans reward dishonest politicians with their support? How is it possible that so many Americans believe all the lies and deception and vote for whoever promises the greatest financial benefit? Why do they not care about what best serves God or the nation? The challenge for Christians is to see through all the lies and false promises and to discern how to vote Christian values. Other lies will not be repeated in this chapter. See chapters on lies and deception during 2008 and 2012 presidential elections.

FAILURE OF CHRISTIAN LEADERS: "All that is needed for evil to triumph is for good men to do nothing."[312] Why are so many Christian leaders such absolute failures at providing moral guidance to Christians in the area of politics and government? First and foremost, some mistakenly believe their first priority should be obedience to the Great Commission, saving souls for Christ. It should be obedience to the Greatest

---

[312] "All that is necessary for the triumph of evil is that good men do nothing." "This is probably the most quoted statement attributed to Burke.... [In] Sergei Bondarchuk's Soviet film adaptation of Leo Tolstoy's book 'War and Peace'... the narrator declares, 'All that is necessary for evil to triumph is for good men to do nothing'." "Edmund Burke," Wikiquote, http://en.wikiquote.org/wiki/Edmund_Burke.

Commandment, loving God with all their heart, mind, soul, and strength. Their lives should be God-centered, not man-centered. Second, they neglect part of the Great Commission: "teaching all that I have commanded you." Third, they fail to fully understand God, overemphasizing His love and neglecting His holiness, which cheapens Christ's death on the cross. Fourth, they try to be invitational, avoiding divisive issues, to welcome non-believers and believers and to maintain peace within their congregations. See chapter on Failure of Christian Leaders for further discussion.

CONCLUSION: VOTING CHRISTIAN VALUES: The 2012 national election is one of the most important elections in the history of the United States, one that will affect the direction of the United States for many years. Accept this challenge and warning as from the LORD.

> And Mordecai told them to answer Esther: "Do not think in your heart that you will escape in the king's palace any more than all the other Jews. For if you remain completely silent at this time, relief and deliverance will arise for the Jews from another place, but you and your father's house will perish. Yet who knows whether you have come to the kingdom for such a time as this?" (Esther 4:13-14, NKJV)[313]

All Americans answer to God, not man, for everything done to ensure the election of men and women who will govern in accordance with God's laws. Every Christian has a duty to vote for the candidates who will best serve God. That is what best serves our nation and all Americans. Not voting is not an option when one must choose between the lesser of evils. Failure to vote for the lesser of evils ensures election of the most evil.

---

[313] Holy Bible, New King James Version. Nashville: Thomas Nelson, Inc., 1982.

The race may be close. Every vote counts. Note this quote from the LGBT (Lesbian Gay Bisexual Transvestite) link on the 2008 Obama campaign website.

> In 2004, George Bush won Nevada by less than 2.5% of voters, New Mexico by less than 1% of voters, and Colorado by less than 100,000 votes. In Ohio, Bush won by just over 100,000 votes -- less than 10 votes per precinct. This time, we can't leave anything to chance. This is your choice: three minutes spent registering to vote -- or four years spent wishing that you had.[314]

No Christian should vote for President Obama. No president has aligned himself more strongly against God and God's laws than President Obama. Alan Keyes, a brilliant, deeply committed African-American Christian, ran against Barack Obama for the U.S. Senate in 2004. In a speech given by Senator Obama on June 28, 2006, posted on Obama's 2008 presidential campaign website, Obama quoted Keys:

> Jesus Christ would not vote for Barack Obama. Christ would not vote for Barack Obama because Barack Obama has behaved in a way that is inconceivable for Christ to have behaved…. Mr. Obama says he's a Christian…and yet he supports a lifestyle that the Bible calls an abomination… Mr. Obama says he's a Christian, but supports the destruction of innocent sacred life.[315]

---

[314] LGBT (Lesbian Gay Bisexual Transvestite) link under "People" on campaign website of Senator Obama, http://pride.barackobama.com (accessed October 7, 2008).

[315] Barack Obama, "Call to Renewal Keynote Address," June 28, 2006, http://www.Barackobama.com/speech/060628-call_to_renewal/print.php.

President Obama and most Democrats strongly align themselves against God and His laws in virtually all areas: appointment of judges, taxes, federal spending, federal debt, marriage, abortion, homosexual rights, freedom of speech, freedom of religion, etc.

No Christian should vote for any Democrat. Christians should not, for example, vote for pro-life Democrats. When Democrats control the House or the Senate, they block legislation based on God's laws. When Democrats have a majority in the Senate, they chair the Senate Judiciary Committee and block any pro-life Christian judges from becoming federal judges or Supreme Court Justices. Empowering Democrats enables them to defeat attempts by Christians to return our nation to the Christian principles upon which it was founded.

Fear of God is the beginning of wisdom (Pr. 9:10; Ps. 111:10. See Job 28:28; Pr. 1:7; 15:33). Americans should fear God, not man, place their trust in God not man, and vote for men who will govern in obedience to His commandments. Christians should seek better understanding of God's laws, and follow Christ, living and voting in obedience to "the will of [the] Father." They should reach out to others, to lead them from darkness to light, from death to life, and challenge them to live and vote Christian values. All this is done in vain if it is reluctant, sacrificial obedience to God's will. Read Psalm 51, written by King David, a man after God's heart, for understanding of what God really wants.

President John F. Kennedy challenged Americans to a higher calling with the words, "Think not what your country can do for you, but what you can do for your country." A much higher calling is: "Think not what God can do for you, but what you can do for God." The highest calling is the Greatest Commandment: "Thou shalt love the Lord thy God with all thy heart, and with all thy soul, and with all thy mind" (Deut. 6:5;

Matt. 22:37-40; Luke 10:27). Jesus said, "I am come that they might have life, and that they might have it more abundantly" (John 10:11, KJV). This abundant life is only possible if one dies to self and lives for Christ.

If you have been blessed by reading this book, then I close by asking three things. First, forgive me for not writing this book sooner and better. Second, join me in loving and serving God by making a difference in our elections. Third, do not thank me for this book, but join me in praising God, for He alone is worthy to be praised! Blessed be the name of the LORD! He is the King of Kings and LORD of Lords! In Him we live and move and have our being! Let us exalt His name together!

BIBLIOGRAPHY

"2012 Values Voter Presidential Voter Guide." Family Research Council Action, http://www.frcaction.org (accessed August 3, 2012).

"Abraham Lincoln Quotes." Thinkexist, http://thinkexist.com/quotes/abraham_lincoln, April 13, 2012.

"Apostles' Creed." Catechism of the Catholic Church. Wikipedia.org., http://en.wikipedia.org/wiki/Apostles%27_Creed.

Balkin, Karen, Ed. The War on Terrorism: Opposing Viewpoints. New York: Thomson Gale, 2005.

Barton, David. The Bible, Voters & the 2008 Election. Aledo, Texas: Wallbuilder Press, 2008.

Bethany Monk. "Same-Sex Marriage to Become Plank in DNC Platform," Citizenlink, July 31, 2012, http://www.citizenlink.com.

"Bill of Rights." U.S. National Archives & Records Administration, http://www.archives.gov/exhibits/charters/constitution.html.

Black, Henry Campbell. Black's Law Dictionary, 5th Ed., 1979, p 766.

Blakely, Jonathan. "One Top GOP Line of Attack: Kagan's Opposition to Military Recruitment at Harvard Law School's Office of Career Services." ABC News, http://abcnews.go.com/blogs/politics/2010/05/one-top-gop-line-of-attack-kagans-opposition-to-military-recruitment-at-harvard-law-schools-office-of-career-services/.

Bondarchuk's, Sergei. Soviet film adaptation of Leo Tolstoy's book War and Peace.

Bracchi, Paul. "It May Have Been a Victory for Free Speech, But Why Did Breakfast Insult of Muslim's Faith Case Ever Come to Court?", DailyMail, http://www.dailymail.co.uk/news/article-1234680/ It-victory-free-speech-did-breakfast-insult=Muslims-faith-case-come-court.html.

Bruce, Mary. "Obama: Voters Face Starkest Contrast Since Johnson-Goldwater." ABC OTUS News, April 10, 2012.

Burke, Edmund. "Edmund Burke," Wikiquote, http://en.wikiquote.org/wiki/Edmund_Burke.

"Can Congress Make Me Buy Health Insurance." Citizenlink, http://www.citizenlink.com/2009/08/24/can-congress-make-me-buy-health-insurance/.

Carpenter, F.B. (1866). "Six Months at the White House," p. 282. Retrieved 2010-02-20. Quoted in "Abraham Lincoln and Religion." TheFreeDictionary, http://encyclopedia.thefreedictionary.com/ Abraham+Lincoln+ and+religion #endnote_rf-17.

Citron, Jamie. "We're Going to be the Edge," October 02, 2008, and "Friends of Barack Visit Ohio," October 06, 2008. LBGT link under "People" at http://pride.barackobama.com.

"Constitution of the United States." U.S. National Archives & Records Administration, http://www.archives.gov/exhibits/charters/constitution.html.

"Declaration of Independence." U.S. National Archives & Records Administration, http://www.archives.gov/exhibits/charters/declaration.html.

"The Developing Threat of Freedom of Conscience." Citizenlink, http://www.citizenlink.com/2011/04/15/the-developing-threat-of-freedom-of-conscience/.

"Effective Tax Rates." Congressional Budget Office, http://www.cbo.gov/ftpdocs/88xx/doc8885/EffectiveTaxRates.shtml.

Foust, Michael. "Obama: If Elected I Will Use the Bully Pulpit for Gay Causes," Baptist Press, Feb 28, 2008, http://www.bpnews.netbpnews.asp?id=27510 as quoted in October 2008 letter by James Dobson at http://www.citizenlink.com.

"FRC Action: Elena Kagan's Pro-Abortion Record is Far Outside the Mainstream." Family Research Council Action, May 19, 2010, http://www.frcaction.org.

Hausknecht, Bruce. "Obamacare Decision Next Week: What's at Stake?", June 22, 2012, http://www.citizenlink.com.

Holy Bible, King James Version. Nashville: Thomas Nelson, Inc., 1982.

Holy Bible, New King James Version. Nashville: Thomas Nelson, Inc., 1982.

Holy Bible, New International Version. Grand Rapids: Zondervan Bible Publishing, 1973, 1978, 1984.

Holy Bible, Today's New International Version. Grand Rapids: Zondervan Bible Publishing, 2001, 2005.

Kornblut, Anne E. and Robert Barnes. "Kagan Would
    Emphasize Supreme Court Moving in New Direction." The
    Washington Post, May 11, 2010,
    http://www.washingtonpost.com/wp-
    dyn/content/article/2010/05/10/AR2010051001116.html.

Kozar, Richard. John McCain: Overcoming Adversity.
    Philadelphia: Chelsea House Publishers, 2002.

Lorinov, "Obamacare: Dissenting Justices Opinion," Lorinov's
    Blog, June 28, 2012,
    http://roblorinov.wordpress.com/2012/06/28/obamacare-
    dissenting-justices-opinion/

Mansfield, Stephen. The Faith of Barack Obama. Nashville,
    Dallas: Thomas Nelson Publisher, 2008.

"March 2008 Action Update." National Journal, March 7, 2008,
    http://nj.nationaljournal.com/voteratings. As cited in Focus
    Action, http://www.citizenlink.org.

Mendell, David. Obama: A Promise of Change. New York:
    HarperCollins Publishers, 2008.

Monk, Bethany. "HHS Contraception Mandate Deadline Falls
    Wednesday," Citizenlink, July 31, 2012,
    http://www.citizenlink.com;

Mulbrandon, Catherine. "How Much Taxes Are Paid by the
    Poor, Middle Class and Rich," VisualiizingEconomics,
    February 2, 2012,
    http://visualizingeconomics.com/2010/02/12/.

"National Right to Life Endorses Governor Mitt Romney,"
    National Right to Life Committee, http://www.nrlc.org.

Obama, Barack. The Audacity of Hope: Thoughts on Reclaiming the American Dream. New York: Crown Publishers, 2006.

Obama, Barack. "Call to Renewal Keynote Address," June 28, 2006. http://www.Barackobama.com.

Obama, Barack. Change We Can Believe In: Barack Obama's Plan to Renew America's Promise. New York: Three Rivers Press, 2008.

Obama, Barack. Dreams from My Father. New York: Three Rivers Press, 1995.

"Obama Distorts His Abortion Record In Third Debate," National Right to Life Committee, October 16, 2008. http://www.nrlc.org (accessed October 22, 2008).

"ObamaCare and the Power to Tax," Wall Street Journal, June 28, 2012, http://online.wsj.com/article/SB10001424052702303561504577495242473319890.html.

"President Obama to Freedom of Religion: Nertz to You!", Family Research Council Action, August 6, 2012, http://www.frcaction.org.

"The Presidential Record on Life: President Barack Obama 2009-present." National Right to Life, http://www.nrlc.org.

"Pro-Life Group Proves That Obama Subsidizes Abortion," Citizenlink, http://www.citizenlink.com/2012/10/29/pro-life-group-proves-that-obamacare-subsidizes-abortion/.

"Report: Rev. Jeremiah Wright Has Affair With Another Man's Wife," Fox News, September 9, 2008. http://FOXNews.com.

Roberts, Chief Justice. "Roberts: Our Decision Isn't About Whether Obamacare Is Sound Policy," Talking Points Memo Livewire, June 28, 2012, http://livewire.talkingpointsmemo.com/entries/roberts-our-decision-isnt-about-whether-obamacare-is.

Roy, Avik. "CBO: Obamacare Will Spend More, Tax More, and Reduce the Deficit Less Than We Previously Thought," Forbes, August 27, 2012, http://www.forbes.com.

Sapet, Karrily. Political Profiles: Barack Obama. Greensboro, North Carolina: Morgan Reynolds Publishing, 2008.

"SCOTUS Obamacare Ruling: The Dissenting Opinion in it's entirety," Patriots for America, June 28, 2012, http://patriotsforamerica.ning.com/forum/topics/scotus-obamacare-ruling-the-dissenting-opinion-in-it-s-entirety.

"Senator Barack Obama Record on Abortion, United States Senate, Illinois State Senate." National Right to Life Committee, http://www.nrlc.org (accessed August 28, 2008).

"Senator John McCain Record on Abortion in the United States Senate." National Right to Life Committee, http://www.nrlc.org (accessed August 28, 2008).

"Senator John Sidney McCain III" and "Senator Barack Hussein Obama, Jr." Project Vote Smart, http://www.votesmart.com (accessed March 22, 2008).

"So-Called Hate Speech," Citizenlink, http://www.citizenlink.com/2010/03/citizenlink-so-called-hate-speech/.

"Sotomayor: A Policy Maker or a Jurist?", Family Research Council Action, May 26, 2009, http://www.frcaction.org.

Stanek, Jill. "Obama Blocked Born Alive Infant Protection Act," April 2, 2008. National Right to Life Committee. http://www.nrlc.org (accessed July 7, 2008).

Steele, Shelby. A Bound Man: Why We Are Excited about Barack Obama and Why He Can't Win. New York: Free Press, 2008.

Stewart, Gail. People in the News: John McCain. New York: Gale, Cengage Learning, 2008.

Street, Paul. Barack Obama and the Future of American Politics. Boulder, Colorado: Paradigm Publishers, 2008.

"Supreme Court Upholds Obama Health-care Reform." Catholic World News, June 28, 2012, http://www.catholicculture.org/news/headlines/index.cfm?storyid=14767.

"Supreme Court's Obamacare Decision: Full Text." The Atlantic, June 28, 2012, http://www.theatlantic.com/politics/archive/2012/06/the-supreme-courts-obamacare-decision-full-text/259102/.

Thompson, Derek. "The Health Care Decision Explained in 1 Paragraph on SCOTUSblog," The Atlantic, June 28, 2012, http://www.theatlantic.com/business/archive/2012/06/the-health-care-decision-explained-in-1-paragraph-on-scotusblog/259097/

Titus, Herbert W. God, Man, and Law: The Biblical Principles. Oak Brook, Illinois: Institute in Basic Life Principles, 1994.

Tobias, Carol. "Statement by Carol Tobias, National Right to Life President," April 12, 2012, State Senate, http://www.nrlc.org.

"UK Pastor Arrested Over Comments on Homosexuality," Citizenlink, http://www.citizenlink.com/2010/05/citizenlink-uk-pastor-arrested-over-comments-on-homosexuality/.

"Values Voter Guide for 2008 Presidential Candidates." Family Research Council Action, http://www.frcaction.org (accessed July 9, 2008).

Van Der Vat, Dan. Pearl Harbor: The Day of Infamy—An Illustrated History. New York: Basic Books, 2001. Introduction by Senator John McCain.

"Vote Scorecard." Family Research Council Action, http://www.frcaction.org (accessed July 9, 2008).

"Vote Scorecard." Family Research Council Action, http://www.frcaction.org (accessed February 17, 2012).

"Vote Scorecard." Focus on the Family Action, http://www.citizenlink.org (accessed July 9, 2008).

"Vote Scorecard." National Right to Life Committee, http://www.nrlc.org (accessed July 7, 2008).

"Vote Scorecard." National Right to Life Committee, http://www.nrlc.org (accessed February 17, 2012).

Wagner, Heather. Barack Obama. New York: Chelsea House Publishers, 2008.

Wells, Catherine. Political Profiles: John McCain. Greensboro, North Carolina: Morgan Reynolds Publishing, 2008.

Whelan, Ed. "Obamacare Dissenting Opinion the Original Majority Opinion?," Kansas Citian, June 28, 2012, http://thekansascitian.blogspot.com/2012/06/obamacare-dissenting-opinion-original.html

"Where Do the Candidates Stand on Life: John McCain, Barack Obama," National Right to Life Committee, http://www.nrlc.org (accessed August 28, 2008).

"Where Do the Candidates Stand on Life: Mitt Romney, Barack Obama," National Right to Life Committee. http://www.nrlc.org.

"Widdecombe and Gay Tory Defend Cornish BB Owners, The Christian Institute, http://www.christian.org.uk/news/widdecombe-and-gay-tory-defend-cornish-bb-owners/.

DECLARATION OF INDEPENDENCE[316]

IN CONGRESS, July 4, 1776.

The unanimous Declaration of the thirteen united States of America,
When in the Course of human events, it becomes necessary for one people to dissolve the political bands which have connected them with another, and to assume among the powers of the earth, the separate and equal station to which the Laws of Nature and of Nature's God entitle them, a decent respect to the opinions of mankind requires that they should declare the causes which impel them to the separation.

We hold these truths to be self-evident, that all men are created equal, that they are endowed by their Creator with certain unalienable Rights, that among these are Life, Liberty and the pursuit of Happiness.--That to secure these rights, Governments are instituted among Men, deriving their just powers from the consent of the governed, --That whenever any Form of Government becomes destructive of these ends, it is the Right of the People to alter or to abolish it, and to institute new Government, laying its foundation on such principles and organizing its powers in such form, as to them shall seem most likely to effect their Safety and Happiness. Prudence, indeed, will dictate that Governments long established should not be changed for light and transient causes; and accordingly all experience hath shewn, that mankind are more disposed to suffer, while evils are sufferable, than to right themselves by abolishing the forms to which they are accustomed. But when a long train of abuses and usurpations, pursuing invariably the same Object evinces a design to reduce them under absolute Despotism, it is their right, it is their duty, to throw off such Government, and to provide new Guards for their future security.--Such has been the patient sufferance of these Colonies; and such is now the necessity which constrains them to alter their former Systems of Government. The history of the present King of Great Britain is a history of repeated injuries and usurpations, all having in direct object the establishment of an absolute Tyranny over these States. To prove this, let Facts be submitted to a candid world.

He has refused his Assent to Laws, the most wholesome and necessary for the public good.

He has forbidden his Governors to pass Laws of immediate and pressing importance, unless suspended in their operation till his

---

[316] U.S. National Archives & Records Administration, "The Charters of Freedom: The Declaration of Independence," http://www.archives.gov/exhibits/charters.

Assent should be obtained; and when so suspended, he has utterly neglected to attend to them.

He has refused to pass other Laws for the accommodation of large districts of people, unless those people would relinquish the right of Representation in the Legislature, a right inestimable to them and formidable to tyrants only.

He has called together legislative bodies at places unusual, uncomfortable, and distant from the depository of their public Records, for the sole purpose of fatiguing them into compliance with his measures.

He has dissolved Representative Houses repeatedly, for opposing with manly firmness his invasions on the rights of the people.

He has refused for a long time, after such dissolutions, to cause others to be elected; whereby the Legislative powers, incapable of Annihilation, have returned to the People at large for their exercise; the State remaining in the mean time exposed to all the dangers of invasion from without, and convulsions within.

He has endeavoured to prevent the population of these States; for that purpose obstructing the Laws for Naturalization of Foreigners; refusing to pass others to encourage their migrations hither, and raising the conditions of new Appropriations of Lands.

He has obstructed the Administration of Justice, by refusing his Assent to Laws for establishing Judiciary powers.

He has made Judges dependent on his Will alone, for the tenure of their offices, and the amount and payment of their salaries.

He has erected a multitude of New Offices, and sent hither swarms of Officers to harrass our people, and eat out their substance.

He has kept among us, in times of peace, Standing Armies without the Consent of our legislatures.

He has affected to render the Military independent of and superior to the Civil power.

He has combined with others to subject us to a jurisdiction foreign to our constitution, and unacknowledged by our laws; giving his Assent to their Acts of pretended Legislation:

For Quartering large bodies of armed troops among us:

For protecting them, by a mock Trial, from punishment for any Murders which they should commit on the Inhabitants of these States:

For cutting off our Trade with all parts of the world:

For imposing Taxes on us without our Consent:

For depriving us in many cases, of the benefits of Trial by Jury:

For transporting us beyond Seas to be tried for pretended offences

For abolishing the free System of English Laws in a neighbouring Province, establishing therein an Arbitrary government, and enlarging its Boundaries so as to render it at once an example and fit instrument for introducing the same absolute rule into these Colonies:

For taking away our Charters, abolishing our most valuable Laws, and altering fundamentally the Forms of our Governments:

For suspending our own Legislatures, and declaring themselves invested with power to legislate for us in all cases whatsoever.

He has abdicated Government here, by declaring us out of his Protection and waging War against us.

He has plundered our seas, ravaged our Coasts, burnt our towns, and destroyed the lives of our people.

He is at this time transporting large Armies of foreign Mercenaries to compleat the works of death, desolation and tyranny, already begun with circumstances of Cruelty & perfidy scarcely paralleled in the most barbarous ages, and totally unworthy the Head of a civilized nation.

He has constrained our fellow Citizens taken Captive on the high Seas to bear Arms against their Country, to become the executioners of their friends and Brethren, or to fall themselves by their Hands.

He has excited domestic insurrections amongst us, and has endeavoured to bring on the inhabitants of our frontiers, the merciless Indian Savages, whose known rule of warfare, is an undistinguished destruction of all ages, sexes and conditions.

In every stage of these Oppressions We have Petitioned for Redress in the most humble terms: Our repeated Petitions have been answered only by repeated injury. A Prince whose character is thus marked by every act which may define a Tyrant, is unfit to be the ruler of a free people.

Nor have We been wanting in attentions to our Brittish brethren. We have warned them from time to time of attempts by their legislature to extend an unwarrantable jurisdiction over us. We have reminded them of the circumstances of our emigration and settlement here. We have appealed to their native justice and magnanimity, and we have conjured them by the ties of our common kindred to disavow these usurpations, which, would inevitably interrupt our connections and correspondence. They too have been deaf to the voice of justice and of consanguinity. We must, therefore, acquiesce in the necessity, which denounces our Separation, and hold them, as we hold the rest of mankind, Enemies in War, in Peace Friends.

We, therefore, the Representatives of the united States of America, in General Congress, Assembled, appealing to the Supreme Judge of the world for the rectitude of our intentions, do, in the Name, and by Authority of the good People of these Colonies, solemnly publish and declare, That these United Colonies are, and of Right ought to be Free and Independent States; that they are Absolved from all Allegiance to the British Crown, and that all political connection between them and the State of Great Britain, is and ought to be totally dissolved; and that as Free and Independent States, they have full Power to levy War, conclude Peace, contract Alliances, establish Commerce, and to do all other Acts and Things which Independent States may of right do. And for the support of this Declaration, with a firm reliance on the protection of divine Providence, we mutually pledge to each other our Lives, our Fortunes and our sacred Honor.

The 56 signatures on the Declaration appear in the positions indicated:

Column 1

Georgia:
Button Gwinnett
Lyman Hall
George Walton
Column 2
North Carolina:
William Hooper
Joseph Hewes
John Penn
South Carolina:
Edward Rutledge
Thomas Heyward, Jr.
Thomas Lynch, Jr.
Arthur Middleton
Column 3
Massachusetts:
John Hancock
Maryland:
Samuel Chase
William Paca
Thomas Stone
Charles Carroll of Carrollton
Virginia:
George Wythe
Richard Henry Lee
Thomas Jefferson

Benjamin Harrison
Thomas Nelson, Jr.
Francis Lightfoot Lee
Carter Braxton
Column 4
Pennsylvania:
Robert Morris
Benjamin Rush
Benjamin Franklin
John Morton
George Clymer
James Smith
George Taylor
James Wilson
George Ross
Delaware:
Caesar Rodney
George Read
Thomas McKean
Column 5
New York:
William Floyd
Philip Livingston
Francis Lewis
Lewis Morris
New Jersey:
Richard Stockton

CONSTITUTION OF THE UNITED STATES[317]

Note: The following text is a transcription of the Constitution in its original form. Items that are [underlined] hyperlinked have since been amended or superseded.

We the People of the United States, in Order to form a more perfect Union, establish Justice, insure domestic Tranquility, provide for the common defence, promote the general Welfare, and secure the Blessings of Liberty to ourselves and our Posterity, do ordain and establish this Constitution for the United States of America.

Article. I.
Section. 1.
All legislative Powers herein granted shall be vested in a Congress of the United States, which shall consist of a Senate and House of Representatives.

Section. 2.
The House of Representatives shall be composed of Members chosen every second Year by the People of the several States, and the Electors in each State shall have the Qualifications requisite for Electors of the most numerous Branch of the State Legislature.
No Person shall be a Representative who shall not have attained to the Age of twenty five Years, and been seven Years a Citizen of the United States, and who shall not, when elected, be an Inhabitant of that State in which he shall be chosen.
Representatives and direct Taxes shall be apportioned among the several States which may be included within this Union, according to their respective Numbers, which shall be determined by adding to the whole Number of free Persons, including those bound to Service for a Term of Years, and excluding Indians not taxed, three fifths of all other Persons. The actual Enumeration shall be made within three Years after the first Meeting of the Congress of the United States, and within every subsequent Term of ten Years, in such Manner as they shall by Law direct. The Number of Representatives shall not exceed one for every thirty Thousand, but each State shall have at Least one Representative; and until such enumeration shall be made, the State of New

[317] U.S. National Archives and Records Administration. "The Charters of Freedom: The Constitution of the United States," http://www.archives.gov/exhibits/charters.

Hampshire shall be entitled to chuse three, Massachusetts eight, Rhode-Island and Providence Plantations one, Connecticut five, New-York six, New Jersey four, Pennsylvania eight, Delaware one, Maryland six, Virginia ten, North Carolina five, South Carolina five, and Georgia three.

When vacancies happen in the Representation from any State, the Executive Authority thereof shall issue Writs of Election to fill such Vacancies.

The House of Representatives shall chuse their Speaker and other Officers; and shall have the sole Power of Impeachment.

Section. 3.

The Senate of the United States shall be composed of two Senators from each State, chosen by the Legislature thereof for six Years; and each Senator shall have one Vote.

Immediately after they shall be assembled in Consequence of the first Election, they shall be divided as equally as may be into three Classes. The Seats of the Senators of the first Class shall be vacated at the Expiration of the second Year, of the second Class at the Expiration of the fourth Year, and of the third Class at the Expiration of the sixth Year, so that one third may be chosen every second Year; and if Vacancies happen by Resignation, or otherwise, during the Recess of the Legislature of any State, the Executive thereof may make temporary Appointments until the next Meeting of the Legislature, which shall then fill such Vacancies.

No Person shall be a Senator who shall not have attained to the Age of thirty Years, and been nine Years a Citizen of the United States, and who shall not, when elected, be an Inhabitant of that State for which he shall be chosen.

The Vice President of the United States shall be President of the Senate, but shall have no Vote, unless they be equally divided.

The Senate shall chuse their other Officers, and also a President pro tempore, in the Absence of the Vice President, or when he shall exercise the Office of President of the United States.

The Senate shall have the sole Power to try all Impeachments. When sitting for that Purpose, they shall be on Oath or Affirmation. When the President of the United States is tried, the Chief Justice shall preside: And no Person shall be convicted without the Concurrence of two thirds of the Members present.

Judgment in Cases of Impeachment shall not extend further than to removal from Office, and disqualification to hold and enjoy any Office of honor, Trust or Profit under the United States: but the Party convicted shall nevertheless be liable and subject to Indictment, Trial, Judgment and Punishment, according to Law.

Section. 4.

The Times, Places and Manner of holding Elections for Senators and Representatives, shall be prescribed in each State by the Legislature thereof; but the Congress may at any time by Law make or alter such Regulations, except as to the Places of chusing Senators.

The Congress shall assemble at least once in every Year, and such Meeting shall <u>be on the first Monday in December,</u> unless they shall by Law appoint a different Day.

Section. 5.

Each House shall be the Judge of the Elections, Returns and Qualifications of its own Members, and a Majority of each shall constitute a Quorum to do Business; but a smaller Number may adjourn from day to day, and may be authorized to compel the Attendance of absent Members, in such Manner, and under such Penalties as each House may provide.

Each House may determine the Rules of its Proceedings, punish its Members for disorderly Behaviour, and, with the Concurrence of two thirds, expel a Member.

Each House shall keep a Journal of its Proceedings, and from time to time publish the same, excepting such Parts as may in their Judgment require Secrecy; and the Yeas and Nays of the Members of either House on any question shall, at the Desire of one fifth of those Present, be entered on the Journal.

Neither House, during the Session of Congress, shall, without the Consent of the other, adjourn for more than three days, nor to any other Place than that in which the two Houses shall be sitting.

Section. 6.

The Senators and Representatives shall receive a Compensation for their Services, to be ascertained by Law, and paid out of the Treasury of the United States. They shall in all Cases, except Treason, Felony and Breach of the Peace, be privileged from Arrest during their Attendance at the Session of their respective Houses, and in going to and returning from the same; and for any Speech or Debate in either House, they shall not be questioned in any other Place.

No Senator or Representative shall, during the Time for which he was elected, be appointed to any civil Office under the Authority of the United States, which shall have been created, or the Emoluments whereof shall have been encreased during such time; and no Person holding any Office under the United States, shall be a Member of either House during his Continuance in Office.

Section. 7.

All Bills for raising Revenue shall originate in the House of Representatives; but the Senate may propose or concur with Amendments as on other Bills.

Every Bill which shall have passed the House of Representatives and the Senate, shall, before it become a Law, be presented to the President of the United States: If he approve he shall sign it, but if not he shall return it, with his Objections to that House in which it shall have originated, who shall enter the Objections at large on their Journal, and proceed to reconsider it. If after such Reconsideration two thirds of that House shall agree to pass the Bill, it shall be sent, together with the Objections, to the other House, by which it shall likewise be reconsidered, and if approved by two thirds of that House, it shall become a Law. But in all such Cases the Votes of both Houses shall be determined by yeas and Nays, and the Names of the Persons voting for and against the Bill shall be entered on the Journal of each House respectively. If any Bill shall not be returned by the President within ten Days (Sundays excepted) after it shall have been presented to him, the Same shall be a Law, in like Manner as if he had signed it, unless the Congress by their Adjournment prevent its Return, in which Case it shall not be a Law.

Every Order, Resolution, or Vote to which the Concurrence of the Senate and House of Representatives may be necessary (except on a question of Adjournment) shall be presented to the President of the United States; and before the Same shall take Effect, shall be approved by him, or being disapproved by him, shall be repassed by two thirds of the Senate and House of Representatives, according to the Rules and Limitations prescribed in the Case of a Bill.

Section. 8.
The Congress shall have Power To lay and collect Taxes, Duties, Imposts and Excises, to pay the Debts and provide for the common Defence and general Welfare of the United States; but all Duties, Imposts and Excises shall be uniform throughout the United States;

To borrow Money on the credit of the United States;

To regulate Commerce with foreign Nations, and among the several States, and with the Indian Tribes;

To establish an uniform Rule of Naturalization, and uniform Laws on the subject of Bankruptcies throughout the United States;

To coin Money, regulate the Value thereof, and of foreign Coin, and fix the Standard of Weights and Measures;

To provide for the Punishment of counterfeiting the Securities and current Coin of the United States;

To establish Post Offices and post Roads;

To promote the Progress of Science and useful Arts, by securing for limited Times to Authors and Inventors the exclusive Right to their respective Writings and Discoveries;

To constitute Tribunals inferior to the supreme Court;

To define and punish Piracies and Felonies committed on the high Seas, and Offences against the Law of Nations;

To declare War, grant Letters of Marque and Reprisal, and make Rules concerning Captures on Land and Water;

To raise and support Armies, but no Appropriation of Money to that Use shall be for a longer Term than two Years;

To provide and maintain a Navy;

To make Rules for the Government and Regulation of the land and naval Forces;

To provide for calling forth the Militia to execute the Laws of the Union, suppress Insurrections and repel Invasions;

To provide for organizing, arming, and disciplining, the Militia, and for governing such Part of them as may be employed in the Service of the United States, reserving to the States respectively, the Appointment of the Officers, and the Authority of training the Militia according to the discipline prescribed by Congress;

To exercise exclusive Legislation in all Cases whatsoever, over such District (not exceeding ten Miles square) as may, by Cession of particular States, and the Acceptance of Congress, become the Seat of the Government of the United States, and to exercise like Authority over all Places purchased by the Consent of the Legislature of the State in which the Same shall be, for the Erection of Forts, Magazines, Arsenals, dock-Yards, and other needful Buildings;--And

To make all Laws which shall be necessary and proper for carrying into Execution the foregoing Powers, and all other Powers vested by this Constitution in the Government of the United States, or in any Department or Officer thereof.

Section. 9.

The Migration or Importation of such Persons as any of the States now existing shall think proper to admit, shall not be prohibited by the Congress prior to the Year one thousand eight hundred and eight, but a Tax or duty may be imposed on such Importation, not exceeding ten dollars for each Person.

The Privilege of the Writ of Habeas Corpus shall not be suspended, unless when in Cases of Rebellion or Invasion the public Safety may require it.

No Bill of Attainder or ex post facto Law shall be passed.

No Capitation, or other direct, Tax shall be laid, <u>unless in Proportion to the Census or enumeration herein before directed to be taken</u>.

No Tax or Duty shall be laid on Articles exported from any State.

No Preference shall be given by any Regulation of Commerce or Revenue to the Ports of one State over those of another; nor shall Vessels bound to, or from, one State, be obliged to enter, clear, or pay Duties in another.

No Money shall be drawn from the Treasury, but in Consequence of Appropriations made by Law; and a regular Statement and Account of the Receipts and Expenditures of all public Money shall be published from time to time.

No Title of Nobility shall be granted by the United States: And no Person holding any Office of Profit or Trust under them, shall, without the Consent of the Congress, accept of any present, Emolument, Office, or Title, of any kind whatever, from any King, Prince, or foreign State.

Section. 10.

No State shall enter into any Treaty, Alliance, or Confederation; grant Letters of Marque and Reprisal; coin Money; emit Bills of Credit; make any Thing but gold and silver Coin a Tender in Payment of Debts; pass any Bill of Attainder, ex post facto Law, or Law impairing the Obligation of Contracts, or grant any Title of Nobility.

No State shall, without the Consent of the Congress, lay any Imposts or Duties on Imports or Exports, except what may be absolutely necessary for executing it's inspection Laws: and the net Produce of all Duties and Imposts, laid by any State on Imports or Exports, shall be for the Use of the Treasury of the United States; and all such Laws shall be subject to the Revision and Controul of the Congress.

No State shall, without the Consent of Congress, lay any Duty of Tonnage, keep Troops, or Ships of War in time of Peace, enter into any Agreement or Compact with another State, or with a foreign Power, or engage in War, unless actually invaded, or in such imminent Danger as will not admit of delay.

Article. II.
Section. 1.
The executive Power shall be vested in a President of the United States of America. He shall hold his Office during the Term of four Years, and, together with the Vice President, chosen for the same Term, be elected, as follows:

Each State shall appoint, in such Manner as the Legislature thereof may direct, a Number of Electors, equal to the whole Number of Senators and Representatives to which the State may be entitled in the Congress: but no Senator or Representative, or Person holding an Office of Trust or Profit under the United States, shall be appointed an Elector.

The Electors shall meet in their respective States, and vote by Ballot for two Persons, of whom one at least shall not be an Inhabitant of the same State with themselves. And they shall make a List of all the Persons voted for, and of the Number of Votes for each; which List they shall sign and certify, and transmit sealed to the Seat of the Government of the United States, directed to the President of the Senate. The President of the Senate shall, in the Presence of the Senate and House of Representatives, open all the Certificates, and the Votes shall then be counted. The Person having the greatest Number of Votes shall be the President, if such Number be a Majority of the whole Number of Electors appointed; and if there be more than one who have such Majority, and have an equal Number of Votes, then the House of Representatives shall immediately chuse by Ballot one of them for President; and if no Person have a Majority, then from the five highest on the List the said House shall in like Manner chuse the President. But in chusing the President, the Votes shall be taken by States, the Representation from each State having one Vote; A quorum for this purpose shall consist of a Member or Members from two thirds of the States, and a Majority of all the States shall be necessary to a Choice. In every Case, after the Choice of the President, the Person having the greatest Number of Votes of the Electors shall be the Vice President. But if there should remain two or more who have equal Votes, the Senate shall chuse from them by Ballot the Vice President. The Congress may determine the Time of chusing the Electors, and the Day on which they shall give their Votes; which Day shall be the same throughout the United States.

No Person except a natural born Citizen, or a Citizen of the United States, at the time of the Adoption of this Constitution, shall be eligible to the Office of President; neither shall any Person be eligible to that Office who shall not have attained to the Age of thirty five Years, and been fourteen Years a Resident within the United States.

In Case of the Removal of the President from Office, or of his Death, Resignation, or Inability to discharge the Powers and Duties of the said Office, the Same shall devolve on the Vice President, and the Congress may by Law provide for the Case of Removal, Death, Resignation or Inability, both of the President and Vice President, declaring what Officer shall then act as President, and such Officer shall act accordingly, until the Disability be removed, or a President shall be elected.

The President shall, at stated Times, receive for his Services, a Compensation, which shall neither be increased nor diminished during the Period for which he shall have been elected, and he shall not receive within that Period any other Emolument from the United States, or any of them.

Before he enter on the Execution of his Office, he shall take the following Oath or Affirmation:--"I do solemnly swear (or affirm) that I will faithfully execute the Office of President of the United States, and will to the best of my Ability, preserve, protect and defend the Constitution of the United States."

Section. 2.

The President shall be Commander in Chief of the Army and Navy of the United States, and of the Militia of the several States, when called into the actual Service of the United States; he may require the Opinion, in writing, of the principal Officer in each of the executive Departments, upon any Subject relating to the Duties of their respective Offices, and he shall have Power to grant Reprieves and Pardons for Offences against the United States, except in Cases of Impeachment.

He shall have Power, by and with the Advice and Consent of the Senate, to make Treaties, provided two thirds of the Senators present concur; and he shall nominate, and by and with the Advice and Consent of the Senate, shall appoint Ambassadors, other public Ministers and Consuls, Judges of the supreme Court, and all other Officers of the United States, whose Appointments are not herein otherwise provided for, and which shall be established by Law: but the Congress may by Law vest the Appointment of such inferior Officers, as they think proper, in the President alone, in the Courts of Law, or in the Heads of Departments.
The President shall have Power to fill up all Vacancies that may happen during the Recess of the Senate, by granting Commissions which shall expire at the End of their next Session.

Section. 3.

He shall from time to time give to the Congress Information of the State of the Union, and recommend to their Consideration such Measures as he shall judge necessary and expedient; he may, on extraordinary Occasions, convene both Houses, or either of them, and in Case of Disagreement between them, with Respect to the Time of Adjournment, he may adjourn them to such Time as he shall think proper; **he shall receive Ambassadors and other public Ministers; he shall take Care that the Laws be faithfully executed**, and shall Commission all the Officers of the United States.

Section. 4.

The President, Vice President and all civil Officers of the United States, shall be removed from Office on Impeachment for, and Conviction of, Treason, Bribery, or other high Crimes and Misdemeanors.

Article III.
Section. 1.

The judicial Power of the United States shall be vested in one supreme Court, and in such inferior Courts as the Congress may from time to time ordain and establish. The Judges, both of the supreme and inferior Courts, shall hold their Offices during good Behaviour, and shall, at stated Times, receive for their Services a Compensation, which shall not be diminished during their Continuance in Office.

Section. 2.

The judicial Power shall extend to all Cases, in Law and Equity, arising under this Constitution, the Laws of the United States, and Treaties made, or which shall be made, under their Authority;--to all Cases affecting Ambassadors, other public Ministers and Consuls;--to all Cases of admiralty and maritime Jurisdiction;--to Controversies to which the United States shall be a Party;--to Controversies between two or more States;-- between a State and Citizens of

another State;--between Citizens of different States;--between Citizens of the same State claiming Lands under Grants of different States, and between a State, or the Citizens thereof, and foreign States, Citizens or Subjects.
In all Cases affecting Ambassadors, other public Ministers and Consuls, and those in which a State shall be Party, the supreme Court shall have original Jurisdiction. In all the other Cases before mentioned, the supreme Court shall have appellate Jurisdiction, both as to Law and Fact, with such Exceptions, and under such Regulations as the Congress shall make.
The Trial of all Crimes, except in Cases of Impeachment, shall be by Jury; and such Trial shall be held in the State where the said Crimes shall have been committed; but when not committed within any State, the Trial shall be at such Place or Places as the Congress may by Law have directed.

Section. 3.
Treason against the United States, shall consist only in levying War against them, or in adhering to their Enemies, giving them Aid and Comfort. No Person shall be convicted of Treason unless on the Testimony of two Witnesses to the same overt Act, or on Confession in open Court.
The Congress shall have Power to declare the Punishment of Treason, but no Attainder of Treason shall work Corruption of Blood, or Forfeiture except during the Life of the Person attainted.

Article. IV.
Section. 1.
Full Faith and Credit shall be given in each State to the public Acts, Records, and judicial Proceedings of every other State. And the Congress may by general Laws prescribe the Manner in which such Acts, Records and Proceedings shall be proved, and the Effect thereof.

Section. 2.
The Citizens of each State shall be entitled to all Privileges and Immunities of Citizens in the several States.
A Person charged in any State with Treason, Felony, or other Crime, who shall flee from Justice, and be found in another State, shall on Demand of the executive Authority of the State from which he fled, be delivered up, to be removed to the State having Jurisdiction of the Crime.
No Person held to Service or Labour in one State, under the Laws thereof, escaping into another, shall, in Consequence of any Law or Regulation therein, be discharged from such Service or Labour, but shall be delivered up on Claim of the Party to whom such Service or Labour may be due.

Section. 3.
New States may be admitted by the Congress into this Union; but no new State shall be formed or erected within the Jurisdiction of any other State; nor

any State be formed by the Junction of two or more States, or Parts of States, without the Consent of the Legislatures of the States concerned as well as of the Congress.

The Congress shall have Power to dispose of and make all needful Rules and Regulations respecting the Territory or other Property belonging to the United States; and nothing in this Constitution shall be so construed as to Prejudice any Claims of the United States, or of any particular State.

Section. 4.

The United States shall guarantee to every State in this Union a Republican Form of Government, and shall protect each of them against Invasion; and on Application of the Legislature, or of the Executive (when the Legislature cannot be convened), against domestic Violence.

Article. V.

The Congress, whenever two thirds of both Houses shall deem it necessary, shall propose Amendments to this Constitution, or, on the Application of the Legislatures of two thirds of the several States, shall call a Convention for proposing Amendments, which, in either Case, shall be valid to all Intents and Purposes, as Part of this Constitution, when ratified by the Legislatures of three fourths of the several States, or by Conventions in three fourths thereof, as the one or the other Mode of Ratification may be proposed by the Congress; Provided that no Amendment which may be made prior to the Year One thousand eight hundred and eight shall in any Manner affect the first and fourth Clauses in the Ninth Section of the first Article; and that no State, without its Consent, shall be deprived of its equal Suffrage in the Senate.

Article. VI.

All Debts contracted and Engagements entered into, before the Adoption of this Constitution, shall be as valid against the United States under this Constitution, as under the Confederation.

This Constitution, and the Laws of the United States which shall be made in Pursuance thereof; and all Treaties made, or which shall be made, under the Authority of the United States, shall be the supreme Law of the Land; and the Judges in every State shall be bound thereby, any Thing in the Constitution or Laws of any State to the Contrary notwithstanding.

The Senators and Representatives before mentioned, and the Members of the several State Legislatures, and all executive and judicial Officers, both of the United States and of the several States, shall be bound by Oath or Affirmation, to support this Constitution; but no religious Test shall ever be required as a Qualification to any Office or public Trust under the United States.

Article. VII.

The Ratification of the Conventions of nine States, shall be sufficient for the Establishment of this Constitution between the States so ratifying the Same.

The Word, "the," being interlined between the seventh and eighth Lines of the first Page, the Word "Thirty" being partly written on an Erazure in the fifteenth Line of the first Page, The Words "is tried" being interlined between the thirty second and thirty third Lines of the first Page and the Word "the" being interlined between the forty third and forty fourth Lines of the second Page.

Attest William Jackson Secretary

Done in Convention by the Unanimous Consent of the States present the Seventeenth Day of September in the Year of our Lord one thousand seven hundred and Eighty seven and of the Independence of the United States of America the Twelfth In witness whereof We have hereunto subscribed our Names,

G°. Washington
Presidt and deputy from Virginia
Delaware
Geo: Read
Gunning Bedford jun
John Dickinson
Richard Bassett
Jaco: Broom
Maryland
James McHenry
Dan of St Thos. Jenifer
Danl. Carroll
Virginia
John Blair
James Madison Jr.
North Carolina
Wm. Blount
Richd. Dobbs Spaight
Hu Williamson
South Carolina
J. Rutledge
Charles Cotesworth Pinckney
Charles Pinckney
Pierce Butler
Georgia
William Few
Abr Baldwin

New Hampshire
John Langdon
Nicholas Gilman
Massachusetts
Nathaniel Gorham
Rufus King
Connecticut
Wm. Saml. Johnson
Roger Sherman
New York
Alexander Hamilton
New Jersey
Wil: Livingston
David Brearley
Wm. Paterson
Jona: Dayton
Pennsylvania
B Franklin
Thomas Mifflin
Robt. Morris
Geo. Clymer
Thos. FitzSimons
Jared Ingersoll
James Wilson
Gouv Morris

BILL OF RIGHTS[318]

The Preamble to The Bill of Rights
Congress of the United States
begun and held at the City of New-York, on
Wednesday the fourth of March, one thousand seven hundred and eighty
nine.

THE Conventions of a number of the States, having at the time of their
adopting the Constitution, expressed a desire, in order to prevent
misconstruction or abuse of its powers, that further declaratory and restrictive
clauses should be added: And as extending the ground of public confidence
in the Government, will best ensure the beneficent ends of its institution.

RESOLVED by the Senate and House of Representatives of the United
States of America, in Congress assembled, two thirds of both Houses
concurring, that the following Articles be proposed to the Legislatures of the
several States, as amendments to the Constitution of the United States, all, or
any of which Articles, when ratified by three fourths of the said Legislatures,
to be valid to all intents and purposes, as part of the said Constitution; viz.

ARTICLES in addition to, and Amendment of the Constitution of the United
States of America, proposed by Congress, and ratified by the Legislatures of
the several States, pursuant to the fifth Article of the original Constitution.

Note: The following text is a transcription of the first ten amendments to the
Constitution in their original form. These amendments were ratified
December 15, 1791, and form what is known as the "Bill of Rights."

Amendment I
Congress shall make no law respecting an establishment of religion, or
prohibiting the free exercise thereof; or abridging the freedom of speech, or
of the press; or the right of the people peaceably to assemble, and to petition
the Government for a redress of grievances.

Amendment II

---

[318] U.S. National Archives and Records Administration, "The Charters of
Freedom: The Bill of Rights," http://www.archives.gov/exhibits/charters.

A well regulated Militia, being necessary to the security of a free State, the right of the people to keep and bear Arms, shall not be infringed.

Amendment III

No Soldier shall, in time of peace be quartered in any house, without the consent of the Owner, nor in time of war, but in a manner to be prescribed by law.

Amendment IV

The right of the people to be secure in their persons, houses, papers, and effects, against unreasonable searches and seizures, shall not be violated, and no Warrants shall issue, but upon probable cause, supported by Oath or affirmation, and particularly describing the place to be searched, and the persons or things to be seized.

Amendment V

No person shall be held to answer for a capital, or otherwise infamous crime, unless on a presentment or indictment of a Grand Jury, except in cases arising in the land or naval forces, or in the Militia, when in actual service in time of War or public danger; nor shall any person be subject for the same offence to be twice put in jeopardy of life or limb; nor shall be compelled in any criminal case to be a witness against himself, nor be deprived of life, liberty, or property, without due process of law; nor shall private property be taken for public use, without just compensation.

Amendment VI

In all criminal prosecutions, the accused shall enjoy the right to a speedy and public trial, by an impartial jury of the State and district wherein the crime shall have been committed, which district shall have been previously ascertained by law, and to be informed of the nature and cause of the accusation; to be confronted with the witnesses against him; to have compulsory process for obtaining witnesses in his favor, and to have the Assistance of Counsel for his defence.

Amendment VII

In Suits at common law, where the value in controversy shall exceed twenty dollars, the right of trial by jury shall be preserved, and no fact tried by a jury, shall be otherwise re-examined in any Court of the United States, than according to the rules of the common law.

Amendment VIII

Excessive bail shall not be required, nor excessive fines imposed, nor cruel and unusual punishments inflicted.

Amendment IX

The enumeration in the Constitution, of certain rights, shall not be construed to deny or disparage others retained by the people.

Amendment X

The powers not delegated to the United States by the Constitution, nor prohibited by it to the States, are reserved to the States respectively, or to the people.

Note: The capitalization and punctuation in this version is from the enrolled original of the Joint Resolution of Congress proposing the <u>Bill of Rights</u>, which is on <u>permanent display in the Rotunda of the National Archives Building</u>, Washington, D.C.